AURANGZEB

The Genesis of Pakistan

Prafull Goradia
Jaganniwas Iyer

Prints Publications Pvt Ltd

Published by

Prints Publications Pvt Ltd
Viraj Tower- 4259/3, Ansari Road,
Darya Ganj, New Delhi-110002, India.
Phone : 91-11-45355555
E-mail: contact@printspublications.com
Website: www.printspublications.com

Edition: 2024

ISBN: 978-81-96577-63-6
Price: Rs. 495/-

Published and Printed by Mr. Pranav Gupta (Managing Director) on behalf of Prints Publications Pvt Ltd, New Delhi.

"वह दीन–ए–हिजाजी का बेबाक बेड़ा
निशां जिसका अक्सा–ए–आलम में पहुँचा
न अम्मान में झिझका न कुलजम में ठिठका
मुजाहिम हुआ कोई खतरा न जिसका
किए पै–सिफर जिसने सातों समुन्दर
वह डूबा दहाने में गंगा के आकर।"

"The fleet of Islam that sailed from Arabia,
Conquering everything from the west to Persia,
The entire world bowed to whose victorious flag,
No danger, fear or obstacle could make it sag,
The Gulf of Amman, nor the Red Sea could hold,
Such was its victorious march, for all to behold,
The sword of Islam that conquered the seven seas,
Alas! Sank when it reached the banks of the Ganges".

—Mohammad Hali

ABOUT THE AUTHORS

PRAFULL GORADIA

Born in Bombay (now Mumbai) in 1937, Prafull Goradia is a doyen of the tea industry, who quit a privileged and affluent existence to plunge into the uncertain world of politics, his real passion and calling ever since he was a boy of ten. He was elected to the Rajya Sabha in 1998 by the Bharatiya Janata Party (BJP).

Prafull Goradia has penned innumerable articles on global and national issues and several books. *Profiles of Tea, Saga of Indian Tea, The Saffron Book, Hindu Masjids, Muslim League's Unfinished Agenda, Anti-Hindus, Fly Me To The Moon, Saffron Reawakening, Had Patel Been Prime Minister, Jinnah Helped Hindus, Population Exchange, India Across and Abound* are some of his important works. Krishna Rajya, co-authored with Jaganniwas Iyer, is a pioneering and seminal work on Krishna as the political unifier and strategist par excellence. His works help contemporary readers view modern India's political journey through an informed lens. He presides over The Indian School in Delhi, reputed for offering modern education with traditional Indian ethos.

JAGANNIWAS IYER

Jaganniwas Iyer is an experienced editor, writer and analyst with comprehensive experience in various publications, research-oriented writing and a columnist on political, historical and strategic topics for various national and regional newspapers in both Hindi and English. He has also translated major works into both Hindi and English and has been part of the editorial team that accomplished the translation of *The Complete Works of Deendayal Upadhyay*—the progenitor of the ideology of Integral Humanism—under the aegis of the Deendayal Research Institute (DRI). He is the editor of *Shankarāvataraṇam*, (2005) a major work on the life and philosophy of Shrīmad Ādi Shankarāchārya, under the aegis of the Shrīmad Ādya Jagadguru Shankarāchārya Vedic Shodh Sansthanam, Varanasi. Along with Prafull Goradia, a former Member of Parliament, he is also the co-author of Krishna Rajya, a treatise on the life and role of Shri Krishna as a strategist, political thinker, statesman and unifier of India.

CONTENTS

INHERITOR OF A PERNICIOUS LEGACY

CHAPTER 01

Aurangzeb inherited one of the biggest empires the world has known, rich in resources, territorial extent and also legacy. Even before he shed his mortal coils, he had engineered not only its dissipation but also seeded its eventual ruin and destruction. As such a sweeping judgment is bound to raise eyebrows, it bears iteration here that the history of the Mughal Empire itself bears out the scathing evaluation of history.

The Mughal Empire, considered by many to be one of the classic periods of India's history, was founded in 1526 by one Zahir-ud-Din Muhammad Babar, a warlord with Mongol heritage from Andijan, (Uzbekistan), the oldest city in Central Asia. The empire he established in the Indian subcontinent lasted for a little over three centuries.

By 1650, the Mughal Empire was one of three leading powers of the Islamic world—the so-called "Gunpowder Empires"—which also included the Ottoman Empire and Safavid Persia. At its height, around 1690, the Mughal Empire ruled almost the entire subcontinent of India, controlling four million square kilometres of land and a population of about 160 million.

Map 1: Extent of Mughal Empire from Akbar to Shah Jahan and Auragnzeb

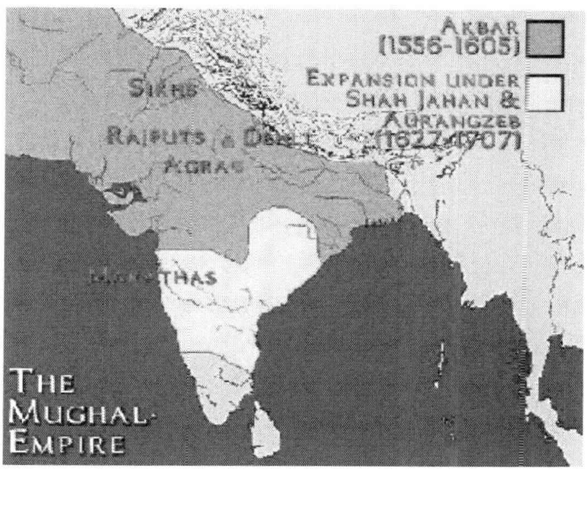

The Organization of the Mughal Empire and its Economic System

The Mughal emperors were despotic rulers. Its rule, as with any despotic system, could be sustained only by the empire's sway over a large number of its ruling elites, which the Mughal empire too had to rely upon. The imperial court included officers, bureaucrats, secretaries, court historians and accountants, who produced astounding documentation of the empire's day-to-day operations. The Mughal elites were organized based on a system that came to be known as the *mansabdari*. This was introduced by Mughal emperor Jalaluddin Akbar (1542-1605). The term *mansab* is Arabic in origin, meaning rank or position; *mansabdari* was the determining yardstick of the rank and status of the empire's officials, both civilian and military. It was a system wherein nobles were granted the right to hold a *jagir* (plot or tract of land, or territory) or revenue assignment (not land) for services rendered by them to the kingdom or empire. However, the direct control over these nobles remained in the hands of the monarch. The *mansabdari* prevalent in the Mughal world was modelled on a military and administrative system developed by the Mongol conqueror Genghis Khan (1162-1227). Being of Turkic and Mongol ancestry, the Mughals borrowed from this system to classify their nobility. The emperor exercised control over the lives of his nobles, from who they married to their education in arithmetic, agriculture, medicine, household management, and the rules of government.

The economic life of the empire Aurangzeb inherited can be described as vibrant. India's economy in the 17th century was buoyant, owing to its linkages with a strong international market trade. Goods produced by farmers and artisans were part of this trade across the country's borders, including the seas. The emperor and his court were supported by taxation and the ownership of a region known as the *Khalisa Sharifa*, which varied in size with the emperor. The rulers also established jagirs—feudal land grants—which were commonly administered by local chieftains, some of whom harboured bigger political ambitions. However, no Mughal *amir* or military governor could morph into a significant satrap, with the notable exception of Bengal, upon which the Mughals themselves came to rely when their period of decline set in. During the reign of his father Emperor Shah Jahan (1627-1658), the Mughal Empire continued to expand moderately. Shah Jahan's sons commanded large armies on different fronts. India at the time was a rich centre of the arts, crafts and architecture, and some of the best of the architects, artisans, craftsmen, painters and writers of the world resided in Shah Jahan's empire. According to economist Angus Maddison, Mughal-era India's share of global gross domestic product (GDP) grew from 22.7% in 1600 to 24.4% in 1700, surpassing China to become the world's largest (*The World Economy Volumes 1–2; 2006; Development Center of the Organization for Economic Co-operation and Development. p. 639*).

It would be easy to believe that the Mughal Empire was one rosy canvas of societal harmony and socioeconomic progress—this is what 'official' history has propagated to generations of Indians—but this was far from the case. Its harmonious life cloaked the sordid reality that the religious intolerance and zealotry that had accompanied the entry of Islamic sultanates into the subcontinent never actually evaporated during the Mughal times. E. Dewick and Murray Titus quote the *Badshahnama*, and inform us that 76 temples in Banaras alone were demolished—on Shah Jahan's orders. Thus, the dormant religious bigotry that would eventually consume the empire was rekindled by this Mughal emperor, who is otherwise famed for the Taj Mahal.

Shah Jahan's path to the Mughal throne was no stroll in the garden. Shahab-al-Din Khurram, as he was known before he became renowned as Emperor Shah Jahan (reign 1628-58), was not a chosen successor to his father Jahangir. The Mughal Empire had no system of primogeniture for the inheritance of power and wealth. On the contrary, the practice of princely sons competing to achieve military successes and consolidating their power at court, often breaking out in rebellions and wars of succession, became an unwritten norm. As an outcome, a forbidding, quite often ominous political climate hung over the Mughal court and domain in the periods of all Mughal emperors, and unmistakably so in the years Prince Khurram was growing up.

The magnificence and architectural grandeur for which history chronicles credit Shah Jahan also exacted a huge cost from the Mughal economy. Aurangzeb inherited an economy that had seen better days, but the 'credit' for beginning the slide into bankruptcy must belong to Shah Jahan. The core of the economy, from Delhi to the Deccan, had begun slipping into ruin while the outward appearance of splendour was maintained somehow. French traveller and writer Francois Bernier after a visit to Bengal reported that parents would castrate their children to turn them into eunuchs and sell them off as slaves to harems, simply in order to survive. The Italian contemporary of Aurangzeb, Nicolo Manucci, who served under Dara Shikoh till the latter's overthrow and demise, has gorier accounts to narrate.

Iconoclasm in Hindu temples, which had become dormant under Akbar (he had his compelling political reasons; notably, the need for military alliances with Rajput clans), surged again under Jahangir and then Shah Jahan. Readers would have seen the *Jahangirnama*'s account of what he did in Banaras. Abdul Hamid Lahori, a bigoted chronicler of Shah Jahan's life, describes in the *Badshahnama* the spree of temple destruction thus: "*It had been brought to the notice of His Majesty (Shah Jahan) that during the late reign many idol temples had been begun, but remained unfinished at* **Banaras, the great stronghold of infidelism.** *The infidels were now desirous of completing them.* **His Majesty, the defender of the faith, gave orders that at Banaras, and throughout all his dominions in every place, all temples that had been begun should be cast down. It was now reported from the province of Allahabad that 76 temples had been destroyed**... *"*

This orgy of destruction unleashed on Hindu temples in Varanasi and Prayagraj (it was Akbar who had imposed the Islamic name Allahabad on the city) was in 1631. Shah Jahan wasn't done yet. In 1635, his generals led an expedition into the Bundela heartland to punish the infidel Jujhar Singh; this was also his son Aurangzeb's first ever military expedition. Sir Jadunath Sarkar tells us what happened during this campaign in his seminal work *Book of Aurangzeb*.

"Shah Jahan's soldiers captured some ladies of the royal Bundela family… Mothers and daughters of kings, were robbed of their religion and forced to lead the infamous life of the Mughal harem. Shah Jahan himself made a triumphal entry into Orchha, the capital of the Bundelas, demolished the lofty and massive temple of Bir Singh Dev, and raised a mosque in its place." Aurangzeb in this campaign against the Bundelas took particular interest in razing Hindu places of worship.

Apart from visiting his jihadi iconoclasm on temples, Shah Jahan also demolished a Sikh gurudwara at Lahore, triggering off the first armed conflict led by Guru Hargobind, whose father Guru Arjan Dev had been captured and tortured to death by Shah Jahan's father Jahangir. Shah Jahan however, came a cropper in his military encounters against the revered sixth Sikh guru.

The roots of the Two-Nation Theory, which came to its fullest bloom in the 20th century under Mohammad Ali Jinnah, the founder of the Islamic state of Pakistan after partitioning India, were laid three centuries earlier by Aurangzeb's father and grandfather.

The lifestyle of the ruling class in India during the Mughal times was extravagant, surpassing that of the European aristocracy. India in the 17th century had an industrial sector producing luxury goods which Europe could not match, though this achievement came about by subjecting the population to a high degree of exploitation, both economic and religious. The standards of living of ordinary people were lower than those of European peasants and their life expectation was shorter. The high degree of exploitation was possible because of the passivity of village society. The social mechanism which kept the villages passive also lowered labour productivity, and provided little incentive to technical progress or productive investment. Mughal India had a good deal to awe Western visitors. From the time of Akbar to Shah Jahan, the court was one of the most opulent as well as influential in the world. Akbar is said to be fairly cosmopolitan and religiously tolerant, an image that is today open to questioning. However, what is undeniable is that none of his successors shared this outlook.

Jalaluddin Akbar's tenure was not all roses and honey, though, and he had to unsheathe the scimitar to cement his hold on the throne, which itself fell into his lap rather fortuitously following a freak victory in the Second Battle of Panipat (1556). He had been brought up by his guardian and mentor Bairam Khan, who was soon removed from the scene by assassination, while on his way to Mecca for the Haj pilgrimage. There were the Mirzas, local Uzbegs, who had to be killed at Akbar's behest after they first conspired and then rebelled against him, including his brother Mirza Mohammad Hakim, who was the ruler of Kabul. Then there was an assassination attempt on Akbar in 1564 while he was returning from the dargah of Hazrat Nizamuddin near Delhi. The would-be assassin, who was caught and beheaded, was a slave of Mirza Sharfuddin, whose rebellion against Akbar had to be put down with force.

While several Rajput states accepted Akbar's suzerainty, Mewar and Marwar—under Udai Singh II and Chandrasen Rathore respectively—elected to remain outside the imperial fold. Udai Singh was the son of the Sisodia ruler, the mighty Rana Sanga, who had fought Babur at the Battle of Khanwa in 1527. As the head of the Sisodia clan, he possessed the highest ritual status of all the Rajput kings in India. Akbar viewed quelling Udai Singh as essential to asserting their imperial authority among the Rajputs. During this period of his reign, Akbar was still a devout Muslim and sought to impress the superiority of his faith over what were regarded by contemporaries as the most prestigious warriors in the then Hindu world.

In 1567, Akbar mounted an invasion of Mewar's Chittor Fort. The fortress-capital of Mewar was of strategic importance as it lay on the shortest route from Agra to Gujarat and was also considered a key to holding the interior parts of Rajputana. Despite heroic Rajput resistance, Chittorgarh fell in February 1568 after a siege of four months. The fall of Chittor was proclaimed by Akbar as "the victory of Islam over infidels [*i.e.*, non-Muslims]". In his *Fatahnama* (dispatches announcing victory) issued on March 9, 1575 conveying his news of victory, Akbar wrote: "With the help of our blood-thirsty sword we have erased the signs of infidelity in their minds and destroyed the temples in those places and all over Hindustan". Not only that, Akbar, a descendant of Timur had the surviving defenders and 30,000 non-combatants massacred and their heads displayed upon towers erected throughout the region to demonstrate his authority.

The conquest of Chittorgarh was followed up by a Mughal attack on the Ranthambore Fort in 1568. But despite many Rajput kings submitting to Akbar, the house of Mewar continued to resist him. Udai Singh's son and successor, the legendary Maharana Pratap, soon faced the Mughals in the Battle of Haldighati in 1576. Though the Maharana had to opt for a tactical retreat at Haldighati, all of Akbar's might failed to quell him. The Haldighati setback notwithstanding, Pratap continued to constantly wage war against the Mughals and was successful in retaining most of his kingdom during Akbar's reign, becoming a national symbol of undying Hindu defiance of Islamic rule.

Literature and painting flourished; there were magnificent palaces and mosques at Agra, Delhi, Fatehpur Sikri, and Lahore. The nobility lived in walled castles with harems, gardens fountains and large retinues of slaves and servants. They had huge wardrobes of splendid garments in fine cotton and silk.

Succession in the Mughal Domain

Although each classic period Mughal ruler was the son of his predecessor, the succession was by no means one of primogeniture—the eldest did not necessarily inherit his father's throne. In the Mughal world, every son had an equal share in his father's patrimony, and all males within a ruling group had a right to succeed to the throne, creating an open-ended, if contentious, system. Each son was semi-independent of his father and received semi-permanent territorial holdings when he was deemed old enough to manage them. There were often fierce battles among the princes when a ruler died. The rule of succession could be summed up by the Persian phrase *takht ya takhta* (the throne or funeral bier).

Babar was a refugee from the fierce dynastic struggles in Central Asia; his uncles and other warlords had deprived him of rule over the Silk Road cities of Samarqand (Samarkand) and Fergana (in Uzbekistan). Babur was able to establish a base in Kabul, though, from which he turned south and conquered Delhi. Babur called his dynasty "Timurid", but it is better known as the Mughal Dynasty, which is a Persian rendering of the word "Mongol".

Though Babar also defeated the Rana Sanga in the Battle of Khanwa in 1527 after Panipat (1526), he was not able to conquer Rajputana, home of the warlike Rajputs. He ruled over a substantial part of northern India, though. Babar died in 1530 at the age of 47. His eldest son Humayan warded off an attempt to seat his aunt's husband as emperor and assumed the throne. Babar's body was taken to Kabul, Afghanistan, nine years after his death, and buried in the Bagh-e-Babar.

Humayan was no leader. In 1540, the Pashtun ruler Sher Shah Suri defeated and deposed Humayan. The second Mughal ruler regained his throne only with aid from Shah Tamasp of Persia in 1555, a year before his death. Humayun managed to somewhat expand on the domain Babar had conquered. He died after a fall down the stairs of the royal library, and his 13-year-old son Akbar was crowned. Akbar defeated the remnants of the Pashtuns and brought some previously unquelled Hindu regions under Mughal control. He also gained control over most Rajputs through diplomacy and matrimonial alliances.

Akbar was a patron of literature, poetry, architecture, science, and painting. Although a committed Muslim, Akbar during the latter part of his reign is said to have encouraged religious tolerance and sought wisdom from holy men of all faiths. He became known as Akbar the Great.

Akbar's son Jahangir ruled the Mughal Empire from 1605 until 1627, inheriting the peace and prosperity his father's reign had bequeathed. In 1611, Khurram's father Jahangir, then emperor of the Mughal realm, married Nur Jahan, daughter of a Persian aristocrat Mirza Ghiyas Beg, who later was adorned with the title Itmad-ud-Daula. Jahangir's affection and trust in Nur Jahan enabled her to wield an extraordinary amount of power in the affairs of state. As time wore on, Jahangir's addiction to opium and alcohol smoothened Nur Jahan's path to the exertion of her influence.

The Mughal state gave absolute power to the emperor, and those who exercised influence over the emperor gained immense influence and prestige. Nur Jahan placed various members of her family in high positions throughout the court and administrative offices. Her brother Asaf Khan was appointed Grand Wazir (minister) to Jahangir. Nur Jahan arranged her daughter Mehr-un-Nissa Begum's marriage to Shaharyar, Jahangir's youngest son by another woman. Shaharyar was Jahangir's preferred heir to the Mughal throne; this too was no assured succession. Khurram was a prince of no less promise, and looked like garnering the support of a sufficient number of Mughal courtiers and noblemen. Nur Jahan arranged for the marriage of Arjumand Bano—later known in history as Mumtaz Mahal or the Lady of the Taj— her niece and daughter of her brother the Grand Wazir Asaf Khan, to Khurram. Nur Jahan wanted her influence on the Mughal throne to extend even after Jahangir's passing, one way or the other, irrespective of who would acquire Jahangir's seat, though her preference was for Shahryar.

However, it was Nur Jahan's influence over Jahangir that Khurram resented, and which would set the stage for play of intrigue. Moreover, he was angered at having to play second fiddle to her favourite Shahryar, his half-brother and Nur Jahan's son-in-law. During Jahangir's tenure when the Persians laid siege to Kandahar (in today's Afghanistan), Nur Jahan, at the helm of the affairs, ordered Prince Khurram to march to Kandahar, but he refused. His refusal to obey Nur Jahan's orders bore a cost—Kandahar fell to the Persians after a forty-five-day siege, never again to be recovered by the Mughal Empire. Khurram feared that in his absence Nur Jahan would attempt to poison his father against him and prevail upon Jahangir to name Shahryar the heir in his place. The apprehension was sufficient to drive Khurram to rebel against his father rather than fight the Persians.

The path to succeeding Emperor Jahangir would be a blood-soaked contest. Nur Jahan wanted her son-in-law Shaharyar to become emperor after Jahangir. This was certain to invite a challenge and soon enough, a rebellious Khurram made his first attempt at a throne-grab, leading a rebel army in 1623 against his father and Nur Jahan, only to suffer defeat. In 1627, upon Jahangir's demise, Nur Jahan's brother Asaf—whose daughter Arjumand was Khurram's consort—threw in his lot with his son-in-law and moved quickly to forestall his sister's plans to install Shaharyar as the next Mughal emperor. Asaf manouevred his own palace intrigues to ensure Khurram's succession to the throne. Shaharyar, Jahangir's youngest son suffered defeat, captivity, blinding and finally execution at the hands of a victorious Khurram, who also put to death his nephews Dawar and Garshasp, sons of Khurram's brother Prince Khusrau, who had been murdered earlier; his cousins Tahmuras and Hoshang, sons of the late Prince Daniyal Mirza (son of Mughal Emperor Akbar, Shah Jahan's grandfather). Khurram, assuming the title of Shah Jahan, meaning Emperor of the World, was clearly taking no chances in ensuring there would be no rival for the throne. Shah Jahan's karma of disposing off his brothers, cousins and nephews would come back to visit him in his own old age.

This aspect of Shah Jahan's life and career might surprise many who have been led to believe the fifth Mughal monarch to be a ruler who introduced refinement and grandeur in 17th century India. But the opulence and glitter of the Mughal court and palace, and of the royal family could not mask the darker and gradually increasing ominousness of Mughal rule. The supposedly tolerant Akbar's reign was arguably an interregnum. The reversal to zealotry, began during Jahangir's period, with destruction of Hindu temples and the torturous murder of the fifth Sikh Guru Arjan Dev. The *Jahangirnama*, the autobiography of this fourth Mughal king, describes his iconoclastic actions at Banaras (Varanasi), the holiest of holy cities of Hindus, in the following words:

"I am here led to relate that at the city of Banaras, a temple had been erected by Raja Maun Sing, which cost him the sum of nearly thirty-six lakhs of five *methkaly ashrefies*. The principal idol in this temple had on its head a tiara or cap, enriched with jewels of amount of three lakhs of ahsrefies. He had placed in this temple, moreover, as the associates or ministering servants of the principal idol, four other images of solid gold, each covered with a tiara, in the like manner enriched with precious stones. It was the belief of these

Jehennemites that a dead Hindu, provided when he had been alive, he was a worshipper, when laid before this idol would be restored to life. As I could not possibly give credit to such a pretence, I employed a confidential person to ascertain the truth; and as I justly supposed, the whole was detected to be an impudent imposture. Of this discovery I availed myself, and I made it my plea for throwing down this temple which was the scene of this imposture; and on the spot, with the very same materials, I erected the great mosque, because the very name of Islam was proscribed at Banaras, and with God's blessing, it is my design, if I live, to fill it full with true believers" (*Jahangirnama*; pages 14 and 15). In the same memoir, Jahangir admitted that it was not possible to kill all the Hindus in this land, a reality his father Akbar too had learnt in his lifetime.

Thus, it did not take long for the era of darkness to return after a brief interlude of the Akbarian years. Jahangir wasted little time in reverting to the ways of the earlier Islamic invaders and iconoclasts, and his son and successor Shah Jahan, otherwise famed for the Taj Mahal, reintroduced the hated *jaziya* (religious tax imposed by a Muslim state on non-Muslim subjects; in reality, a ransom to be paid to the state for merely being allowed to live). E. Dewick and Murray Titus in their work *Indian Islam* (1979, Munshiram Manoharlal Publishers; page 24), quoting the *Badshahnama*, write that 76 temples in Banaras alone were demolished on Shah Jahan's orders. Shah Jahan was later forced to withdraw the *jaziya* only because of fierce Hindu resistance, but that lies outside the scope of this work.

It was Nur Jahan, Jahangir's queen and the de facto ruler of the Mughal domain in her alcoholic and wayward husband's time, who eventually proved to be the concealed dynamo that set off the chain of events that culminated in the decay and fall of the Mughal Empire a century after her husband sat on the throne after Akbar's passing. She was certainly more decisive and proactive than her husband, and there can be little doubting that she was indeed the real power behind the throne for over a decade. Nur Jahan wielded a level of power and influence unprecedented for any Mughal female figure, empress or otherwise. She was granted honours and privileges none of her predecessors or successors ever enjoyed. She had the authority to issue coinage struck in her name. The sole reason Nur Jahan came to have such pre-eminence was because of her husband's incurable addiction to hunting, alcohol and opium, plus his frequent ill-health.

Born as Mehr-un-Nissa in 1577 in Kandahar, present-day Afghanistan, Nur Jahan came from a Persian family. She was the second daughter and fourth child of the Persian aristocrat Mirza Ghiyas Beg and his wife Asmat Begum. Owing to a reversal in his fortunes, Ghiyas Beg was forced to quit his native Persia and relocate to India where he found employment under Mughal Emperor Akbar. Mehr-un-Nissa was born en route in Kandahar. She was fortunate to receive a good education, becoming fluent in Persian and Arabic, and well-versed in art, literature, music and dance. In 1594, only seventeen years old, Nur Jahan married her first husband Ali Quli Istajlu, also known as Sherafgun Khan, a marriage said to be arranged by Akbar himself. Sherafgun served both Akbar and Jahangir.

Sherafgun was killed in 1607, after it was rumoured that he had refused to obey a summons from the Governor of Bengal, took part in anti-state activities and attacked the governor when he came to escort Sherafgan to court. Akbar's successor Jahangir has been suspected of arranging Sherafgun's death because the former was said to have fallen in love with Nur Jahan and wanted to add her to his harem, though there are conflicting accounts of this episode.

There are thick allegations of an early affection between Nur Jahan and Emperor Jahangir before Nur Jahan's first marriage to Sherafgun. In 1611, Nur Jahan met Emperor Jahangir at the palace's *meena bazaar* during the Persian festival of Nowruz, which celebrates the coming of the new year. Jahangir proposed immediately and they were married on 25 May of the same year. Nur Jahan was thirty-four years old at the time of her second marriage and she would be Jahangir's twentieth and last legal wife. He gave her the title of *Nur Mahal* (Light of the Palace) upon their marriage in 1611 and *Nur Jahan* ("Light of the World) five years later in 1616. Jahangir's affection and trust in Nur Jahan led to her acquiring a great deal of power in affairs of state. His addiction to opium and alcohol made it easier for Nur Jahan to exert her influence. His trust in her was so great that he gave her the highest symbol of power and determination of the decrees of the empire—his imperial seal, implying that her perusal and consent were necessary before any document or order received legal validity. Little wonder that she not only wielded imperial authority, but was also recognized as the real force behind the Mughal throne. It was, however, soon to become her undoing.

By 1620, Jahangir's health had begun to decline perceptibly. Nur Jahan's anxiety to to consolidate her hold over the throne and also secure her future now grew. Tensions between Nur Jahan and Jahangir's third son, the crowned

Prince Khurram (later Shah Jahan) increased, leading to the usual outbreak into intrigue and conflict for succession to the Mughal throne. It was Khurram who prevailed in a blood-soaked tussle, killing his brothers Shahryar and Khusrau. Nur Jahan was the loser, and she was placed under arrest by her son-in-law, where she spent the rest of her days in the company of her widowed daughter Ladli Begum (Shahryar Mirza's wife). She died in Lahore in 1645 and was interred at the Shahdara Bagh mausoleum.

Jahangir was succeeded by his son, Prince Shahabuddin Khurram also known as Shah Jahan, as we have seen. The 36-year-old Shah Jahan inherited an incredible empire in 1627, but any joy he felt would be short-lived. Just four years later, his beloved wife, Mumtaz Mahal, died during the birth of their 14th child. The emperor went into deep mourning and was not seen in public for a year. As an expression of his love, or so it is said, Shah Jahan commissioned the building of a magnificent tomb for his dear wife. Constructed of white marble, the Taj Mahal is touted as the crowning achievement of Mughal architecture.

Map 2: Since the 1600s, that is Jehangir's time, there were European trading posts in India

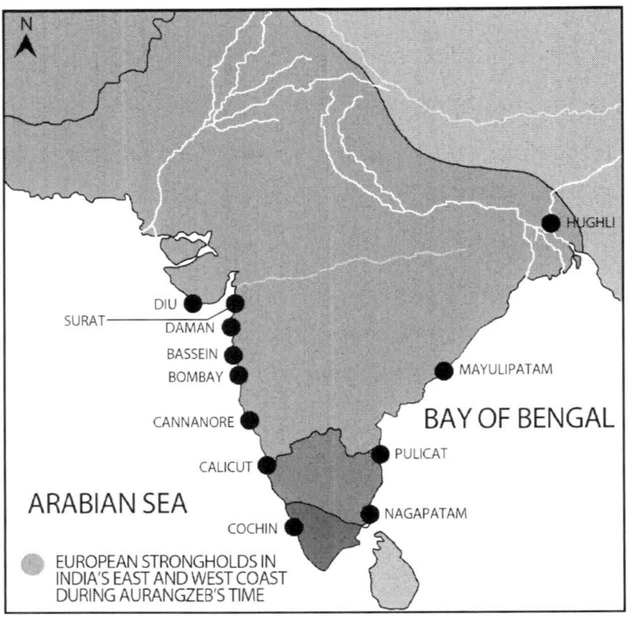

The empire, as noted, was founded by Babar, an adventurer and fortune seeker from Central Asia. Zahiruddin Babar was a direct descendant of Timur Lang (also called Tamerlane in the West) on his father's side, and of the Mongol conqueror Ghengis Khan on his mother's side. Babar, a native of Ferghana in Uzbekistan, was ousted from his native domains by one Sheybani Khan and invaded Afghanistan and then India. His victory in the First Battle of Panipat (1526) gave him control of a portion of northern India but the founder of the Mughal Empire died in Kabul a mere four years later, in 1530. Babar's son Humayun succeeded him, but the inherent instability of the kingdom Babar had founded became evident in his son's time. Humayun was defeated and driven into exile from India by Sher Shah Suri, a local Afghan warlord. Babar Son's could return to Delhi only in 1555 and died the same year after an accidental fall from the stairs.

The Mughal Dynasty left a large and visible mark on India. Regrettably, in the ultimate analysis, it proved to be debilitating one. It would be no exaggeration at all to state that the 'great' Mughals only paved the way for the takeover of India by European colonial powers in the 18th and 19th centuries, Britain in particular.

As our brief look at the Mughal lineage Babar downwards shows, the postulate that there was a monolithic Mughal rule over *all* of India from 1526, the year Babar grabbed Delhi following the First Battle of Panipat till 1857, when the dynasty's last figurehead incumbent Bahadur Shah Zafar was dethroned and packed off to Burma to die in exile, is basically fiction. Sadly, because of the ideological stranglehold of a non-India and often anti-Indian elite over the polity after 1947, this fiction has been successfully passed off as history. Fewer masquerades have been as successful.

Our sources for this conclusion are historical, chiefly Muslim and European annals, plus of course the incomparable Sir Jadunath Sarkar. From Babar to Aurangzeb and beyond, till the edifice of Mughal rule finally collapsed and met its natural end, one does not come across any instance where its rulers were even minimally interested in safeguarding and conserving the independence and integrity of India, leave alone advancing it. Since the 12th century CE, i.e., the onset of the medieval age, India had fallen victim to Islamic onslaughts and rule, first by the Ghaznavids and Ghurids, the Slave Dynasty, the so-called Delhi Sultanate and then the Mughal empire. All of these states were without exception, an uncontrolled domain of religious despotism and imperial aggrandizement. The Mughal-era state was the largest manifestation of this grotesque architecture.

While Babar did not live long after hi triumph in India, his successors ensconced themselves here permanently, Akbar onwards. Humayun became a fugitive after being ousted from Delhi and had to seek refuge in Persia before returning to India in 1555. His son Akbar and his successors then sat on the Mughal throne till its eventual decay and collapse. But as far as the polity was concerned, Mughal *Badshahs* were nothing more than indulgent, wanton and despotic rulers. Also, they were not merely kings in the temporal sense, but 'protectors' and agents of Islam's religious expansion in infidel lands. This expansionist tenet was intrinsic, and mandated the oppression of all non-Muslims living in their domain. Islamic sultanates operated in accordance with the law of the Sharia. The adherents of the faith claim a divine status for it, supposedly having come down from Allah himself. but the application of any law, religious or secular is after all in the hands of human agency(ies). The argument of interpretation does not hold water in this case; *ijtihad*, or interpretation, which is a product of the interaction of a multitude of opinions and views, debate and reasoning, was outlawed by the faith of the rulers a mere century after its origin and *taqlid* (orthodoxy) was firmly battened down on its adherents. Sharia law and its application in the Mughal domain was no different. It rested solely in the hands of a special category—the ruler and the clergy, in this case the Qazis. As was bound to happen, the interpretation of supposedly divine laws was whimsical, arbitrary and unscrupulous. Non-Muslim subjects of the Mughal Empire had to count their blessings if they ever had to seek recourse to the empire's officials for even a semblance of justice. Appearing before the *Badshah* for any justice could be fatal or beneficial, the likelihood of the former being greater.

The state, as a political entity and as an unescapable state of affairs for the ordinary subject, was the nature of the state in Mughal times. This absolute despotism created a state of fear. Respect for the ruler did exist, but this was a respect enforced through fear. In sharp contrast, Hindu kings respected the people and in turn, *earned* respect and deference through their character and conduct, which was at all times supposed to be in adherence to dharma. The one thing Hindu rulers truly feared was being regarded as a ruler who disobeyed or violated dharma. The maintenance of an environment of fear and enforcing necessitated the maintenance of a large, standing military force even in *peacetime*. But the concept of 'peacetime' itself was a misnomer— the

Mughal Empire did not let non-Mughal domains live in peace because of its aggrandizing and expansionist nature. This was indeed the case from Babar to Aurangzeb, with any difference being of degree and not of nature. Insatiable expansion did not let any real peace prevail in India and in turn, the Mughal Empire itself did not know any peace. It was constantly at war with itself and the country over which it lorded, until its wheels began coming off during Aurangzeb's reign.

Absolute political power concentrated in the hands of a despot produced the most pernicious outcomes on the Indian people and nation. The cumulative effect of Mughal rule was to thwart India's progress by several centuries. Accumulated learning and knowledge of centuries were not only destroyed but ground to an almost permanent halt. Hindu Bharat produced generations of scholars, astrologers, astronomers, mathematicians, musicians and poets, and continued to do so, albeit with lesser frequency amidst a hostile medieval period of warfare, conquest and persecution, but *not a single university or institution of excellence was produced throughout the 'great' or 'glorious' Mughal rule. in fact, the last Indian university was Nalanda, which became a victim of the rapine unleashed by Khiljian raider Bahkhtiyar Khilji in 1240. The next universities in India could come up only in 1857, after more than six centuries, 617 years to be precise, at Bombay, Calcutta and Madras under the East India Company after the Mughals had crumbled and their 'empire' had been taken down.*

The Mughal Empire, totalitarian in its nature, created a climate wherein any vestige of self-respect became alien to the subjects that resided in it. The debasement of human character can be rightly called one of the lasting ill-effects of Mughal rule. From officials and *mansabdars* to the man on the street, even basic safety, let alone any economic progress, depended only slavery and obsequiousness to the ruler of the day. Under the regime of Akbar 'the Great', the sheer number of personnel employed only for the personal services of the emperor was one of the features of the economic life of his reign that stood out, albeit obnoxiously. Some of those in the employ of the *Badshah* were free men, while others were slaves (slavery was a sordid, inhuman fact of Muslim rule), but the tasks assigned to both categories of workers were interchangeable. Akbar set the standard in most matters, and anyone who occupied or aspired to a position at his court had to follow these rules as far as his means allowed. The imperial household and its *zanankhana* (ladies' apartments) contained more than 5,000 ladies, each of whom had separate apartments. They were served by an adequate staff of servants, and watched in successive circles by female guards, eunuchs, Rajputs, and the porters at the gates, apart from the troops stationed on all four sides of the buildings. Supplies for the household were obtained from distant sources, regardless of the amount of workforce required. Wherever the Emperor might be, water for his use was brought from the Ganges, while ice came daily by post carriages and by *harkaras* (runners) from the snowy mountains to Lahore (the city was one of the three Mughal capitals, the other two being Agra and Delhi), and fruit was supplied regularly from Kashmir and Kabul, and even from more distant sources, such as Badakhshan and Samarqand.

Things got worse…and worser…as the despotisms of Jahangir, Shah Jahan and Aurangzeb followed. To imagine that any refinement, culture or learning in such an environment could grow is to live in delusion.

The criminal misuse of productive resources and human abilities for the wanton sensual indulgences and pursuits of its *badshahs* became one of the most visible visages of the Mughal Empire, apart from its expansionist nature and incessant hostility to the country, especially those parts that lay outside its influence and domination, not to speak of the debilitating effect on the economy. It goes without saying that the insatiable hunger of the Mughal emperors for personal luxuries on a gargantuan scale had to obviously be financed by their citizenry. Affluence does flow as an outcome of an economy that is flourishing, and in turn provides stimuli to further economic progress and advancement, but one cannot find any evidence to show that the Mughals had any elementary knowledge of this fundamental principle of economics. Their emperors had a limitless craving for sensual enjoyment and expanding the empire's domains in pursuit of their greed and religious zealotry. The only way such an empire and the lifestyle of its wayward and wanton monarchs could be financed was through predatory taxation, which grew proportionately with Mughal expansionism and the self-aggrandizement of its *Badshahs*.

The rule of Akbar (1556-1605), eulogized as "the great", was a stark picture of the economic reality of the country in his time. Serfdom was generally the lot of ordinary village labourers, who could earn a little more than the bare minimum necessary for subsistence, and that too in favourable seasons and/or circumstances. When conditions turned adverse, the choice was often between the certainty of starvation at home and the probability of starvation on the roadside or in the jungle. If Akbar's regime had any system to keep villages functional in tough times, we do not know of it from any Mughal-era literature—one must ignore the modern-day eulogies and novels about the 'great' Akbar and his supposedly utopian reign. There were instances of people selling off their own children when the stock of food was exhausted, and living off the land too became tortuous, a state of affairs that grew acute in Shah Jahan's time and morphed into a castration industry, a flourishing enterprise especially in Bengal.

A look at some job descriptions can said to be a reasonably accurate measure of what enterprise and work had become in the Mughal realm. There were 'jobs' (if at all one could call them that) like spittoon-bearer, cup-bearer, umbrella-bearer, ice-bearer, servants specially appointed to serve a specific delicacy, a large staff employed for hunting, hawking, pigeon-flying, trainers who sharpened the fighting instincts of cocks, rams, frogs and even spiders. Then there were servants whose only job was to drive away flies that threatened to approach the handsome sultan or aristocrat. *In brief, the employment market under the Mughals was one where slaves had to carry out the above-mentioned functions and any other their masters decreed.*

While this sordid economic reality was the state of affairs since the time of the so-called Delhi sultanate, we have to bear in mind that the Mughal Empire covered a much larger territory. As an empire, it lasted for nearly two centuries. While its panegyrists continue to sing paeans about its 'glory' and how India attained the 'zenith of prosperity', it was actually a saga of economic vandalism, driven by life-sucking taxation, an edifice that could not be sustained for long. Even the few positive things done during Akbar's reign was squandered away in a most profligate way by his debauched son, Jahangir, whose interest in governance was minimal, if any. Such responsibility was outsourced by this pleasure-loving badshah the administration to his venal begum Noor Jahan and her brother Asaf Khan, who had become the Grand Wazir, but was more akin to a Mughal-era Rasputin in wielding influence over the court and state affairs. We have accounts by Muslim chroniclers, quite unambiguous, of how the sibling duo wrecked the empire's economy. One telling measure of how the southward spiral of the Mughal Empire's finances began reaching its nadir—in Aurangzeb's time—was Mughal naval power becoming a joke. This vacuum in naval power was filled, thankfully, by Shivaji, who built up a formidable naval force along India's western coast. This was a period when Aurangzeb's corrupt officials were busy selling *farmans* to European traders.

By 1700, Aurangzeb had lost effective control over the economy and administration of three important port cities of India: Calcutta (or Bengal in general), Machilipatnam and Surat—i.e., both the eastern and western coasts. His *amirs* and *umraos* paid him the customary respect, exhibited the requisite fear and deposited revenue. However, the deposit of this revenue was within their own domain, and very little, if any, reached the coffers in Agra/Delhi. The *amirs*, sensing the opportunity became mini-despots in their own little domains they had carved out for themselves. India's downslide under the Mughals was not without its attendant costs. European powers did not let go of the opportunity this state of affairs provided to make inroads into the country, first through (unfair) trade and intruding into the political arena to begin carving out their 'spheres of influence'. This also led to frequent outbreaks of violence with the local populace. There were several instances when Aurangzeb's Muslim governors would accept bribes, liquor and women from European mercantilists to 'settle' these clashes. Needless to add, it weren't the natives who got any justice.

Leo Amery, the Secretary of State for the Colonies, describes the situation thus:

"[This] is a picture of the Mughal Empire on the eve of its dissolution, still apparently intact, but showing everywhere the cracks and fissures which were soon to bring the whole fabric tumbling down in wreckage. We see the aged…Aurangzib in his camp, with his immediate entourage of self-seeking, venal, luxury-loving and incompetent ministers, in the midst of a vast army, utterly worthless from the fighting point of view… besieging Maratha forts only to be reoccupied (by the enemy) as soon as the army has marched on elsewhere. Meanwhile the fabric of government, sustained only by an endless stream of Imperial letters and by the services of some 4,000 spies, becomes weaker everywhere. An alien government in the hands of Turks and Persians, with Persian as its official language, it has lost the hold…over the Hindu population as the result of Aurangzib's fanatical persecution of the Hindu religion and extrusion of the Hindus from all positions of responsibility. The facade is still there and actually covers a wider area of India than ever before, but end is near… A bare fifty years will separate the death of Aurangzib from Clive's victory at Plassey. The Mughal avatar in India ends and the British raj begins."

This is one of the most lucid assessments of both the alien regimes, Mughal and British, provided by an Englishman. R.C. Majumdar, the doyen of Indian history describes the same thing from the Indian point of view:

"The official history of the freedom movement starts with the premise that India lost independence only in the 18th century and had thus an experience of subjection to a foreign power for only two centuries. Real history, on the other hand, teaches us that the major part of India lost independence about five centuries before, and merely changed masters in the 18th century."

The scenario described above should not be surprising when one recognizes the fact that the Mughal Empire was Indian only in its geographic presence. Else, there was nothing Indian about it. It was in reality, a sultanate of Islamic despots who cared neither for the country's political independence nor its territorial integrity. Both are not recognized in Islamic doctrine; Islam does recognize geographical borders. The venality of the Mughal state only paved the way for the colonial conquest of India by the East India Company. It were the Marathas, under Chhatrapati Shivaji and later the Peshwas who adhered to avowed goal of recovering the lost Hindu Rashtra, the original Hindu civilizational state.

The Mughal Empire was unarguably a regime of foreigners, by foreigners and for those foreigners. In fact, this was so from the time of the so-called Slave Dynasty and Delhi Sultanate, from the time of Iltutmish to Aurangzeb's reign, which like that of all his predecessors was soaked in blood. Sultans or Mughals, these rulers stuffed their administration with alien Muslims.

They broadly belonged to two categories; one thronged India from Central Asia, mostly adventurers, freebooters and former aristocrats whose careers had been wrecked at home, relatives of the sultan or his clan and sundry mercenaries looking to make fortunes via shortcut. For that matter, Mughal founder Babar, who came from Andijan in Uzbekistan, was the son of a Ferghana warlord who had been ousted and driven out of his realm by rivals. The second category was also of foreign Muslims or their descendants who had already settled in India and had been serving in various capacities in the administration of the sultans.

We may look at the demographic details of the employed personnel under Akbar the supposedly great. Mooreland has this to say: "The [administrative] Service was not by any means confined to men of Indian nationality, and *in*

Akbar's time it was predominantly foreign. Akbar himself was a foreigner—the Omrahs consist mostly of adventurers from different nations who entice one another to Court (Bernier)..." (italics added).

Some other numbers prove the point: *70 percent* of senior officials of Akbar's regime came from Muslim families that had come with Humayun from Afghanistan. They were rewarded and promoted by Akbar after he became the *Badshah*. Of the remaining 30 percent, *more than half* were Muslims, both Indian and foreign. Only the remainder were Hindus.

In the *forty* long years of his reign, Akbar appointed a grand total of the following numbers of Hindus in his administration: *twenty-one*. Of this, seventeen were Rajputs. These appointments were part of his calculated move to consolidate his hold over Rajputana. The remaining four Hindus include the following: Raja Mahesh Das, more popularly known as Birbal, Raja Todar Mal and his son, and finally, a Khatri official whose name unknown.

Aurangzeb seized the throne and had all of his brothers executed after a protracted succession struggle in 1658. At the time, the ailing Shah Jahan was still alive, but Aurangzeb had him confined to Agra Fort. Shah Jahan spent his declining years gazing out at the Taj and died in 1666. The ruthless Aurangzeb proved to be the last of the notable Mughals. His enforcement of Islam, banning even music in the empire (which made many Hindu rites impossible to perform) set in motion the chain of events that eventually consumed the Mughal Empire, as we shall see.

CHAPTER 02

COMPLEX PERSONA, FRAYED POLITY

Muhiuddin Mohammad Aurangzeb (1618-1707), lord of the Mughal Empire from 1658 till his death was a highly complex persona. More than 310 years after he breathed his last in the Deccan in Maharashtra, his ghost continues to hover over the realm of politics, culture and religion in the Indian subcontinent, which at the best of times is a heady enough matrix, testing and often besting those caught up in its vortexes.

Why is mention or study of Aurangzeb important today? The answer is to be sought not in the fanciful and politically correct, whitewashed or romantic portrayals of this particular Mughal emperor or indeed the Mughal Empire itself, but in the legacy that Aurangzeb birthed, which continues to stalk the land he ruled for half a century. The closer and more pertinent reason for a reappraisal of Aurangzeb is the aftermath of what this particular Mughal ruler did and left behind in his lifetime, which continues to influence the course of the subcontinent's history.

Of the subcontinent's history, one of the most pertinent and lingering queries is what would have been the course of events if Aurangzeb, who called himself Alamgir, had never become the emperor? If the Mughal throne had passed on from his father Shah Jahan to his brother Dara Shikoh, widely eulogized as tolerant, given to syncretism and accommodating of diverse faiths and ways of life, would India have been a markedly different place? Then there is conjectural intellectualism about how South Asia itself would have taken a turn different than the one it did towards the middle of the 17th century. More to the point, what scholars and interpreters refer to is the continuing interreligious strife between Hindus and Muslims that continues to this day.

That the personal biography of Aurangzeb is also India's history for some seven decades bears little iteration, though it is an important epoch in its annals. Most historians and writers of the history of this period, not to mention a horde of panegyrists, are wont to credit him with having achieved the largest territorial expanse of any Indian empire before the advent of the British, but this is at best only a half-truth and also highly misleading. While the Mughal sceptre wielded formal authority from Kabul to Khulna and Kashmir to Karnataka under Aurangzeb, the fraying of the empire had begun even as he rode to power over the corpses of his brothers and after deposing his father, the famed Shah Jahan. The Mughal Empire in the middle of the 17th century might have been governed on the direct orders of the emperor, administered by the appointees of the crown, and not by vassal kings or nawabs, but the embers that would consume it were already glowing. Apologists would be quick to point to the geographical spread of Aurangzeb's domain, but in stark contrast to the empires of Chandragupta Maurya, Samudragupta or Vikramaditya, rebellions and revolts stalked Alamgir throughout his reign. Some revolts were incubated even before Aurangzeb strode to the throne in a blood-soaked epoch. The decay and disruption that would eventually consume the Mughal Empire was arguably intrinsic to its very setup, but it remained submerged during the period of Akbar and Jahangir. It however, began rearing its head not long after Shah Jahan took over and under his son who succeeded him, the administration's breakdown, manifested by the mighty empire's increasing failure to maintain order and hold the realm together became apparent.

The irony is that the emperor under whose watch this happened is even today eulogized as a 'Great Mughal'.

Descriptions of Aurangzeb as "great" must occupy the category of incredulousness. Of his influence and dominance for a substantial part of 17th century India, there can be little doubt, yet the complexity of his persona was in no small measure responsible for the unraveling of the Mughals. To quote Sir Jadunath Sarkar, undoubtedly the most detailed biographer of Aurangzeb: "Why was it so? (Meaning, the downfall of the Mughal Empire set in motion under Aurangzeb) The ruler was free from vice, stupidity and sloth. His intellectual keenness was proverbial, and at the same time he took to the business of governing with all the ardour which men usually display in the pursuit of pleasure. In industry and attention to public affairs, he could not be surpassed by any clerk. His patience and perseverance were as remarkable as his love of discipline and order. In private life, he was simple and abstemious like a hermit. He faced the privations of a campaign or a forced march as uncomplainingly as the most seasoned private. No terror could daunt his heart, nor weakness or pity melt it. Of the wisdom of the ancient which can be gathered from books, he was a master. He had, besides, undergone a long and successful probation in war and diplomacy in his father's lifetime".

Yet, the culmination of the fifty-year reign of such a ruler was not a greater and better empire that would go on to greater or loftier heights, but total failure and the end—albeit gradual—of the empire itself. Therein lies the complexity of Aurangzeb's persona. An emperor who was so zealously determined to preserve his domain lived to see the seeding of its eventual ruin—and admitted as much in his correspondence during his final days. The kingdom over which he exercised absolute control for half a century saw *six* Mughal 'emperors' in the span of the next eleven years, a testimony to badly frayed polity Aurangzeb left behind him. The irony is compounded by the fact that the over-centralized, gargantuan edifice Aurangzeb presided over in his time itself became the cause of its demise.

The reign of Aurangzeb must also stand out for two marked epochal developments in the history of India—the total and irreversible break of the Rajputs from the Mughal Empire, transforming from once-dependable allies to implacable enemies, and more potently, the rise of the Marathas as not only an independent kingdom that challenged Mughal supremacy, but who went on to become the nemesis of the Mughals even in the north of India. Both happened under Aurangzeb's watch, but more to the point, the sixth Mughal emperor was undeniably responsible for birthing both factors. The next people who became armed opponents of Aurangzeb's empire were the Sikhs. These determining factors of the 18th century, which exerted their influence on, and shaped Indian history well into the 19th century, were set in motion by Aurangzeb. The Rajputs erased the long-hovering Mughal shadow from Rajputana. The Sikhs asserted their faith and independence in the Punjab, ending Mughal presence there. However, it were the Marathas who not only thwarted the southward expansion of the Mughals, but also drove them back all the way to the north, ultimately decimating them even in Delhi and Agra, and reducing them to taxpaying vassals of Pune. Though this ignominy was to visit the house of Timur three decades after Aurangzeb's passing, he bears no small responsibility in fathering it.

Aurangzeb's reign is touted by his apologists as one of maximum territorial expanse. Yet, in that very reign, when the Mughal crescent had supposedly become a full moon, the waning had already begun. India's political sky was beginning to see the hues of a new dawn, in which the Mughals would be no longer visible. Apart from the Rajput and Sikh reassertion and the Maratha ascendancy and later supremacy over much of the subcontinent, the future masters of India had begun finding a fertile and sound footing in it. The British East India Company, present in India since Aurangzeb's grandfather Jahangir's period, was already growing in influence and power. Madras and Bombay became the presidencies of the Company in 1653 and 1687 respectively. Calcutta was founded in 1690; all this while Aurangzeb was busy disposing of his brothers to become the emperor, or irretrievably stuck in the Deccan quagmire, trying to quell an enemy who was to ultimately overwhelm him and his empire itself. He remained oblivious to these developments elsewhere in his realm. The East India Company from Leadenhall Street formed a dominion within the Mughal Empire, fortified its possessions to a degree that enabled it to withstand even the strongest imperial onslaught, and also began its first initiatives in local government and legislation, which would one day form the fulcrum of its empire in India, one whose legacy lives on and governs even modern India. It would go on to build an empire and administration that still has no parallel in world history. All this happened under Aurangzeb, and he was unable to do anything about it. Worse, it is doubtful if he could even comprehend what was happening in the world around him. This comes out as ironical for a ruler whose intelligence and political cunning in outwitting his domestic rivals had not been in doubt.

The mid-17th century, when this supposedly great Mughal came to office was already beginning to reveal the Mughal Empire, which Babar had founded and Akbar had really made an empire, as being rotten at its very core. Exertion had given his dynasty the grand edifice, and Jahangir and Shah Jahan Akbar's had done their bit to extend and embellish it. While it appeared glittering from the outside, the starry countenance cloaked the reality that it was ready to tumble like a house of cards at the first serious push, whether native or foreign. The 17th century scorched on, but the imperial power found itself increasingly unable to exert its authority. The Mughals, once feared, now themselves became fearful of their Maratha and Rajput adversaries. The royal treasury was drying up, and replenishment wasn't happening. The empire had no moral aura to boast of, but its moral turpitude became apparent in this century, a debilitation far more serious than the material one. Mughal rule had ceased to command the respect of its subjects, much less deference; its public servants had thrown all honesty to the winds; its ministerial officials lacked ability, while statesmanship was the last thing one associated with the ruling family's princes, with the possible exception of the refined Jahan Ara, Shah Jahan's eldest daughter and Aurangzeb's sister.

Empires are built and held on force, its most visible and potent instrument being the army. The Mughal army from Akbar to Shah Jahan and Aurangzeb's early term dictated terms to the rest of India; when the twilight of the 17th century had to yet to set in, it realized that it was a defeated force. Nowhere was this more evident than in Assam, Rajasthan and finally the Deccan; it were the Mughals that recoiled from their foes and not the other way round. Aurangzeb, who in his heyday was known for not yielding an inch, kept chastising his sons in letter after letter, in a desperate attempt to turn the tide of fate. The Mughal Empire reached a point where it was ripe for either disarray or dissolution.

The complexity of Aurangzeb as an individual is by no means limited to the political realm. It spans his personal, religious and cultural outlook, which forms the subject of this study.

Intelligence, Shrewdness—and Poor Judgment

The sixth offspring of Mughal Emperor Shahabuddin Muhammad Khurram Shah Jahan and his wife Begum Arjumand Banoo—more known in history as Mumtaz Mahal—Muhiuddin Mohammad Aurangzeb was unusual in several respects. Aurangzeb was born on October 24, 1618 (15 Ziqada, 1027, AH) at Dahod in Gujarat when the then Mughal Emperor Jahangir was on his way from Gujarat to Agra. Jahangir had just suppressed an attempted revival of the Ahmednagar sultanate by Malik Ambar. The emperor's son Prince Khurram (Shah Jahan) and his wife Mumtaz were part of this royal entourage on its way to the Mughal capital. Aurangzeb's birth could not be immediately celebrated at the place of his birth in a style befitting India's ruling family; a grander commemoration had to wait until the royal party reached Ujjain, the capital of the province of Malwa, which neighbours Gujarat.

Aurangzeb was noted for his courage from his early age. He was also endowed with intelligence, sharp thinking ability and an excellent memory. His life till the age of ten was not a settled one. His father Khurram's relationship with Emperor Jahangir was not a happy one. Under the heady influence of his beautiful but imperious wife Nur Jahan, Jahangir deprived Prince Khurram of his royal titles and fiefdoms, also driving him into rebellion. Shah Jahan's revolt against his father did not yield fruit and after sustaining a defeat at Bilochpura (near Agra) in 1623, he had to flee to current-day Telangana, Orissa and Bengal, then turning to Jaunpur in Uttar Pradesh en route to the Deccan. Shah Jahan was finally forced to submit to his father, but his pardon came at a price. He had to place his eldest son Dara Shikoh and third son Aurangzeb in Jahangir's custody at Lahore in the year 1626. This effectively meant that Empress Nur Jahan would be in charge of their fate for their period of glorified captivity. It was only after Jahangir passed away the following year and Shah Jahan ascended the Mughal throne—in a bloody saga in which Khurram murdered his brother Shaharyar and Khusrau (earlier), cousins Tahmuras and Hoshang, sons of Daniyal Mirza (Emperor Akbar's third son) and nephews Dawar and Garshasp (sons of Shah Jahan's formerly executed brother Prince Khusrau) and imprisoned his stepmother Nur Jahan in Lahore—that he was able to free his sons from their captivity. Any semblance of a normal adolescence for Aurangzeb thus arrived only with palace intrigue and fratricide, his childhood having being consumed in confinement. Intrigue and fratricide went on shape him for the rest of his life.

Aurangzeb's life was somewhat settled by the time he was ten, after these tumultuous couple of years of tussle between his father and grandfather. The young prince's early education, in keeping with his Sunni family's tradition, was strictly Islamic. One Sadullah Khan, who rose to be a *wazir* (minister) of Shah Jahan, was one of Aurangzeb's teachers. One Mir Mohammad Hashim, who had spent twelve years in Mecca and Medina studying his religion's theology, became Aurangzeb's tutor and remained in his service till the end of Shah Jahan's reign.

His natural keenness of mind drove Aurangzeb to grasp what he read and learnt. He turned out to be a thorough memorizer of both the Qur'an and the Hadith, mastering them both. The *Masir-e-Alamgiri* or *Alamgirnama* says that he could quote readily from both. He was a scholar of Arabic and Persian, which he could speak fluently and write in. Growing up in Agra, Delhi plus occasional visits to Lahore, the language he was familiar with was the Hindi of that age, namely, Brajbhasha-infused Hindi, which Aurangzeb could speak with remarkable fluency. He could also recite popular sayings in Hindi readily. Though Persian was the Mughal court's language, much work, even in the private lives of the ruling dynasty, was conducted in Hindi. Later in his youth when he had to serve in Kandahar in Afghanistan and Balkh in Central Asia, Aurangzeb also acquired mastery over the Turkish language, or Chagtai Turki to be precise.

In written language too, Aurangzeb was much more endowed than his predecessors on the Mughal throne. He could write Arabic in a quick *naskh* hand, and would write out the Quran, considered an act of piety among Muslims. Two copies of Aurangzeb's handwritten Quran were presented to Mecca and Medina, richly bound and illuminated, while a third is preserved at the tomb of Nizamuddin Auliya in Delhi. It is said that some other copies of the Aurangzeb-written Quran exist in some unknown corners of India.

While Aurangzeb's copying of the Quran might be of interest to a lot of academicians and pursuers of history, the emperor laboured at it, spending much time not because of any aesthetic bent of mind, but because he considered it sinful to "eat the bread of idleness" and was a stickler to the principle of having to earn one's bread through labour. Aside of his Quran-copying, Aurangzeb also used to stitch caps himself, which would be sold and the earnings ostensibly be recorded as the emperor's breadwinning work. Admirable as this might appear to puritan and panegyrist, this penchant for clericalism defined Aurangzeb for his practically his entire life.

Not that Aurangzeb's Quranic exertions lent him any literary taste. The Mughal emperor wrote letters and engaged in regular correspondence till the very end of his life, also quoting verses to lay stress on his communication. But Aurangzeb was no lover of poetry or literature. His historian says in the *Masir-e-Alamgiri* (pages 531-532): "The Emperor did not like to hear useless poetry, still less laudatory remarks. But he made an exception in favour of poems containing good counsel". It wasn't poetry alone he had a disdain for; music drew his ire, as it is deemed 'un-Islamic'. A mere ten years after coming to power in 1658, Aurangzeb banished music from his court. He however, had a liking for fine chinaware, and bowls, cups and chalices made of these came aplenty to him in the form of presents from noblemen and other royal courts. Aurangzeb however, had no liking for any fine architecture. No edifice of any architectural grandness came up in his tenure of fifty years. The mosques that came up under his watch were mostly erected on the ruins of desecrated or destroyed Hindu temples, most notably Mathura and Kashi (Varanasi), and even today poison socio-political and civilizational relations in India to a debilitating degree. But they are certainly not marked for any architectural beauty, not even Aurangzeb's own tomb at Aurangabad in Maharashtra. The mosques were erected to mark his victories, along with the many *sarais* (inns) that came up along the routes he and his army traversed. They however, remain mere structures of brick and mortar which either quickly decayed, or have remained to effect social decay.

Shah Jahan's third son was blessed with a near-photographic memory. Of him it was reputed that he never forgot a face he had once seen, and his ability to remember events and people was remarkable. In intrigues, of the palace kind or otherwise, or in diplomacy overt and covert, Aurangzeb was one formidable adversary as they come in the annals of history.

Theology consumed Aurangzeb, not aesthetics or refinement; in fact, he memorized the entire Quran, quite a remarkable feat. Not unnaturally, Aurangzeb preferred the company of the dervish (Muslim saint) to the intellectual. Intellectualism under his watch would end up as a vulnerable, if not endangered pursuit. So would all other nobler endeavours of life. But as we shall see in subsequent chapters, it was not just lack of intellectualism Aurangzeb suffered from. The sixth Mughal ruler, who ruled over a domain larger than any of his forebears, was exceptionally marked for lack of anything remotely approaching a visionary outlook. While this by itself might be construed as an ordinary enough failing for most rulers who have strode the corridors of time—or have simply marked time, were one to be less charitable—in Aurangzeb's case, his all-too-frequent categorization as a 'Great Mughal' must call this particular attribute into serious question. If Aurangzeb is to be termed a Great Mughal (Sir Jadunath Sarkar in fact, calls him the greatest of the Great Mughals), it might arguably be so for the extent of territory he ruled over and the sheer length of his tenure—half a century. Else, the legacy of ruin and dissolution he left behind belie any notion of greatness.

Aurangzeb, or Alamgir, as he titled himself after grabbing the Mughal throne in 1658, was not lacking in intelligence or shrewdness. Yet, both of these qualities failed to produce in him a great judge of humans or situations. The outcome was the denouement of the empire his ancestor Babar had founded and great-grandfather Akbar had built and expanded.

To be fair, Aurangzeb began his formal reign in 1658 without much of the fanatical religiosity that has become the calling card of his identity today. It might seem ironic today, but Alamgir in office began not with any imperious religious *firman* (royal order), but with remission of taxes; some eighty or so levies and cesses of various kinds. There was a sound and practical reason too, for remitting these taxes, as around 1660-61, there was a famine of intense severity. But this royal order remained only an order, as some leading historians of the age, most notably James Tod (Volume I, page 310) inform us that "the royal prohibition had no effect". Local officials continued to collect all the prohibited taxes for their own benefit. In fact, they exacted more than the previous rates by way of transit duties, with the net result being goods in transit having to pay more than double their cost price. This required closed monitoring of the empire's tax machinery and its workforce, something Aurangzeb's administration was not cut out for. There is little evidence to suggest that Aurangzeb himself was adequately seized of the seriousness of this problem and what long-term debilitating effects this could have on his empire's finances and day-to-day functioning.

Possibly, Aurangzeb's judgment could have been clouded by the fact that wars of conquest launched soon after his ascension began bringing in spoils to fill the royal treasury. The Mughals were successful in annexing Cooch Behar in 1661 and Garhgaon, the capital of the Ahoms in Assam in 1662. Though they failed to nab the Ahom king, the Mughals secured a handsome booty in gold, silver and elephants plus some territory. Such territorial and monetary acquisitions elsewhere swelled the Mughal coffers and Aurangzeb could afford to gloss over the lack of administration in his realm. But all this would prove pyrrhic in the long run. Assam itself could be held for only four years by the Mughals. A Mughal army under Raja Ram Singh, the son of Aurangzeb's ablest general Mirza Raja Jai Singh, was finally defeated at Saraighat in 1667-68. The Mughals lost Guwahati too, to the Ahoms in 1681. Aurangzeb's famed military shrewdness proved a failure here.

Civil administration had broken down in the Mughal domain during the war of succession launched by Shah Jahan's four sons for the Mughal throne, in which Aurangzeb clinched the issue at the Battle of Samugarh against his eldest brother Dara Shikoh in May 1658. Unfettered local officials of the Mughal Empire would oppress the weak, unleashing disorder and turmoil in many places. The problem was a plain and simple matter of cultivators of crops and fruits losing their produce to robbery by the powerful or the ravages of war, which again were wrought by the imperial army on the march and those who resisted it.

A brief look at the Mughal system of revenue collection that prevailed in Aurangzeb's time would be instructive to understand how an unjust system was further aggravated. Inland transit duties could accurately be categorized as the lubricant of the Mughal machinery, particularly its war machine. The nature of these duties levied reveals somewhat the kind of revenue administration in force at the time of Aurangzeb's coming to power. At every ford, ferry, hill pass or provincial boundary, a toll equivalent to one-tenth of the value of goods was exacted on the merchandise that passed through these points. This was meant as a fee for guarding those routes. But this soon opened the gates for unauthorized exaction of toll, which led to oppression. In popular parlance, a *raahdaar*, meaning guard of the road, soon degenerated into a *raahjan*, meaning a brigand. *Raahjani* or dacoity still remains a term of common use in Hindi. Agra, Lahore, Delhi, and Burhanpur, the larger cities of the empire, had a duty called *pandari*. This was levied on all items of food and drink brought for sale from outside.

It is estimated by Sir Jadunath Sarkar and other historians that these major cities of the empire could shell out 25 lakh rupees a year from the *raahdaari*. This excludes the collections made under the supervision of the zamindars and jagirdars. Then there were the perks of the underling officials of the Mughal system. The total loss to India's business class annually could easily be put at around a crore of rupees, or 25 per cent of the gross land revenue of the state. This was the state of affairs when Aurangzeb came to power, and little of his measures succeeded in mitigating the situation. Worse, his alternatives centered not around improving governance or increasing administrative efficacy, but raising the state's revenue through conquests or puritanical and religious impositions on Hindus.

It can well be argued that Aurangzeb tried to begin the administrative chapter of his reign with all the right intentions. Among his first acts in governance was the abolition of the *raahdari* and *pandari* levies, which to put it bluntly, were plain thievery by his officials. But herein lies the rub. Such abolitions are rendered no more than lip service unless attended by the punitive might of the state. This early Aurangzebian *firman* called for sustained and meticulous follow-up. The emperor issued—not orders, but *requests*—to zamindars and jagirdars to implement this order in their respective domains. It was done, at least for a period of time and also allowed a freer flow of corn and grains to places adversely affected by the scarcity, also leading to a fall in grain prices. This happier state of affairs lasted till about 1660-61, but there was scanty rainfall for a succession of years thereafter. If any major disaster did not follow, it was only because dearth of foodgrains in one place was met by transferring surplus to other places.

But none of these measures served to strengthen the administration or even make it sound. The *Zawabit-e-Alamgiri*, a revenue officers' guide book, written around 1691, makes mention of the various cesses abolished by Aurangzeb. Though the Mughal historian Khafi Khan says that about eighty levies were abolished by the emperor, he actually mentions only fourteen of them by their various names. Khafi Khan, who has no pretensions to be being a neutral or unbiased historian, himself admits that despite Aurangzeb's *firman* of cess-abolishment, these continued to be illegally levied in the Mughal Empire's far-off provinces. Obviously, the local underlings had no fear of this secret defiance of their master's orders. The panegyrist Khafi Khan himself admits: "Of all the sovereigns of the House of Timur—nay, of all the sovereigns of Delhi—no one, since Sikandar Lodi, has ever been apparently so distinguished for devotion, austerity and justice. In courage, long suffering and sound judgment, he was unrivalled. But from reverence for the injunctions of the law, he did not make use of punishment and without punishment, the administration of a country cannot be maintained. Dissensions had risen among his nobles through rivalry. So, every plan and project that he formed came to little good; and every enterprise which he undertook was long in execution and failed in its object" (*The Oxford History of India by* Vincent A. Smith; page 425).

There we are. An emperor who had not the slightest hesitation in employing brutal force to slaughter his brothers on the way to the throne, depose his father and throw him into cruel confinement, and unleash religious persecution of his non-Muslim subjects in myriad ways, was either unable or unwilling to act with firmness in matters of governance.

The reasons for such poor judgment in even mundane administration, let alone governance, are not difficult to identify, although no historian seems to have particularly dwelt on this. Aurangzeb followed, to a great degree, a policy of favouring Muslims in the employment of various posts and responsibilities of his kingdom. While this made no difference as far as matters of theology or religion might be concerned, no state administration, or even that of a large firm, can run on the basis of such policies. In Aurangzeb's empire, the impartial handling of finances was a task beyond his co-religionists and depended on Hindu officials, particularly the traditional mercantile castes. It had been a tested co-existence put in place by his great-grandfather Akbar.

Alamgir, blindsided by his religiosity, paid little attention to this crucial aspect. Nor was he able to exercise any sound judgment as to the ill-effects such a deleterious policy might have in the long run. At every interval of his reign, we find Aurangzeb plunging the Mughal Empire into long-drawn out wars, which drew initial success, but were disastrous failures viewed in both strategic and military terms. As we shall see, Aurangzeb's lack of judgment went on to write the finis of the empire itself.

CHAPTER 03

BIGOTRY BEGAN IN BUNDELKHAND

When one looks at the career and conduct of Muhiuddin Mohammad Aurangzeb, far too often called a "Great Mughal", one is struck by a notable factor—this 'Great' Mughal was devoid of any vision. Not that his predecessors or successors, with the arguable exception of Jalaluddin Akbar, were any better.

The lack of any overarching vision of this supposedly great Mughal becomes evident from Aurangzeb's very first stint at holding any significant office. This was his persecution of war against the Bundela Rajputs in 1635; a campaign the prince was tasked with when was only 16 years of age. The Bundelas had grown in power during the times of Mughal emperors Jahangir and Shah Jahan, Aurangzeb's grandfather and father respectively. Bir Singh Bundela, chieftain of this clan, had been Jahangir's confidante and had been entrusted by the Mughal emperor to slay Abul Fazl, a favourite minister of Jahangir's father the great Akbar. There was no favour Jahangir could refuse this Bundela, who grew in wealth and power sufficient to be able to levy contributions from neighbouring princes, on his own authority. Clearly, the Mughal administrations of both Jahangir and Shah Jahan had grown weaker, though the opulence of the court retained its sheen.

Bir Singh Bundela's son Jhujhar Singh had risen against Shah Jahan, raiding and plundering Mughal domains south of Agra. Constrained to act against him, Shah Jahan sent a 10-000 strong Mughal army with 1,000 cavalry to be commanded by three generals but under the authority of Prince Aurangzeb, who was instructed to remain far from actual battle. The rebel Bundelas were overpowered after fierce resistance, in which the Mughal army suffered not inconsiderable casualties.

Aurangzeb played little role in the actual fighting, but was much active in making two sons and one grandson of the fallen Jhujhar Singh captive and forcibly converting them to Islam. Another son Udaybhan and a minister Shyam Dawa, who refused to give up their religion to save their lives were murdered in cold blood. Religion taking precedence over anything else, including politics, was to become the defining characteristic of Aurangzeb's life and reign. The Bundela War was just the beginning, but the young Muhiuddin lost no time in demonstrating this particular trait. The Bundela resistance under Jhujhar Singh had been fierce; in fact, the Bundela War was a protracted one, stretching to two years. Those among Jhujhar's womenfolk who were unfortunate to be captured alive were forcibly deprived of their religion and then thrown into the hellishness of the slavery of the Mughal harem. Chivalry to women was not known to the alien jihadi invaders, and Aurangzeb during the first military campaign of his life only reinforced this.

Aurangzeb was not done with his exploits in the Bundela territory yet; he entered its capital Orchha, sent request to his father Shah Jahan to visit the newly conquered domain at Datia and Orchha, the capital of the Bundelas. Here, Shah Jahan ordered the demolition of a lofty and massive temple that had been built by the late Bir Singh Bundela. This grand temple wasn't the only Hindu place of worship to suffer Islamic desecration. Aurangzeb would go on to repeat such deeds throughout the domain he would later usurp.

If this typical jihadi treatment meted out to defeated foes was intended to stamp out the Bundelas forever, it must be stated without hesitation that Aurangzeb's first military outing sowed the seeds of a spectacular failure. The Mughal prince showed zilch inclination to win over the Bundelas through any act of magnanimity, instead inviting the emperor to preside over a jihadi destruction of ancient Hindu temples. Politically and militarily too, Aurangzeb displayed a remarkable lack of vision. The Bundelas suffered greatly under the marauding Mughals, with their king murdered, womenfolk enslaved and sent off to Shah Jahan's harem and sons of the fallen king either converted or slaughtered. Yet, this failed to cow them into submission. They regrouped under a brave warrior chieftain Champat Rai of Mahoba, crowned Jhujhar Singh's infant son Prithviraj their new ruler and kept up the war against the Mughals—a war that would continue till the end of the 17th century and culminate in the first half of the 18th only with the complete effacement of Mughal rule from Bundelkhand. It was the brave Champat Rai's son, the intrepid Chhatrasal—who also went on to gain the tutelage of that nemesis of the Mughals, Chhatrapati Shivaji— who was destined to write the final chapter in this long drawn-out saga. The credit for the end of Mughal rule in Bundelkhand belongs to Aurangzeb, whose roots he laid in the first assignment of his career.

The Bundela War, as mentioned above, was Aurangzeb's first outing in as military campaign for his father's empire. He was only seventeen when Shah Jahan sent him to Bundelkhand to subdue this clan of Rajputs who had risen against the Mughal Empire. As such, this was supposed to be a military campaign in which the young Mughal prince would be blooded. Contemporary Mughal accounts of the Bundelkhand campaign are glowing in praise for Aurangzeb, but the fact is that the prince himself played no significant part in the fighting. Emperor Shah Jahan had appointed him the nominal chief of the expedition, but he was to stay in the rear during the course of the campaign. Three Mughal generals were in charge of the actual conduct of the hostilities against the Bundelas. They were to advise Aurangzeb about the military operation, but had to act only in consultation with him. In other words, Aurangzeb was given the decisive say. But if this campaign was intended to be Aurangzeb's baptism by fire, an unbiased evaluation has to be that this 'baptism' was performed at quite a safe distance from the fire. Throughout the conduct of hostilities against the rebellious Bundelas, his generals kept Aurangzeb miles behind the actual fighting lines.

The customary eulogies aside, the only achievement for Aurangzeb was a first-hand experience in implementing his iconoclastic puritanism. But it was a campaign that that would one day rebound on the Mughal Empire itself. More telling is the fact that Aurangzeb had implemented a jihadi doctrine he had already internalized; namely, desecration of a beaten enemy's religion, womenfolk and all sacred space, but had failed in evolving any military doctrine that might have stood the Mughal armed edifice in good stead.

Thus, anti-non-Muslim religious bias and indeed, cruelty was on display in the young Aurangzeb's very first military campaign, which was the war against the Rajputs of the Bundela clan, as they had risen against the Mughal Empire in Shah Jahan's time.

The cause of the Bundela Rajputs' grievance against the Mughal Empire was Mughal Emperor Shah Jahan's military expedition against Bir Singh's son Jhujhar Singh whose supposed offence was leaving for his kingdom without the emperor's permission (Sir Jadunath Sarkar; *History of Aurangzeb*). A 35,000 strong Mughal army sent to teach the Bundelas raided and plundered Bundela territory, forcing Jhujhar Singh to submit, but the seeds of confrontation between the Mughals and Bundelas had been sown. The Bundelas under Jhujhar could not be kept subdued for long and Shah Jahan had to send another 20,000 strong Mughal army with 1,000 cavalry to be commanded by three generals who were placed under the authority of Prince Aurangzeb. Shah Jahan's third son was to remain at a distance from the scene of actual hostilities. The rebel Bundelas could be overpowered only after fierce resistance, and the invading Mughal army did not get off lightly.

But Aurangzeb's own role in actual combat in his career's first military operation was minimal. Jhujhar Singh himself fell in battle, but his two sons and one grandson were unfortunate in being captured alive, following which Aurangzeb became quite active in forcibly converting them to Islam. The fallen Jhujhar had another son Udaybhan and a minister Shyam Dawa; both steadfastly refused to convert to Islam to save their lives. As we have noted, they were murdered in cold blood.

The genocide of the resisting Bundelas was not the only jihadi act on Aurangzeb's part. The Bundelas under Jhujhar Singh had demonstrated vicious resistance. The Mughal war to punish Bundelkhand turned out to be a protracted one, stretching to two years. The Mughals, Aurangzeb particularly, vented their anger against not only their foes on the battlefield but against Bundela womenfolk too. Those women of the Jhujhar family who were unfortunate to be captured alive were forcibly converted to Islam and then thrown into the hell of the Mughal harem. Chivalry to womenfolk of a defeated enemy is not part of the jihadi mentality, and Aurangzeb during his first ever military campaign underscored this fact in a forcible way. Religious persecution became the defining characteristic of Aurangzeb's life and reign.

The Bundela War was only the beginning. The young Muhiuddin, who was quick in demonstrating this particular trait of his nature, would go on to make it his signature tune in life.

Slaughtering steadfast Hindus who refused to bow and dishonouring and enslaving their womenfolk weren't the only exploits of Aurangzeb in the Bundela territory. Under him, the victorious Mughal army entered its capital Orccha; Aurangzeb sent word to his father Shah Jahan, requesting to visit the newly conquered domain at Datia and Orchha. Here, Shah Jahan ordered the demolition of a lofty and massive temple that had been built by clan's patriarch, the late Bir Singh Bundela. This grand temple wasn't the only Hindu place of worship to suffer Islamic desecration. Aurangzeb would go on to repeat such deeds throughout the domain he would later usurp.

Aurangzeb's first military outing of his life thus saw the implementation of a jihadi doctrine he had already internalized. This doctrine mandated the desecration of a beaten enemy's religion, womenfolk and all sacred spaces.

CHAPTER 04

RELIGION SCORED OVER GOVERNANCE

Gujarat and the Deccan

Towards the closing years of Akbar's reign, the Mughal Empire's frontiers had begun extending beyond the river Narmada into the south. Akbar had conquered Ahmadnagar in 1600, although Mughal hold over the Deccan remained tenuous at best. The Deccan was too large to be fully conquered, leave alone properly governed. Akbar might have militarily overwhelmed the old kingdoms, but its local officials refused to bow to the command of his dynasty. They either set up puppet princes as a smokescreen to effect the pursuit of their own ambitions, or in the case of the sultanates of Bijapur and Golconda, even annexed territories in their immediate neighbourhood.

The Mughal foray into the South was also not a smooth one. Central and southern India had been overrun by the earlier Delhi Sultanates but had regained their independence relatively quickly. Akbar had spent much of his reign in conquering and pacifying northern and northwestern India, including Afghanistan, though Kabul and Kandahar were never completely absorbed. Mughal relations with the Afghan tribes and territory were ridden with conflict and animosity throughout their history—the Mughals themselves had barely escaped being extinguished by the Afghans led by a Hindu king Hemachandra in the Second Battle of Panipat (1556). On the other hand, Afghans remained in perennial conflict with the great empire of Persia; Mughal rule over Kandahar and Kabul during the time of Akbar, Jahangir and Shah Jahan, fragile though, allowed the Persians to be free enough to keep a potentially dangerous Ottoman Empire to its northwest, at bay. Persia for its part deterred any nomadic invasion from Central Asia, allowing the Mughals in India to devote more energies and resources to a southward expansion.

But southward expansion for the Mughals was never easy, and in the subsequent turn of events, turned out to be their grave. Jahangir's advance into the Deccan was not only stalled, but also beaten back. A capable leader and administrator Malik Ambar rose in the Deccan, rising to greatness. Ambar attacked and defeated the Mughals in 1620, driving them as far northwards as Burhanpur (in Madhya Pradesh today). This was a crisis severe enough to dispatch the then prince Shah Jahan to the Deccan with a strong army. Shah Jahan's vigorous campaign against Bijapur and Golconda made them submit, but only after a lengthy effort. The Mughals employed ruthless tactics against the civilian populace, but though Bijapur was forced to yield politically, the opposition the Mughals had stoked refused to die. Aurangzeb, during his governorship of the Deccan, would only intensify it, in fact, helping to write the epitaph of the empire itself. Most notably, for Shah Jahan's Mughals, one of the toughest adversaries to crack was Shahji Bhonsale, the most trusted warrior and general of the Bijapur Adilshahi sultanate, whose son Shivaji would one day prove to be Mughals' doom.

However, Shah Jahan's siege in the Deccan ended with treaties and agreements with both Bijapur and Golconda. Their partial submission to the Mughals barred further southward aggression on the part of Aurangzeb, who was authorized by his father to enrich himself by extending his dominion over other parts of Maharashtra. His elder brother Shuja (Shah Jahan's second son) had failed to capture a fortress in the Deccan when deputed there in 1632. Aurangzeb pressed on vigorously, but his zeal was unaccompanied by any minimal outlook for better governance in the Deccan. Instead, his soldiers and commanders freely indulged in plunder of the properties and sometimes womenfolk of the soldiers of the Bijapur and Golconda sultanates that had been forced to cede territory and rights to the Mughals. Kheloji Bhonsale, a cousin of Shahji Bhonsale and a proud and fearless warrior of the Nizamshahi sultanate, was harassed and later murdered. These were among the many incidents in Aurangzeb's viceroyalty of the Deccan from 1636 to 1644, which ended in disgrace and dismissal. Historians, both of the Mughal court and latter-days ones, are divided over the reasons for this sacking, but Aurangzeb's own letters say that he 'resigned' in protest at his father's incessant partiality to Dara Shikhoh, the eldest of the brothers, and Dara's persistent hostility.

Aurangzeb then was given charge of Gujarat in 1644, where he remained till 1647. The province was rife with turbulence and Aurangzeb in a span of less than two years displayed both firmness and administrative capability, particularly in dealing with robber tribes and rebels. In 1544, he converted a newly built temple of Chintaman into a mosque *(Mirat-i-Ahmadi*, page 222). He also reportedly, desecrated the temple by slaughtering a cow in it (source: *Gazetteer of the Bombay Presidency* (Volume I, Part I, page 280).

Central Asia and Afghanistan

Aurangzeb was soon handling the empire's Afghan affairs, and a war in the Central Asian province of Balkh, where his younger brother Mohammad Murad Baksh, Shah Jahan's youngest son, had left without imperial consent after being sent there. Aurangzeb was given a sizeable army by Shah Jahan, of about 25,000, but found himself fighting a guerilla war against the Uzbeks and Turks of Balkh and Badakshan. In the end, it was Aurangzeb's religious puritanism that carried the day. In the middle of a battle, he got down from his elephant to perform his mandatory *namaz*; the enemy army of Bukhara and its king were astonished, with the Bukhara ruler Abdul Aziz exclaiming: "To fight with such a man is to court one's ruin".

But such displays of religiosity notwithstanding, the Mughal losses in Central Asia were enormous. 10,000 of its 25,000 strong army sent on this campaign perished, along with elephants, horses and camels. Many died in the rain and snow. The Mughal Empire expended over four crore rupees over a period of two years. Its army was trained for conventional war, while the Uzbeks and Turks fought by no rules. Not surprisingly, the Mughals suffered retreat at many places. The outcome of this war was at best a stalemate. Aurangzeb's obstinacy in continuing the fighting only made many in the Mughal army sick of their Central Asian stay which they looked upon as an exile; the homesick men wanted to return to India as soon as possible. Some high-ranking commanders in the Mughal army actually worked to thwart Aurangzeb, as they feared that any Mughal success would only whet Aurangzeb's or Shah Jahan's appetite for further inroads into Central Asia and the troops would have to stay on in Transoxiana for years. On the other hand, a failure would hasten their return back home. But even in retreat, the Mughals had no peace, constantly harassed and plundered by the Balochs, Hazaras and Uzbeks. At the end of Shah Jahan's Balkh campaign, of which Aurangzeb was given charge of, not an inch of territory was added to the Mughal Empire nor was any change of regime effected.

Map 3 : Mughal empire's northern boundaries in 1730s (Nadir Shah time)

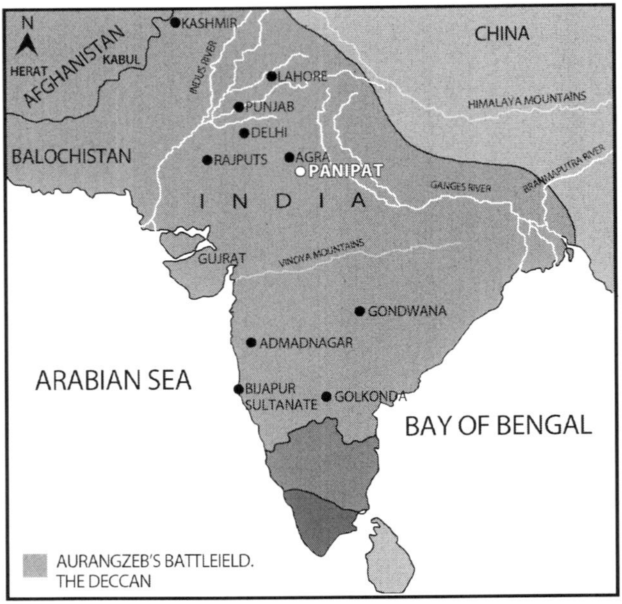

More serious to the Mughals was the loss of Kandahar. This was more damaging than just the loss of territory. Aurangzeb's ancestor Babar had first captured its fortress when he had made Afghanistan his base after being ousted from his native Fergana. It had fallen to the marauding Persians in Akbar's time although he had been able to retrieve it, only for his son and successor Jahangir to lose it. Shah Jahan had been fortunate as the then Persian ruler of Kandahar Ali Mardan Khan surrendered it to the Mughals in 1638 and himself entered the service of the Mughal Empire as a noble. But this was a temporary truce between the Mughals and Persians, as the latter launched a fresh offensive in 1648, forcing Shah Jahan to send Aurangzeb to relieve the beleaguered fortress.

Aurangzeb, for all his soldierly qualities and military acumen, proved spectacularly unsuccessful in saving Kandahar. He led an army without much artillery to take on his adversaries whereas the Persians, owing to their long periods of war with the Turkish Ottoman Empire had mastered the use of large cannons and guns. Kandahar fell to the Persians in February 1649, with Aurangzeb proving unable to save it, despite leading counterattacks between May and September that year. Mughal prestige could not countenance such a loss and Aurangzeb was once again tasked in 1652 with recovering Kandahar. He commanded an army of some 50,000 to 60,000 troops and besides, spent close to 2 crore rupees in his endeavour to wrest back Kandahar, all to no avail. Kandahar was lost to the Mughal Empire and with this defeat, Mughal prestige took a serious blow. Worse, the Mughal Empire for the rest of its existence would live in fear of Persia, also making Afghanistan a festering problem for the Indian subcontinent that continues till this day.

This was not only a military defeat for Aurangzeb; it also led to him falling out of favour with Emperor Shah Jahan, whose acrimonious correspondence with his third son summed it up: "I greatly wonder how you could not capture the fort in spite of such preparations". Shah Jahan went on to question his competence to do the job and ordered him to proceed to the Deccan. Aurangzeb's loss of his military reputation in the desolate Afghan mountains only served to further whet his aggression. But it also further eroded his reasoning, which would go on to have debilitating consequences for the empire itself.

Aurangzeb had earlier been called to lead the Mughal army in Balkh in Central Asia and later Kandahar in Afghanistan, expeditions that lasted from 1647 to 1652. Balkh and Kandahar were costly failures from the point of view of not only Mughal prestige but also India's political influence and military prestige. Some battlefield successes in Balkh notwithstanding, the Mughal army under Aurangzeb was continually harassed and punished by the guerilla warfare conducted by the Uzbeks and Turkomans of Bukhara and Balkh. About the only achievement of note for Aurangzeb was to win the admiration of the opposing Bukhara troops and their king Abdul Aziz, for his act of offering his customary namaz right in the middle of the battlefield in June 1647, spreading out his prayer mat between the two armies. The Bukhara army halted hostilities and their king proclaimed out loud, "To fight with such a man is to court one's ruin".

While his act of Islamic zealotry might have been a proud advertisement for his faith, drawing the drooling admiration of his co-religionist adversaries in Central Asia, it did absolutely nothing to raise either the Mughal army's morale in that long, grueling and fruitless campaign, nor could add any territory to the Mughal Empire. The Uzbek war against the Mughals had taken on the form of a national uprising, not a mere trial of strength between two rulers or commanders. The Uzbeks did not depend on any individual leader in their confrontation with the Mughals. Peace negotiations were imperative if the war-weary Mughals were to return home with any modicum of self-respect. The winter of 1647 was approaching and the Mughals were short of food, supplies and winter clothing.

Aurangzeb's Islamic zealotry failed to mitigate any of these problems the imperial army encountered. His army endured untold hardships on its retreat to Afghanistan in the south, forced to pass throw snow-filled mountain passes paved with hardened ice; many animals and men perished on the way back. The Mughal army lost 10,000 lives including men and animals. The Mughal treasury expended four crore rupees in two years in Central Asia, obtaining a revenue of Rs.22 lakhs only. For all his Islamic fervor, Aurangzeb failed in adding an inch to the Mughal domain, or even replacing an incumbent ruler with an ally or compliant vassal.

The failure of the Central Asian adventure was followed by an even costly failure in Afghanistan, where the Mughal army under Aurangzeb strove to defeat Shia Persia under Shah Abbas II. It was a trial of strength between India under the Mughals and Persia for control of Kabul and Kandahar, and indeed Afghanistan. Aurangzeb not only failed to dislodge the Persians from Kandahar but also ended his siege in defeat. The Mughal defeat in Afghanistan in 1652 was more than a military defeat. It meant the loss of Afghanistan to the Indian empire and made Persia forever a constant and feared adversary of the Mughals.

THE AFGHAN MESS—AURANGZEB'S CONTRIBUTION

CHAPTER 05

It would come as a surprise to many that the political, military and religious sectarian imbroglio in Afghanistan, India's neighbour, has had its roots in the politics and internecine rivalry of the Mughal Empire in India, which effectively lasted during the 16th and 17th centuries. In particular, one Mughal had made a dubious contribution to the handling of the affairs of Afghanistan that continues to have ripple effects in the Indian subcontinent and indeed the globe, in the form of the seemingly intractable Afghan problem. That individual was the sixth Mughal Emperor Aurangzeb.

The Persian Safavid Empire, which ruled Persia (modern-day Iran) from 1501 to 1736 had territorial claims over Kandahar since the reign of Persian emperor Shah Tamasp (1514-1576). The second Mughal ruler Humayun, Babar's son and Akbar's father, was overthrown by the Afghan ruler Sher Shah Suri in 1540 and had to flee India. Humayun was given not only refuge and protection by Shah Tahmasp, but also support in his bid to win back his lost throne in India. Shah Tamasp supplied Humayun with precious cavalry. This support was not however, free; Humayun was forced to allow Safavid Persia to capture Kandahar in Afghanistan. Not only that, Humayun was also compelled to wear a twelve-pointed conical cap, which symbolized the Shia sect of Islam. The Mughals were orthodox Sunnis by faith; given the Shia-Sunni conflict, which began with Islam's founding, this was an insolent challenge to Mughal orthodoxy. Yet, Humayun had no choice but to comply. But the empire of Persia would go on to cast a very long and lasting shadow over the Mughals.

The Mughal saga in Afghanistan began with the arrival of the Turkic invader Babar, who driven out of his native Fergana in Samarqand in Central Asia, seized Kabul en route to his incursion into India. Kabul and Kandahar remained in Mughal possession till Humayun's time. Succeeding Humayun in 1556, Akbar was preoccupied with domestic concerns and did not leave his capital Fatehpur Sikri on a military campaign until 1581, when Punjab was again invaded by his brother, Mirza Muhammad Hakim. Akbar expelled his brother to Kabul and this time pressed on, determined to end the threat from

Muhammad Hakim once and for all. To spur on his Mughal army soldiers to fight in a cold and inhospitable Afghanistan, Akbar provided them with pay eight months in advance. In August 1581, Akbar was successful in seizing Kabul and taking up residence at his grandfather Babur's old citadel. His brother had fled into the mountains. Akbar left Kabul in the hands of his sister, Bakht-un-Nisa Begum, and returned to India. He pardoned his brother, who took up the facto charge of the Mughal administration in Kabul; Bakht-un-Nisa continued to be the official governor. A few years later, in 1585, Muhammad Hakim died and Kabul passed into the hands of Akbar once again, and was officially incorporated as a province of the Mughal Empire.

But this Kabul expedition was just the beginning of a long period of engagement, often fruitless and debilitating, over the northern frontiers of the Mughal Empire. For thirteen years, beginning in 1585, Akbar remained in the north, shifting his capital to Lahore in the Punjab while dealing with challenges from beyond the Khyber Pass. The gravest threat came from the Uzbeks, the tribe that had driven his grandfather, Babur, out of their native Central Asia. They had seized Badakhshan and Balkh from Akbar's distant Timurid relatives, and whose Uzbek troops now posed a serious challenge to the northwestern frontiers of the Mughal Empire. The Afghan tribes on the border were also restless, partly on account of the hostility of the Yusufzais of Bajaur and Swat, and partly owing to the activity of a new religious Roshaniyya sect. The Uzbeks were also known to be subsidizing the Afghan marauders.

In 1586, Akbar negotiated a pact with the Uzbeks in which the Mughals agreed to remain neutral during the Uzbek invasion of Safavid-held Khorasan. In return, the Uzbeks agreed to refrain from supporting, subsidizing, or offering refuge to the Afghan tribes hostile to the Mughals. Thus freed, Akbar began a series of campaigns to pacify the Yusufzais and other rebels. Akbar ordered Zain Khan to lead an expedition against the Afghan tribes. Raja Mahesh Das, more known as Birbal, famous for his wisdom and wit, and a renowned minister in Akbar's court, was also given military command. This Mughal expedition turned out to be a disaster, and on its retreat from the mountains, Birbal and his entourage were ambushed and killed by the Yuzufzai Afghans at the Malandarai Pass in February 1586. Akbar immediately fielded new armies to reinvade the Yusufzai lands under the command of Raja Todar Mal. Over the next six years, the Mughals somehow contained the Yusufzais in the mountain valleys, and forced the submission of many chiefs in Swat and

Bajaur. Dozens of forts were built and occupied to secure the region. Akbar during his reign managed to retain and clamp firm military control over the Afghan tribes.

Despite his pact with the Uzbeks, Akbar nurtured a secret hope of reconquering Central Asia from today's Afghanistan. However, Badakshan and Balkh remained firmly part of the Uzbek dominions. There was only a transient occupation of the two provinces by the Mughals under his grandson, Shah Jahan, in the mid-17th century. Akbar managed to subdue the last of the rebellious Afghan tribes by 1600. The Roshaniyya movement was firmly suppressed. The Afridi and Orakzai tribes, which had risen up under the Roshaniyyas, were subjugated, with the movement's leaders captured and driven into exile. Mughal rule over the present Afghanistan was made secure.

But Afghanistan would not let Mughal India rest in peace. Subsequently, conflicts emerged in the region during the reign of Akbar's son and successor Mughal emperor Jahangir. In 1622, taking advantage of the Mughal preoccupation in the southern Deccan, Safavid Persia besieged and captured the fortress of Kandahar. Emperor Jahangir sent his son Khurram (later Shah Jahan) to retake Kandahar. But Kandahar fell to the Persians, which was a serious blow to Mughal prestige.

Both Kabul and Kandahar returned to Mughal control only in 1638, when a Kurdish turncoat Ali Mardan Khan handed Kandahar over to Shah Jahan, who was by then Mughal Emperor. It was considered vital for the Mughal empire that the twin 'gateway-cities' to India, i.e., Kabul and Kandahar, remain under Mughal rule, for two primary reasons. Firstly, the Mughal Empire in India was often viewed by them as a painfully small compensation for the loss of their ancient capital—Samarqand—which they had been driven out of by the Uzbeks. Beyond the internal administrative agendas, the Mughals always kept it a priority to expand the western frontier of the empire. Secondly, Central Asian trade provided the Mughals with warhorses, without which not only would its military forces be incapacitated, but could also potentially spark internal revolts and foreign invasions. Kandahar in particular was at the crossroads of a number of major commercial trade routes in Central Asia. The two cities were thus the subject of deep strategic concern. Jahangir and Shah Jahan downwards, the Mughal military machine had not demonstrated any competence in handling this threat.

In 1639, the armies of Shah Shafi of Persia had captured Bamiyan and were poised to attack Kandahar next. Worse was to come. In February 1646, Shah Jahan dispatched an army of 60,000 to Kabul, and thence to Badakshan and Balkh, with his son Murad Baksh as the commander-in-chief. This was done in support of Nazr Muhammad and his son, Abdul Aziz, against the Timurid ruler of Balkh. However, Nazr Muhammad and Abdul Aziz betrayed the Mughals after the end of the campaign, and fled to Isfahan. Shah Jahan, from 1645 onwards, spent three years in the Punjab and Afghanistan, locked in a tussle with the Safavids. Following Murad's military failure in Afghanistan, the emperor was now forced to send his third son Aurangzeb with a sizeable army to reconquer Kabul and Kandahar.

Mughal India faced a vexing dilemma of how to cobble a victory in Afghanistan without the military exertion that also carried the risks of humiliation when Aurangzeb embarked on his mission to retrieve Afghanistan. Persia loomed as a rival in the northwest. The possession of Kandahar, frequently changing hands between India's Mughals and Persia's Safavids, was actually beneficial to both powers. Mughal India held its restive Afghan citizens, particularly the unruly tribes, in check, which left the Persians free to deal with a dangerous Ottoman Empire to their west. A capable Persia deterred any invasion from Central Asia, thus allowing the Mughals to commit more attention and resources to a southward expansion. Any all-out war with Persia would have been a disaster.

But Safavid control over Kabul and Kandahar had now become a matter of prestige. The subsequent Balkh campaign in 1647 against them was led by Aurangzeb. The increasingly abortive trans-Oxus Mughal adventure had to be somehow salvaged. Shah Jahan had to sack the wayward and failed Murad and appoint Aurangzeb as the governor and commander-in-chief of Balkh and Badakshan. Aurangzeb proceeded from Gujarat and met his father at Lahore before setting forth on his Afghan assignment. He had by then transformed into a disciplined and good soldier, but also an aloof individual, vehement in his reactions to people and situations, full of morbid suspicion and mistrust of just about anyone, but above all, a fanatic religious zealot.

Aurangzeb's posting in Afghanistan did not carry across-the-board approval in his own family. His father Shah Jahan had already gauged this sinister turn in the making of the persona of his third son, but believed he could deploy it for his military objectives. Shah Jahan's eldest son and his favourite Dara Shikhoh, who by now had come to hate Aurangzeb, tried his best to persuade his father to hold Aurangzeb's aggressive proclivities in check. But there was no rescinding of the emperor's decision to send Aurangzeb northwestward.

Balkh and Badakshan, apart from being inhospitable Central Asia terrain, were also poor in monetary takeaways. Neither of these Central Asian provinces could yield the salary of even a third-rate Mughal peer, unlike Gujarat, the Deccan or Bengal. The resources to support any invading army had to be somehow dug out from the Mughal treasury and/or provinces elsewhere in its realm. The Mughal army present in these Central Asian territories had to endure unrelenting guerilla attacks from the Uzbeks, Turks and Mongols, who had formed a coalition against the Mughal invaders. Maintaining regular supplies to Mughal troops from India's plains across the Hindu Kush Mountain ranges was itself a hopeless task. Aurangzeb had already inherited a debacle by the time he stepped in.

If the Central Asian and Afghan mission was a militarily daunting one, Aurangzeb's conduct of his army's operations was hardly flattering. Concerted guerilla attacks forced Aurangzeb to withdraw the Mughal army in order to defend Balkh. As against 60,000 troops assigned to Murad a year earlier, Aurangzeb had only 25,000 fighting men at his disposal. Moreover, the Mughal and Rajput contingents of his army would by no means fight under a unified command. The Rajputs marched and fought under Raja Jai Singh, while the Mughals were led by Ali Mardan Khan. These religious faultlines might have been glossed over in the heat of the campaign, but would go on to prove the undoing of the empire itself one day. Aurangzeb, far from having any plan or outlook to address this issue, couldn't care less.

Despite a superiority of muskets and troop discipline, the Mughals found themselves increasingly harassed by Uzbek guerilla attacks. Only the tendency of the Central Asians to indulge in loot and plunder even amidst battle staved off what would have been a rout for the Mughal army. Aurangzeb's religious fanaticism, more than soldierly skill was on display. On one particular day, during a particularly fierce battle, Aurangzeb spread his prayer rug in the middle of the battlefield to recite his evening prayers. The Bukhara army gazed at this spectacle agape, while their prince Abdul Aziz stopped hostilities saying, "To fight with such a man is to court one's ruin". But while Aurangzeb's overt display of his Islamic zeal might have won the day for the Mughals, the outcome was actually a stalemate. The Central Asians had not crushed the invading Mughal army, but Aurangzeb's troops were exhausted. No one wanted to stay on in Balkh and Badakshan. Mughal prestige demanded that the king of Badakshan sue for peace, but their king Nazar Mohammad Khan himself was afraid of possible treachery from Aurangzeb's side.

Aurangzeb finally negotiated some settlement with Nazar Mohammad's grandsons, but the Mughal retreat from Central Asia became a nightmare. Uzbeks, Turks, Mongols and Hazaras all attacked the retreating Mughals, cutting off their supply lines and freely plundering them. Mughal soldiers fell to their deaths from steep precipices; horses, mules, camels and elephants perished in the snow and ferocious winter. Aurangzeb had to somehow reach Kabul to take up the Kandahar leg of his assignment, but his passage there was made a caravan of hell. More than 10,000 soldiers of the Mughal army perished, not to speak of the animals that died. Aurangzeb expended four crores rupees in this Central Asian campaign, and the end of it, failed to annex an inch of territory, nor effect any change of regime or even gain an ally for the Mughal Empire. He had though, won the admiration of his Mughal soldiers for his indefatigable energy on the battlefield, unrelenting religious zealotry and compelling his soldiers to drive on to the point of exhaustion. While these might be admirable for an individual, in military situations with no clear-cut pathways or solutions, religiosity masquerading as statesmanship or leadership can only postpone the eventual denouement.

A bigger disaster for Mughal India now lay in wait for them at Kandahar.

Till Kandahar firmly remained a part of any empire in Delhi, it was an indispensable first line of defence. Anyone who wishes to be the master of Kabul has to be able to control Kandahar and Herat. Encouraged by the Mughal reversal in Central Asia, Shah Abbas II in December 1648 marched from Isfahan with an army of 40,000. Shah Jahan had been made to believe by his courtiers that any attack by the Persians in winter was unlikely and as a result, the Mughal emperor delayed any counter-preparations. The Mughal army was most unwilling for a harsh and punishing winter march to strengthen Kabul's defences; its march to Kabul was put off till spring 1649. Shah Abbas II however, was not unwilling in the least. He and his host showed up in Kandahar on December 16, 1648.

The Persians were not only highly motivated under their king, whose presence spurred them to great exertion; they were also superior in their artillery, as the Mughal army was to ruefully discover. By February 1649, the Mughal garrison in Kandahar fortress began to lose heart. On the 11th of that month, Kandahar simply capitulated to Shah Abbas II, after a siege of a mere 57 days. The blow to Mughal prestige couldn't be adequately described.

The disaster of the Balkh campaign had already gravely weakened the Mughals' position on the frontier. The short duration of the Kandahar siege—two months—was a testament to the vulnerability of the Mughals in Afghanistan. Emperor Shah Jahan now ordered Aurangzeb to proceed from Multan where he had been appointed governor and wrest Kandahar back from the Persians. Aurangzeb reached Ghazni in April 1649, but a severe shortage of grains and fodder rendered any further advance impossible. He gathered whatever provisions he could to push on, somehow reaching Kandahar in May 1649, to begin a siege of the fort now in Persian hands. His attempted first assault of the fort, by Rajputs under Raja Man Singh of Gwalior, was repulsed by deadly fire from Persian muskets with heavy losses inflicted on the attacking party.

Strangely, although Aurangzeb had come to lay siege to Kandahar to smoke the Persians out, he was woefully lacking in firepower. The train of artillery he had with him was not only inadequate in number of guns but also quite inferior to the artillery the Persians had with them. For instance, the besieging Mughal army did not have a single piece of large cannon; the Persians had many such pieces. Their big guns were manned by skilful gunners, while Aurangzeb's firepower was contemptible in comparison. Mughal attempts to lay mines near the fort were demolished by the Persian defenders, whose bigger cannons blew up any mines before they could be laid close to the fort. Aurangzeb spent over three months near the Kandahar fort, but obeying Shah Jahan's command, retreated from the town. The fierce Afghan winter was thickening and would surely consume his troops.

The failure of the 1649 siege under Aurangzeb threw Shah Jahan into consternation and he vowed to recover Kandahar "whatever the cost". And it was a great cost indeed. In 1652, Aurangzeb once again marched to Kandahar, this time with 60,000 troops and a war chest of two crore rupees. Bigger and larger cannons had been cast in the Mughal armoury, besides bribing Baloch chiefs in order to purchase their loyalty. Battle was joined with the Persians in May 1652, but Aurangzeb's battle formation and plan of attack was such that any element of surprise was completely lost and Persian gunners and musketeers easily picked off the Mughal attackers. Here again, it were the Rajputs who carried the bulk of the assault and bore the maximum casualties. The only faint hope of retaking Kandahar was to somehow reach the fortress' walls and lay some mines, but the excellent Persian artillery would by no means permit that. The Mughal gunners turned out to be bad marksmen, and in some cases ignorant of how to handle big cannons, two of which burst because of overloading and blew their handlers to pieces. The defending Persian artillery rained deadly fire.

By the end of June 1652, it was apparent that the Mughals would never breach Kandahar fort. There was no question of mounting any armed assault before a single breach had been made. By July, Shah Jahan issued orders for abandoning the siege, ignoring Aurangzeb's plea for some more time and fresh preparations. The caustic correspondence between father and son tells it all. Shah Jahan wrote to Aurangzeb: "I wonder how you could not capture the fort in spite of such vast preparations". In his defence, Aurangzeb begged to be allowed to stay on Afghanistan and even offered to give up his viceroyalty of the Deccan now offered to him, to be allowed to participate in any endeavour to retake Kandahar. But Shah Jahan's reply was withering: "Had I considered you competent to take Kandahar, I would not have recalled your army. Every man can perform some work. It is a wise saying that men of experience need no instruction."

To add insult to injury, Dara Shikoh and his partisans did not let go of this opportunity to fill the emperor's ears with anti-Aurangzeb narrative. He had lost the emperor's favour and confidence. A third Mughal siege of Kandahar was launched in 1653 under Dara, which too met with failure. But the fall of Kandahar was no ordinary military defeat; it was a body blow to Mughal prestige, which from that moment in history, lived in dread of Persia. Mughal India would go on to suffer Persian invasions and intervention from then on. More significantly, the Mughal failure under Aurangzeb laid the foundation for what we today refer to as the "Afghan problem", which has stalked Imperial Britain, the Soviet Union and the USA. No small credit goes to Aurangzeb for this.

THE DECCAN

CHAPTER 06

Mughal expansionism into the Deccan, stalled after Akbar's initial foray, now began again under Shah Jahan after his father Jahangir's feeble attempts at enforcing Mughal control over the south of India were stalled and even beaten back by the southern Golconda and Bijapur sultanates. After assuming power on the throne of Delhi, Shah Jahan strove hard to subdue both these sultanates, which after long drawn out shadow wars, settled for a status of semi-vassalhood under the Mughals; while Golconda capitulated first, Bijapur never fully did, forcing the Mughals to agree to a negotiated peace.

After Shah Jahan returned to Agra, he appointed Aurangzeb as the new viceroy of the Deccan in July 1636; a posting that would play no small role in the latter's course of life and also that of the Mughal Empire itself. The Deccan in fact, was destined to become the nemesis of the Mughals.

Aurangzeb's first viceroyalty of the Deccan lasted from 1636 to 1644 but ended in demotion and dismissal, deprived of his rank and allowance. While Mughal court historians give all kinds of reasons for this takedown, one of Aurangzeb's own letters says he resigned in protest against "the persistent hostility of Dara Shikoh" and "the emperor's partiality towards his eldest son" (*Adab-e-Alamgiri*; 177a). This according to Aurangzeb, deprived him of the emperor's confidence and support, rendering him unable to govern the Deccan with self-respect or effectively. He was later dispatched to Gujarat as Governor after being restored to favour by Shah Jahan.

Following his ignominious showing in Afghanistan, Aurangzeb was transferred by Shah Jahan as Governor of the Deccan for a second time. Aurangzeb took up his second Deccan posting in January 1653. He lost little time in displaying his religious fanaticism on his non-Muslim subjects. In his own admission in the form of a letter to his grandson Bicar Bakht written in old age (*Adab-e-Alamgiri*), the Mughal emperor said: "The village of Sattara near Aurangabad was my hunting ground. Here on top of a hill stood a temple with an image of Khande Rai. By God's grace I demolished it and forbade temple dancers to ply their shameful profession". This was just one among the innumerous instances of his iconoclasm.

While in the Deccan, Aurangzeb strove hard to demonstrate his administrative skill and energy, but his second stint in the Deccan was marked more by his religious outlook and behaviour than by his administrative acumen or achievements. He was particularly unfriendly towards Rajputs, something that came to the notice of Emperor Shah Jahan at Agra. Upon being rebuked for this behaviuor Aurangzeb somewhat pretended to make amends by recommending a Rajput, Rao Karan, for an administrative post in his domain (*Adab-e-Alamgiri*; 29a). But it was evident that there was little love lost between the Mughal prince and the Rajputs.

If there be any lingering doubts as to his religious bigotry, Aurangzeb himself provides proof in the following letter he wrote to his prime minister Sadullah Khan, while being the Governor of the Deccan for a second time:

"The Brahman Chhabila Ram, the *kanungo* of property tax of the city of Bidar, had uttered improper words with reference to the Prophet. After investigation and verification of the charge by order of the Emperor, Zulfiqar Khan and other officers of the place had beheaded him, as was required by justice. Now, the scholar Mulla Muhan has written to me that the brothers of the accursed misbeliever, out of bigotry, have sought justice at the imperial court against Shaikh Mohammad Maula, the lord justice, and Shaikh Abdul Mani, the ecclesiastical judge of the province. I, therefore, remind you of this affair, as it is proper for all Muslims to do their utmost to assert the rules of the Prophet's religion, and it is the duty of kings and nobles to protect the scholars of Islam in enforcing the injunctions of the holy law. You should exert yourself more than your peers to close the road of the complaint of this wretched tribe (to the emperor's feet) and to take care of the letters (i.e., explanations) of the guardians of the honour of the faith". (*Adab-e-Alamgiri*; 101a)

Alamgir's second innings in the Deccan was not known for any administrative efficiency, leave alone achievement. In fact, even in during his first viceroyalty of the southern region, the Mughal administration there failed to alleviate the lot of the common people, leave alone bring any prosperity to them. The only arguable relief was that the people of the region got to enjoy some respite after half a century of war with Bijapur, Ahmednagar and Golconda, because of the Mughals being able to exert some measure of military control. There was no promotion of agriculture afresh under Mughal administration, nor could the peasantry enjoy any significant relief. The Mughals did not bring any fresh lands under tillage. Far from it, much of the earlier cultivated soil lapsed into the jungles. Cultivators too declined in number and resources, while the revenue declined in a considerable way.

This state of affairs in the Deccan was the understandable outcome of a string of short-lived viceroyalties, staffed mostly by unworthy viceroys and incompetent officials and underlings, who were more often than not, corrupt. The one or two incumbents who were efficient were also pitiless in the exaction of revenue from the local populace. One Khan-e-Dauran, who succeeded Aurangzeb as the Deccan viceroy, was so merciless in collecting revenue by force even in harder times that he was murdered just a year into his tenure. His killing was celebrated by the people as deliverance.

Zealotry masquerading as governance in the Deccan—not that the Mughal record was better anywhere else in India—would go on to have more serious consequences for their empire. The Deccan, a very large territory interspersed with many forests, not settled uniformly or organized, was hardly the easiest of places to administer. Across the eastern and western borders of the Deccan lay two powerful states; namely, Bijapur and Golconda, whose relationship with the Delhi-Agra-based Mughal Empire was hostile, necessitating the stationing of large Mughal forces in the Deccan on a permanent footing, which was yet another drain on the imperial treasury apart from the huge administrative expenses. Soil in the Deccan was sterile in comparison with the much more fertile plains of northern India; rainfall too in the Deccan part of southern India was variable and erratic. Added to this were bad harvests and scarcities, and it was a tough job collecting a minimum standard of revenue. Political stewardship in the Deccan demanded a balanced and unbiased mind and temperament, and Shah Jahan's third son, whose outlook was conditioned by the strictures of his religion, was hardly the candidate.

One of Aurangzeb's ministers and close confidants, Mir Jumla, was notorious for looting the rich temples of south India and appropriating their vast treasures. Huge temple idols of gold and copper were uprooted and taken away in large numbers. Mir Jumla, who was earlier in the service of the Golconda sultanate, was won over by Aurangzeb, whose interest in this Persian Shia adventurer and fortune-seeker was more because of the former's acumen for money-making and political intrigue and not any administrative abilities. Moreover, Aurangzeb longed to conquer the rich state of Golconda and there could be no better insider to aid his quest than Mir Jumla. Although Golconda and Bijapur had a semblance of agreement with the Mughal Empire, Aurangzeb's hostility to them stemmed from the fact that they were

Shia sultanates. A long and costly war with these sultanates taxed the Mughal energies considerably, and culminated with Golconda agreeing to pay a costly indemnity in return for peace.

Aurangzeb's harsh treatment of both Golconda and Raja Ranga Rayal of Karnataka Mugal rule was demonstrative of the stark fact that beneath all its outward opulence, Mugal rule was nothing more than a barely disguised dacoity. His unrelenting aggression against Bijapur, the other southern Shia sultanate, went on to become fatal for the empire itself. Shah Jahan's eldest son Dara Shikoh, ever the picture of moderation, had constantly played a restraining role at the imperial court when it came to the issue of political relations with kingdoms or states not directly under Mughal rule. The Mughal policy of accommodation towards them, allowing them to exist and flourish albeit with some imposed conditions underwritten by treaties, actually acted as a buffer against the silent turbulence of the Deccan and particularly the growing discontent of the Hindus.

The Deccan had enough people to join soldiering and besides, its lack of fertility forced many to take up a martial way of life as the only likely means of livelihood. Thus, the raising of large armies in this region was not a difficult task. Hitherto, the direct beneficiaries of such readymade hardy and natural soldiers—mostly the Hindu Marathas who would go on to rewrite India's history—were the Nizamshahi of Ahmednagar, the Adilshahi of Bijapur-Karnataka and the Qutubshahi of Golconda-Hyderabad. Dara Shikoh, with his constant advocacy of peace and non-interference with the southern Deccan sultanates ironically sustained two Muslim buffer states that acted as protection for the Mughals' southern frontiers for nearly a century. Shah Jahan, heeding Dara's way of diplomatic relations with distant kingdoms, kept this architecture intact. In effect, these large southern Shia sultanates kept the torrent of mounting Hindu wrath in check, much like a dam. Aurangzeb, by first tormenting them and later extinguishing these states, demolished that dam. The torrent that escaped those confines would go on to crystallize in the form of the insurmountable Marathas, which consumed the Mughals in that very Deccan where Aurangzeb's religious zealotry was playing itself out during his viceroyalty of the region.

DARA SHIKOH AND AURANGZEB—THE SAGA OF WHAT MIGHT HAVE BEEN

CHAPTER 07

Between two princes, a gentleman given thoroughly to mysticism, syncretism and a genuine desire for intra-faith accord and accommodation, and other, a ruthless, unscrupulous and treacherous puritan implacably wedded to obscurantist, intolerant religious expansionism, the choice of the future ruler of India ought not to have been a choice at all. Tragically, it was the latter who prevailed in the contest that would shape India's future for generations, while the former not only fell by the wayside but was also brutally eliminated.

The name of Dara Shikoh, the eldest of Mughal Emperor Shah Jahan's four sons who survived into adulthood, has become synonymous with tragic endings to grand tales. Dara Shikoh can easily be categorized as a man born in the wrong period of history; or alternatively, a man far too ahead of his times. Either way, he was a complete misfit in the Islamic world of his day. Had he been born in another realm, the world might possibly have heard of a saintly Dara Shikoh. But within the harsh and unrelenting world of medieval realpolitik, Dara was a doomed figure.

There are students of history, alternative-history enthusiasts and the if-sters and but-sters of history who hold the view that had Dara Shikoh fulfilled his promise and inherited the Mughal empire instead of Aurganzeb, then India today would have remained a united nation.

But Dara Shikoh, the poet, writer, architect, philosopher, scholar and artist did not win the game of thrones—the throne in this case being the Peacock Throne. He was fated to be born, live and act in a geopolitical landscape where brute force and unscrupulous tactics sweep away noble intentions. Dara Shikoh also had the misfortune of being born in a family where the overthrow of fathers by their sons was the norm rather than the exception, where daughters too were imprisoned for backing the wrong brother, and holding children hostage was something over which not many in the same family batted an eyelid, if at all. The probability of Dara prevailing in the contest for the throne of the House of Timur was next to zero, although he had the blessings of his father Shah Jahan.

The eldest son and the heir apparent to the Mughal throne, Muhammad Dara Shikoh was born on March 11, 1615 in Ajmer, Rajasthan. Dara was the first son and third offspring of Shahabuddin Muhammad Khurram, later known as Shah Jahan and his second wife, Arjumand Bano, known more as Mumtaz Mahal. He was named by his father; 'Dara' means owner of wealth or star in Persian while the second part of his name is commonly spelled in two ways: Shikoh (terror) or Shukoh (majesty or grandeur). Thus, Dara's full name can be translated as "Of the Terror of Darius" or "Of the Grandeur of Darius", respectively.

Dara was born when his grandfather Jahangir still occupied the Mughal throne as emperor. Even as a lad, Dara was no stranger to the intrigues and plotting of the Mughal court. His father Shah Jahan strove to rebel against Jahangir. The rebellion came a cropper, and Dara and Aurangzeb were sent as hostages to Jahangir's court to ensure Khurram wouldn't dare to be smart in the future. Jahangir now wanted to impose shackles on his son's further ambitions. Khurram's sons and the emperor's grandchildren, now royal hostages at the palace, were kept under the watchful eye of their step-grandmother, Nur Jahan, herself an ambitious woman, and as most historical accounts testify, the real driver of the Mughal regime while her husband consumed himself in sensuous pursuits, particularly his indulgence of the bottle and weed. The then child Dara could meet his father only at the age of thirteen when his father prince Khurram was crowned Emperor Shah Jahan. Possibly, captivity and seclusion at a very early age made Dara grow into a sensitive human being. It however, made his younger brother grow up to become the exact opposite—cold, insensitive, suspicious, fearful, cunning, treacherous and hardhearted.

The eldest son among his four brothers (seven siblings survived into adulthood), Dara Shikoh was his father Shah Jahan's favourite and was groomed to be the future ruler of the Mughal Empire. But Shah Jahan's actions and his doting over Dara belied such expectations. Dara's brothers were deputed to far-off provinces as governors, but the emperor's chosen one was kept within the imperial court. His home became his citadel. It was to later become his prison.

Being kept away from distant, dusty and often dangerous provinces and arduous tasks of administration enabled Dara Shikoh was able to invest his time in spiritual pursuits. He developed a keen interest and proficiency in Sufi mysticism and the Quran at a young age. At the age of twenty-five, Dara wrote his first book, *Safinat-ul-Awliya*, detailing the lives of the Prophet and his family, the Caliphs of Islam and of saints belonging to the five major Sufi orders then popular in India. The Mughal prince was later initiated into the Kadiri order of Sufis by his *pir* (spiritual guide) Mulla Shah. A devout follower, Dara later on in his life commissioned shrines for his *pir* and Miyan Mir in Lahore (Miyan Mir was the *pir* of Mulla Shah).

While he excelled at his scholarly and spiritual pursuits, Dara completely neglected his *rajadharma*, epitomizing indecisiveness and inept leadership, and giving rise to a political failure of enormous proportions which paved the way for his bigoted sibling Aurangzeb's usurpation of the empire's throne. Dara has been described by his contemporaries as one who "seemed doomed never to succeed in any enterprise" (Bernier), and from several contemporaneous accounts he appears to have displayed surprising naïveté for an heir apparent in judging people at key moments in his life. Historians of a later, more modern era have upheld this view of the Crown Prince of the Mughal Empire. Sir Jadunath Sarkar, for example, remarks: "As a ruler of men in troubled times, he [Dara Shikoh] must have been a failure."

The oneness of God (Tawhid) was one idea and thought that came to exercise a dominant hold on Dara's thinking. He believed that the "utterances of God elucidate and explain one another" (Dara Shikoh; *Sirr-e-Akbar*) and thus desired to read all the revealed books within his reach. His studies led him to the conclusion that the 'Truth' was not the exclusive property of any particular or 'chosen' race but could be found in all religions and at all times (Dara Shikoh; *Shathiyat*). He believed that there must be a common source of all revealed scripture, what is referred to as *Umm-ul-Kitab* (mother of the book) in the Quran.

Dara Shikoh therefore, can be justifiably called part of a significant literary movement for the adaptation of Islam to the spiritual traditions of India. There were Muslim rulers in the past who had ordered the translation of various Sanskrit works into Persian in order to increase the Muslim understanding of Hinduism. An example of this is Dara's own great-grandfather Emperor Akbar's Maktab Khana (translation bureau), which produced translations of the *Ramayana*, *Mahabharata* and the *Yoga Vashistha*.

Dara's interactions with religions other than the one he was born into wasn't confined to only reading the literature of other religions. He also sought out and conversed with the learned men of those faiths. *Mukalima-i-Dara Shikuh wa Baba Lal* captures a spiritual discussion between Dara Shikoh and Baba Lal, later recognized to be Lal Dayal, a Hindu mystic from Punjab. The conversation records Dara's curiosity about various aspects of the Hindu religion and the ascetic life it encourages. The Sufi prince later referred to Baba Lal as one of the 'perfects,' stating that "there are *arifs* and 'perfects' in every community though whose grace God grants salvation to that community."

Dara's scholarly and spiritual pursuits brought him particularly close to pursuing the unity of Hinduism and Islam, something that was of great significance to him and occupied the better part of his life. In this particular outlook, he enjoyed a close and supportive relationship with his sister Jahanara who was the First Lady of the empire after the death of their mother. Dara's wife Nadira Begum was also helpful and encouraging in these efforts.

As a scholar, he pursued this theme for many years, helped by the great library he created in the Kashmiri Gate area of Delhi, probably having several hundred thousand books, manuscripts and other documents. He obtained the help of many holy individuals and scholars in this effort, contributing also to the translation of the Upanishads into Persian. He himself penned books on spirituality, mysticism and inter-faith unity, perhaps the most important of which is a treatise on the integrity of Vedantism and Sufism, titled *Majma-ul-Bahrain* (The Confluence of Two Seas) in 1654-55.

Dara was a patron of artists and scholars, extending his generous help without any discrimination, helping spread the message of tolerance, harmony and compassion being central to religion and spirituality. He was a friend of the seventh Sikh Guru Har Rai. A messenger of peace and reconciliation, he used his influence with his father Shah Jahan to prevent bloodshed in Mewar and Garhwal.

Such was Dara's inexperience in the ways of the world that he went on to commit one blunder after another in quick succession during a period that saw the unfolding of a bloody war of succession between the children of Shah Jahan. Dara Shikoh, as we have noted, was well-read, knew several languages, and had a philosophical bent of mind, plus genuinely believed in and strove for religious tolerance, harmony and a blend of faiths, undoubtedly advantages for any aspiring public leader. But he lacked in some of the crucial skills that were absolutely essential for an administrator of his era and circumstances.

Dara Shikoh was out of his depth in the art of warfare, strategies and political manoeuvering, which were indispensable in his age (arguably, in all ages). Shah Jahan doted on his eldest son, and kept him confined to the safe and cozy environs of the Mughal capital Agra. While Aurangzeb led his first military campaign at the age of 17 (and was a success), Dara's first military outing was the Mughal expedition to try and retrieve Kandahar, which had passed into Persian control. After Aurangzeb too had failed in 1652 in wresting Kandahar from Persian invader Shah Abbas-II, Shah Jahan sent Dara Shikoh to try and do what previous Mughal attempts had failed to. Dara rode out on his Kandahar campaign when he was on the threshold of 40, which was shockingly late in an age where any aspirant had to earn his spurs in his teens or at the most, early twenties, if he had to be taken seriously in a power struggle. Dara's Kandahar attempt in the spring of 1653 ended in failure. His lack of soldiering, incompetence as a military commander and inability to obtain the obedience and respect of his army became glaringly apparent. He delegated many of his tasks to his advisers, who often fought each other for his favour. The Mughal commanders also resented the prince favouring his advisers and over more experienced military veterans, generating discontent in the Mughal army. Dara would order and then countermand ill-fated assaults on the Kandahar fortress; by September 1653, the Mughal army was forced to retreat from Afghanistan, its campaign having ended in a defeat.

Critics have accused Dara Shikoh of being a little too idealistic—which he certainly was—so much so that his idealism would often cloud his otherwise clear-headed and analytical thinking that comes only naturally to a scholar, which he definitely was. The philosopher prince was not a practical being, utterly lacking the shrewdness of the politician. He made his decisions based on his idealism-driven faculty of judgment, disregarding the warnings and well-meaning counsels of those close to him. The inevitable result of this combination of peculiar dispositions was a series of personal and political debacles.

Experience of war and governing provinces and regions where he was deputed helped Aurangzeb become battle-hardened campaigner and also a much better and shrewder judge of human ability and nature, qualities that

Dara Shikoh lacked, as he was shielded from any military initiative by his father. When Dara did pick up the sword, it was a shade too late in the day. And if ineptness, lack of political instincts and ruthlessness were not enough, Dara's tactlessness in snubbing and occasionally insulting courtiers and noblemen in the Mughal durbar had a calamitous effect on his own career—and life.

Hatred between Dara Shikhoh and Aurangzeb was birthed right in their childhood. It came to the fore for the first time, in Aurangzeb's mind, in the summer of 1633, when he had to face a maddened elephant charging at him. Watching elephant fights was a royal pastime and Shah Jahan, Dara Shikhoh and Aurangzeb on this occasion of June 7 that year had gathered with the courtiers and soldiers on the banks of the Yamuna to savour the entertainment. Two mighty war-trained pachyderms, Sindkar and Surat Sundar clashed, but the former suddenly broke loose and charged at the young Aurangzeb, who was mounted on a horse perilously close. The Mughal prince hurled his spear at the charging Sindkar, which missed the beast as it continued to hunker down on him. The unthinkable would have happened any moment, but just then, the other huge tusker Surat Sundar, incensed at its adversary breaking away caught up with it, giving the royal soldiers enough time to drag away the emperor's third son to safety. Everyone, not least Emperor Shah Jahan was shaken and relieved, but Aurangzeb later wrote of this near-fatal encounter and his providential escape: "There is no shame in dying as death casts its shadow even over emperors. The shame lies in what my brothers did not do".

The veracity or otherwise of Aurangzeb's accusation against his brothers, viewed solely through the prism of what happened on the said occasion, must be placed in the category of calumny and little else. For those reading the account of this episode as it happened, Aurangzeb's grouse might make it seem that all his three brothers were present doing nothing, or worse, deliberately did not rush to his rescue. The reality of that incident tells us otherwise. Of Shah Jahan's four sons, Dara, the eldest, was quite some distance away and could not have possibly reached Aurangzeb who had been thrown to the ground as his horse had been knocked down by a hefty. by a hefty blow of Sindkar's trunk. The emperor's second son Shuja was not present on the occasion for some unknown reason. Aurangzeb was the third and the youngest, Murad Baksh, was too tender in years to have realistically done anything. Aurangzeb spoke of "my brothers", but in reality, his ire was reserved for only one of them—the eldest. He hated Dara, and that was it. The sentiment did not take long in percolating into the realm of mutuality.

Dara's liberal and tolerant outlook without doubt, was beyond tolerance for Aurangzeb, though the latter was careful not to display his Islamist zealotry until the time, as he perceived, was ripe. Shah Jahan's incessant doting of his eldest son and continual snubbing of the third one added fuel to fire. Not only was Dara's rank elevated in the durbar without any real achievement to show for it, even his sons Suleiman and Siphir were endowed with *mansabs* (military ranks denoting a commander's place in the hierarchy) higher than Aurangzeb. While the latter's failed Kandahar campaign earned him a lot of opprobrium from his father Shah Jahan, Dara Shikoh, already designated "Shahzada Buland Iqbal" (Prince of High Fortune) in 1642, was raised to the status of "Shah-e-Buland Iqbal" (King of High Fortune) in 1654 by the emperor. This, despite his own disastrous shot at the reconquest of Kandahar in 1653. It was inevitable that Shah Jahan's most favoured son and the most hated one would soon measure swords for the game of the Mughal throne.

The animosity between the two brothers was such that both Dara Shikoh and Aurangzeb could barely be in the same city together. Suspicious and fearful of his third son, Shah Jahan took care to keep Aurangzeb posted as governor of Mughal provinces; Aurangzeb's stints were mainly in Gujarat and the Deccan. But his youth was spent in governing faraway provinces that were not always peaceful and subservient, which contributed to his evolvement as a battle-hardened veteran. Dara spent most of his life, or rather practically all of it, in the safe and luxurious environs of the empire's capital Agra and occasionally Delhi. The mismatch couldn't have been starker when it came to a showdown.

The final showdown was not very long in coming.

In September 1657, Emperor Shah Jahan took ill from strangury, brought on by excessive sexual indulgence. His customary practice of *Jharokha Darshan* (wherein kings and monarchs would appear at the balcony of their palace or fortress to address their subjects. This was a medieval Hindu practice, an essential and direct way of communicating with the people. This Hindu practice was adopted by the third Mughal ruler Akbar and continued under Jahangir and Shah Jahan, but Aurangzeb dispensed with it in the 11th year of his reign on the grounds that it was un-Islamic and a form of idol worship.) was halted, setting off the rumour mill that the *Badshah* had perhaps shed his ghost. Shops were closed in the bazaars around Delhi. Dara Shikoh, already anointed the regent, lost no time in stepping into his father's duties. Only Dara and his sister Jahanara—both their father's most favoured offspring—were allowed any physical access to him. The stage was set for the transition of power—or so it seemed. Shah Jahan was able to recover somewhat from his ailment and become mobile, but his dip in health eventually proved costly for him. Dara's de facto takeover was by no means going to be countenanced by his brothers, and the animosity—and open hostility—was not long in bursting into the open.

The emperor's second son Prince Shah Shuja, then the viceroy of Bengal and Orissa rebelled against his father, declaring himself the new emperor with the fancy self-bestowed title of Shuja-ud-Daulah. Murad Baksh, the fourth son crowned himself emperor at Surat and even received an ambassador from faraway Turkey. In contrast to both Shuja and Murad, Aurangzeb did not declare his emperorship but engaged in a busy secret correspondence with Murad, and, to a lesser extent, with Shuja. Letters written in cipher encased in bamboo tubes passed from runner to runner over special relay posts newly established between Ahmedabad and Aurangabad. Aurangzeb and Murad agreed to joint action against their brothers and agreed to divide the Mughal territory amongst themselves. However, Aurangzeb was only playing for his Murad's support for claiming the throne solely for himself. He would later execute Murad, typical of Mughal fratricide for the throne.

Dara Shikoh forbade any news travelling out of his sick father's palace chambers, which only fuelled further rumours that the worst might have happened at Agra. Shah Jahan's eldest daughter Jahanara supported Dara Shikoh all her life and sided with him in this fratricidal war, while the younger sister Roshanara (a vicious lady given to religious zealotry) ran a secret support network for Aurangzeb in Agra right under the emperor's nose. Shuja's army marched westwards from Bengal but was halted by an imperial army sent under the command of Prince Suleiman Shikoh, Dara's elder son and Mirza Raja Jai Singh of the House of Amer, the venerable and seasoned Rajput vassal-general of Shah Jahan. The two belligerents clashed at Bahadurpur, eight kilometres northeast of Banaras, and Shuja was routed by Suleiman-led imperial Mughal army, and forced to flee eastwards. Dara's victory against his brother Shuja turned to be a hollow one, as a substantial portion of the imperial army had been dispatched eastwards of Agra, leaving him weaker to face the more serious threat that was developing in the southwest.

That was none other than Aurangzeb. On February 5, 1658, Aurangzeb set out from Aurangabad on his mission to grab the Mughal *takht* (throne). By April 3, he crossed the Namada River towards Ujjain. On April 13, learning that Murad, the youngest of the four brothers, had reached a place not far away from him, Aurangzeb sent word to him to march quickly. The next day, the combined forces of Aurangzeb and Murad camped at Dharmatpur on the western bank of the Gambhira River.

The knives were now out, and had begun flashing.

Dara Shikoh, not the best of military commanders by a long shot, was now in action mode. By February 1658 he ordered Raja Jaswant Singh of Marwar, another Mughal vassal, to lead an imperial Mughal army to confront the challenger, i.e., his own brother. Jaswant Singh's forced reached Malwa hurriedly, but the Raja was in the dark about the enemy's movements. He first blocked Karchraud near Ujjain to give battle to Murad but the latter avoided battle by prudently taking a detour around Karchraud and joined Aurangzeb. Jaswant soon found out that Aurangzeb was already in Malwa, which threw the Jodhpur king into some consternation. He tried to parley with Aurangzeb under the impression that the imperial army's strength would be enough to dissuade both princes to give up their rebellion and return to their respective domains.

Shah Jahan's orders to this Rajput vassal king were to do everything possible to make Aurangzeb and Murad retreat, and if that failed, use force against them. The army he led was numerically larger, but stricken by discordance among its several Rajput chieftains who came from different clans, divided by hereditary feuds and perceptions of status and honour. The more serious division was between the Muslim and Hindu soldiers. Though nominally part of one single army, they did not see eye to eye. The best of generals could not wield them together into a single fighting unit. Rajputs in the service of the Mughal empire would stake even their lives for the Mughal emperors' campaigns, but wouldn't fight together with the Muslim soldiers of the army, neither would Muslim soldiers of any Mughal force willingly take orders from a Rajput superior. They hadn't done so during the times of Akbar and Jahangir, not during the failed Mughal campaigns in Afghanistan from 1649-53, and they wouldn't do so now. The feeling was mutual.

If Shah Jahan's choice of Jaswant Singh as the commander to lead the Mughal army to force Aurangzeb into submission left much to be desired, Dara Shikoh, who was the man in charge issuing those orders, was little better, if at all. Jaswant Singh's personal valour was never in question, but he lived and fought by the ancient Kshatriya code of war, which had no place in war with a totally alien enemy.

Jaswant's tactics at Malwa were woeful, to say the least. His choice of battleground was bad; the place was so cramped that his infantry and horsemen could not manoeuvre freely, nor gather momentum for a charge. The ground was narrow and uneven, ditches and swamps flanking it on both sides. One account of the battle tells us that Jaswant deliberately had water poured on 200 yards of ground in front of him and trodden it into mud, evidently to arrest the enemy's charge. His position was also surrounded by trenches dug the previous day, as the usual precaution against night attacks. The effect of all this was that the imperial army seemed to be standing on an island, awaiting a siege rather than launching an assault on a challenger. He failed to send timely help to the divisions that needed it most, and the once the battle began, lost control over his forces. The Jodhpur King in this particular battle looked a mere divisional leader and not the supreme commander of the Mughal forces deputed by its official crown prince.

The crowning ignominy of Jaswant Singh's command was his despisal of artillery. One of his chiefs, Askaran Das Singh (father of the renowned Durgadas Rathore) advised him to attack the European gunners who manned the artillery pieces of Aurangzeb's army in a night raid and eliminate them, so as to save the Rajputs from facing enemy cannon in an open combat, but his boss would have none of it. For him, attacking an unarmed foe was below Rajput dignity! European gunners were at a premium due to their proficiency in handling cannons, and a quick surprise raid on Aurangzeb's battery at night would have rendered his park of artillery virtually useless the next day, as Mughal cannoneers weren't good at handling these heavy pieces of artillery (they had woefully demonstrated this in Kandahar), and especially in a crunch situation. But Rajputs like Jaswant Singh stubbornly stuck to the old and outmoded Kshatriya codes of one-to-one combat, which ensured that disaster would befall him—and Dara Shikoh in the bargain.

The faceoff at Dharmatpur began on April 15, 1658. The battle began with the usual discharge of artillery and muskets at long range. The distance gradually decreased, as Aurangzeb's army advanced slowly, keeping its regular formation. The Rajputs were soon engaged in a close hand-to-hand combat, but their narrow and dense positions, unable to manoeuvre, were easy targets for the enemy's archers and muskets. Though the imperial army's losses mounted steadily, the intrepid, bordering on foolhardy valour of his Rajput commanders would have won the day for Dara Shikoh had only Jaswant himself not been a stubborn adherent to obsolete notions of chivalry in combat. The burst of the Rajput charge, with the war cry of "Ram, Ram" on Aurangzeb's artillery was that like of the dash of ferocious tigers. Despite the fusillade of Aurangzeb's gunners and their grim resistance, his artillery chief Murshid Quli Khan and innumerable others were dispatched to their makers by the Rajputs. The artillery division was scattered, though the guns remained intact.

But alas! Jaswant's men could not do the job for their master. Rajput losses were daunting enough, and moreover, the Rajput contingent of the 'official' Mughal army comprised of almost entirely light cavalry, while Aurangzeb's army had heavy mail-clad cavalry. Jaswant Singh, who fought resolutely for four hours, was himself prepared to rush headlong to martyrdom in keeping with Rajput tradition, carrying his sword into enemy ranks, but was dissuaded from doing so and led away to safety. Moreover, the fierce Rajput attack failed to generate the required mass needed to produce a favourable outcome, divided as they themselves were into mutually unfriendly clans. Thus, Sisodias, Rathores, Hadas, Gaurs and Medtas fought loyally and unflinchingly, but not as one unit. The more serious facet was the behaviour of the imperial Mughal army's Muslim soldiers under the supervision of Qasim Khan. They deliberately rendered no help to the Rajputs who had swarmed Aurangzeb's units. The challenger had little difficulty in employing his reserves, whereas the imperial army stood handicapped on this count. The Battle of Dharmat was soon over; Aurangzeb was the victor. After the battle, he gave vent to his zealotry. Muslim prisoners of the imperial army were spared and in fact, treated kindly, while Hindu survivors were slaughtered.

It was a taste of things to come.

Historian Jadunath Sarkar says about the Battle of Dharmatpur: "Far greater than material gains was the moral prestige secured by Aurangzeb. Dharmat became the omen of his future success in the opinion of his followers and of the people at large throughout the empire. At one blow he had brought Dara down from a position of immense superiority to one of equality with his own, or even lower".

The victor of Dharmatpur now marched towards Agra, while Shah Jahan and the Mughal capital were thrown into consternation. The next clash between Dara, the chosen heir and Aurangzeb, the wannabe, would decide the fate of India for centuries to come.

It came ten miles east of Agra, south of the Yamuna—at Samugarh.

Dara Shikoh, or rather his representative Raja Jaswant Singh had lost the Battle of Dharmat, leaving the south of the Mughal capital vulnerable. The defeated imperial Mughal army now retreated towards Samugarh, about 10 miles (16 km) east of Agra, south of the Yamuna. Aurangzeb and his army then flanked Dara's fortified line along the Chambal river. In Agra, Shah Jahan, having recovered somewhat from his debilitating illness came out of the Red Fort to bless his son he doted on so much, who was now going to lead the imperial Mughal army to confront his rebellious challenger son he hated. But the challenger was now advancing towards the Mughal capital and threatened to end Shah Jahan's reign.

Left to himself, Shah Jahan wouldn't have wanted this internecine familial war at all and still hoped for a diplomatic end to this strife, now boiling with undisguised hatred. But the ability of his perceived imperial stature staving off a final showdown was largely imaginary—his own imagination. Mughal courtiers advised the emperor to somehow avoid this clash, as it would bring nothing but disgrace upon the family and empire, but Dara Shikoh scorned such talk. They could stay out of this if they were so unwilling to fight, the Shahzada Buland Iqbal taunted them. He and Chhatrasal Singh Hada, an intrepid Rajput warrior in Mughal service, were enough to send Aurangzeb and his men packing, Dara boasted. The foreign Muslims in the imperial army, mostly Persian and Central Asian mercenaries, resented this demeanour of Dara and secretly resolved to desert to Aurangzeb. Dara could carry on with his Rajput friends—in reality, his only friends.

This was by no means the only act of Dara's tactlessness. Earlier in the durbar, he had poured scorn on the veteran and highly respected Mirza Raja Jai Singh, who tried to soothe an agitated Shah Jahan, by exclaiming, "Raja saheb, I know you're a great warrior, but honestly, just look at your own face in the mirror. Really, *shakal se aap mirasi* (a sect of singing and dancing Muslim fakirs) *lagte hain* (you look like a street dancer)". Any self-respecting Rajput would have unsheathed his blade at such stinging contumely, and the utterer's head would have rolled. Jai Singh was mature and cool-headed, but he had his revenge on Dara later. He dissuaded Jodhpur ruler Jaswant Singh from going to Dara's aid after the latter's defeat and flight, and himself pursued a fugitive Dara upon Aurangzeb's orders. 151 years after Samugarh, in January 1809, French emperor Napoleon Bonaparte insulted de Talleyrand, one of the most versatile, skilled and influenced diplomats in European history—who was instrumental in bringing him to power in 1799—publicly in front of his marshals. Bonaparte's scatological rebuke about his (by then former) minister of foreign affairs was, "He's shit in a silk stocking. I could easily break him like a glass, but it's not worth the trouble". Talleyrand restricted himself to a cold retort, "Pity that so great a man should have been so badly brought up". Charles Maurice de Talleyrand Perigord then aligned himself with the House of Bourbon, becoming one of the key agents in their restoration. He also became France's chief negotiator at the Congress of Vienna in 1815, which had been convened by the European powers acting in concert to take down Napoleon for good.

Dara's parting from his father, as he led his 60,000-strong army out of the Agra fort to put down the looming challenge, was poignant. Drumbeat and clamour accompanied the Mughal crown prince as he strode out of the Diwan-e-Aam (Hall of the Public) after declaring that it would be "*Ya takht ya takhta* (either the throne or the funeral bier), while Shah Jahan raised his frail arms in the direction of Mecca to seek Allah's benediction for his son. Neither father nor son could know that this was the last time they would see each other in the mortal world.

An advance division of Dara's army had reached Dholpur on May 9, to guard the ferries of the Chambal. Dara and his forces reached the place on May 22 and seized all the fords of the Chambal. He wanted to gain time for his son Suleiman Shikoh, victorious against his uncle Shah Shuja, to join the imperial army. Dara ought to have waited for Suleiman to reach Agra first, but committed haste in sallying forth. Now, after reaching Dholpur he learnt to his dismay that Aurangzeb had already crossed the Chambal forty miles east of Dholpur, as he had come to know of a hitherto unknown ford. With his rear exposed to peril, Dara and his army had to fall back towards Agra and encamped close to the plain of Samugarh, where he would confront Aurangzeb.

Aurangzeb's forces, some 45,000 strong, arrived near Samugarh on May 28, tired and worn out by a forced march. The imperial Mughal army had the advantage of numbers. Dara rode out as if to offer battle, but halted his advance midway, as though the mere warning of his approach would scare Aurangzeb into withdrawing. It was a fatal error; a tired Aurangzebian force, worn out after a long march across a waterless plain on a scorching May afternoon, could have been made short work of. But Dara was not a natural warrior. He was not a coward, but was not equal to the demands of strategy or tactics. While their leader hesitated to move, the soldiers lost confidence in him. The blazing sun played havoc with his troops clad in steel and armour, not to mention the horses and elephants. Aurangzeb easily guessed Dara's lack of resolve and ruthlessness, and did not waste this opportunity to rest his troops for the evening, while Dara's soldiers wilted under the blaze. Dara himself retreated to his camp by sundown, which dealt a consequential blow to the morale of his troops. Their master had come face to face with the enemy, without even wanting to deal the mortal blow.

Dara's troops. What, or rather, who were they? The imperial army was a mix of Mughals and Rajputs, but it were the latter who were really and totally devoted to his interests. The Mughals, mostly under Khalilullah Khan, had already been corrupted and won over by Aurangzeb, and were the Trojan horses in Dara's army. His artillery and cavalry formations were formidable, but were arranged in a faulty way; the artillery wasn't dispersed but deployed in one place. Dara occupied the centre of his army formation, seated atop an elephant. But mutual jealousy and hostility between the Hindus (Rajputs) and Muslims (Mughals) of Dara's army was barely concealed. Moreover, Dara Shikoh himself, a liberal in matters of religion, was nothing more than a kafir (infidel) for the zealot Muslims of his day. There were plenty of them in the army he led; in fact, too many of them.

Aurangzeb too rode an elephant, with his right and left flanks adequately marshalled. Hostilities commenced at eight on the morning of May 29. After the opening skirmishes between both armies, Dara went on the offensive when he spotted Aurangzeb's banner atop the latter's elephant. Dara's artillery discharged all their first shots in one go, but inflicted little damage. Aurangzeb's guns did reply, but saved their firepower for later on. Come noon, and the Mughal crown prince's loyal left-wing commander Rustam Khan led a most impetuous charge into Aurangzeb's artillery unit, his men killing many of Aurangzeb's commanders. But Rustam Khan was himself wounded by a musket shot and died a hero's death.

Shah Jahan's youngest son Murad (his sole pervious military performance had been a spectacular failure in Afghanistan), himself a wannabe Mughal emperor (having proclaimed himself as such) now fighting in Aurangzeb's army, launched a fierce attack on Dara's Rajput contingent, but was repelled by the even fiercer Rajput counter-attack. Though many among them fell in this skirmish, Murad himself fell in grave danger of being slain by the Rajputs, whose furious charge eviscerated his unit. The Rajputs, glimpsing a semblance of victory, now fell upon the centre of the Aurangzeb host. The Samugarh battle had by now become a carnage. The legendary Rajput valour now shone, literally, like crimson on the battlefield. The daredevil Raja Ram Singh Rathore, on horseback, rocketed his mount at Aurangzeb's elephant and attempted to cut the ropes that held the rebel Mughal's howdah, to throw Aurangzeb down and end his tale. It is said that Aurangzeb himself was stupefied by this Hindu warrior's out-of-the-world bravery and shouted to his soldiers to spare the Raja's life, but a badly wounded Rathore perished in his final charge.

Dara Shikoh, learning of the death of the best of his generals now resolved to personally lead the assault into enemy ranks, but alas! His inexperience in war, ignorance of battle tactics and the deadly betrayal by his own ranks was about to seal his doom. His charging elephant was now surrounded by Aurangzeb's men, but the Mughal crown prince did not lose heart. Despite Aurangzeb's much superior marshalling of his forces and gradually forcing Dara into a corner, the rebel challenger was himself soon imperilled Dara was inept in warfare, but no coward. Though he was by now despairing of victory, he resolved to kill Aurangzeb then and there. Aurangzeb's protecting bodyguards scattered as Dara pressed on despite enemy cannon fire, but now came the betrayal. The compromised Khalilullah Khan, fearful that despite everything, Dara might still prevail, made only a show of fighting; many of his soldiers crossed over to Aurangzeb. Dara himself was on the verge of overrunning Aurangzeb's forces; the latter had demonstrated tactical superiority throughout the day and had tapped the great advantage of religious cohesion among his ranks, but was now down to the last of his reserves. An unwavering final charge by the Shahzada Buland Iqbal could have closed the chapter in his favour, but this was not destined to be. The traitorous Khalilullah Khan falsely proclaimed that the battle was 'won' and all that remained was for the Mughal crown prince to get down and take Aurangzeb prisoner. Driven by fate, Dara abandoned his elephant for a horse.

It wasn't the howdah of his elephant Dara got down from; it was virtually, the throne of Hindustan he abandoned at that moment. His loyal troops that still remained in the arena saw the empty howdah of the elephant, concluded that their master had fallen in battle. Panic set in among them, breaking out in a helter-skelter dispersal. The jubilation in Aurangzeb's army heralded by the sound of kettle-drums, sounded the conclusion.

It was an utter rout for the imperial Mughal army. Dara was inclined to perish on the battlefield, but a few stubbornly loyal retainers grabbed the reins of their master's horse and force-rode him away to safety.

At Agra, Shah Jahan and Jahan Ara learnt of the disaster that had befallen Dara and burst into grief. Wailing burst out in the Mughal harem; mourning and alarm swept the city's streets. A sense of foreboding hovered, as the feeling of the old world ending and a new, portentous one forcing its way inwards inexorably took hold.

Dara himself had little time to grieve over his defeat, and out of shame did not go to show his face to his father. His life was in danger, and a shaken Shah Jahan dispatched orders to the Mughal governor of Delhi to throw open the stores and military resources of the city for Dara, who now fled Agra for Delhi in the small hours of the morning of May 30, accompanied by his wife Nadira Bano, children and loyal attendants. The remainder of his routed and demoralized army joined him at Delhi over the next two days. Emperor Shah Jahan continued to reinforce him with supplies and money, till the victorious Aurangzeb entered Agra in triumph and sealed the road to Delhi. He then put the Agra Fort under siege, imprisoning his father Shah Jahan in the fort. The aged Mughal emperor would never see the outside world again in his lifetime. The eldest sibling, Jahan Ara willingly chose to share her father's captivity, serving him till he lived.

Aurangzeb also learnt that despite his status as prisoner, Shah Jahan was sending secret messages to Dara who was ensconced in Delhi, writing to him to stay put firmly, as there was no dearth of troops or money. He made up his mind to pursue his enemy and end his saga. Right from their childhood, Dara had been their father's favoured one and therefore, pathologically hated by Aurangzeb. Plus, in his own words, "Dara is an infidel to Islam and a friend to the Hindus. He must be extirpated for the sake of the true faith (*sic*) and the peace of the realm" (Aqil 59-61).

Dara knew it would be fatal for him to linger long at Delhi, as his army had received news that Aurangzeb, after his victory at Samugarh, was preparing to move northwards in pursuit. Dara briefly contemplated moving to the impregnable fortress of Allahabad (then held by one of his devoted lieutenants) and join his son Suleiman Shikhoh, who had defeated the second brother Shuja. But the move was fraught with risk, as Aurangzeb in pursuit from the west and a hostile Shuja in the east would have been too much to handle. Dara therefore decided to turn further northwards to the Punjab, to Lahore precisely, whose fort contained much of his wealth, a vast arsenal and ammunition. He instructed his son to join him at Lahore.

Aurangzeb's Mughal army, which had now become the imperial army was in hot chase. Dara Shikoh, meanwhile, built up his army, using his newfound wealth to distribute favours and purchase new weapons. But by August 1658, Aurangzeb reached Lahore. When his army crossed the Sutlej, panic and desertion appeared in Dara's ranks; there was also rank opportunism and treachery aplenty, with many of his men abandoning him to join the victor of Agra. Dara had by now lost confidence in his own self. He abandoned Lahore and proceeded in the direction of Multan. But his pursuer wasn't far behind.

Dara found himself in no position to take an armed stand at Multan and had to flee westwards, even as desertions continued to hit his diminishing army. He managed to reach Sakkar on the western bank of the Indus. He had only 3,000 or so men left with him now, and moreover, his body and spirit had begun to wear out. He then turned towards Siwistan in Balochistan, but many of his remaining retinue refused to join him, fearing the ferocious reputation of the Balochs. He narrowly escaped capture by the pursuing forces of Aurangzeb and reached Thatta, still in Sindh. The Mughal pursuers gave up their mission. They had failed to capture Dara, but by then, defeated militarily, shrunk politically and a ghost of his former self, posed no threat to Aurangzeb. From Sindh, Dara fled towards Kutch, Gujarat. By now, he was a sick, desolate and ruined man, a pale shadow of the once-proud, enlightened and resplendent Mughal prince.

Crossing the Rann of Kutch after November 1658, Dara found hospitality with the Raja of the territory, who also helped him with money and provisions. The fugitive Mughal prince then crossed into Saurashtra, receiving help from the Jam of Nawanagar, who further supplied him with supplies and equipment. Shah Nawaz Khan, the then governor of Ahmedabad, was an enemy of

Aurangzeb, as the latter had also disposed of Murad Baksh, the youngest of the four brothers, after availing of his help in defeating Dara at Samugarh. Murad had been Shah Nawaz's son-in-law. The Ahmedabad governor had little hesitation in joining Dara Shikoh. He opened the fort of Ahmedabad and its immense wealth to Dara, who occupied the city and spent a month there, resting, recovering and rebuilding his army. He mulled over where he ought to turn next, the Deccan or Rajputana. It was to be the latter, as Raja Jaswant Singh invited him to Ajmer. But betrayal stalked him all his life, as he was about to find out yet again.

Aurangzeb succeeded in winning over Jaswant Singh, despite the latter having fought him—unsuccessfully—at Dharmatpur. He did not want this formidable and proud Rajput king to join his enemy. Another conflict with Dara Shikoh was on the cards, and Jaswant Singh's army of over 25,000, with cavalry, was likely to be a decisive factor. The veteran loyalist Mirza Raja Jai Singh, who Dara had mocked as a *mirasi* in Shah Jahan's durbar, now availed of this opportunity to settle scores. He acted as mediator between Jaswant Singh and Aurangzeb.

By the time Aurangzeb arrived at Ajmer, Dara realized to his utter dismay that the Jodhpur raja had let him down. He had no choice than take a stand against his younger brother, now his implacably deadly foe. On April 12, 1659, both brothers clashed again at Deorai, four miles from Ajmer. The battle opened with artillery exchanges between both sides. For a change, Dara's guns rained death on the enemy while Aurangzeb's cannon shots fell on the walls of impregnable trenches that Dara had prepared to shield his troops. Aurangzeb had to call a mid-battle meeting of his commanders on April 14 to take stock of what was becoming a difficult situation.

The imperial Mughal army then opted to make an all-out attack on Dara's trenches. It had the advantage of numbers, having been reinforced by the armies of Mirza Raja Jai Singh and Jaswant Singh. Despite this, the fierce resistance by Dara's musketeers inflicted slaughter on Aurangzeb's ranks. Jai Singh's soldiers entered the fray to deliver the initiative to Aurangzeb's army. Dara's left wing was annihilated, though the right wing held. Unlike at Samugarh, Dara had displayed better tactical acumen and had fought very bravely, but was done in by betrayal of Raja Jaswant Singh on whose help he had relied. The Battle of Deorai was his second defeat to Aurangzeb.

The victorious Mughal dispatched a large force in pursuit of Dara, who now fled first to Medta and then to Gujarat. The Rajput vassal rajas of Aurangzeb now barred every likely path he could take and wrote letters to local chieftains to capture him if he entered their territory. Westwards was the only relatively safe direction, and he once again turned towards Sindh going through Viramgam in Gujarat. Misery and desolation were his only faithful companions; his dear wife Nadira's life was ebbing away by the day. Even his attire was now in tatters. Jai Singh, once a staunch loyalist of Shah Jahan, now in thrall of his new master Aurangzeb rode in hot pursuit of the latter's luckless elder brother through Gujarat.

Dara Shikoh had still not given up all hope of wresting the Mughal throne back from his arch enemy, but this now looked more a wishful dream. He briefly entertained the thought of crossing into Persia to seek the refuge of the Safavid Emperor Shah Abbas II, but Nadira would have none of it. She feared she would be forced to submit to the Persian emperor and become his slave, and flatly refused to join her husband if he were to go to Tehran. Some historians aver that this was another of Dara's blunders; Persia's emperor Shah Tamasp had helped Dara's great-great grandfather Humayun recover the throne of Delhi a hundred years earlier. The Shiite Safavids would most likely have helped Dara unseat Aurangzeb, a fanatical Sunni whom the Persians detested. But fate had deserted Dara. All that remained was for the final curtain to come down.

It came down at Dadar.

This is not to be confused with the bustling, commercially thriving central suburb of Mumbai having the same name, a junction of the western and central zones of today's Indian Railways. The lesser known Dadar lies nine miles away from the western end of the Bolan Pass. Its zamindar was one Malik Jiwan, an Afghan chieftain and mountain robber, who had once been arrested by the governor of Multan and sent in chains to Delhi where then emperor Shah Jahan had sentenced him to be trampled to death by an elephant. Shahzada Buland Iqbal Dara Shikoh had intervened and gotten this condemned prisoner free. He was now sure that Malik Jiwan would repay him by giving him shelter in his hour of dire need. Jiwan did receive Dara at Dadar, but the once-upon-a-time Mughal crown prince had no idea of what lay in store for him next.

Before he reached Dadar, the greatest personal tragedy befell Dara Shikoh. His beloved wife Nadira Banu, suffering from diarrhea succumbed to her illness. She had been on the run along with her husband ever since his flight from Agra. Dara's world collapsed when Nadira shed her mortal frame. Death seemed to rise all around him. He seemed not to know what to do, if anything at all. He arranged for Nadira's body to be buried at Lahore—her last wish was to die and be buried in the soil of India. He then freed his remaining followers and requested them to disperse wherever they wished to and himself proceeded to Dadar to try and secure shelter with Malik Jiwan.

Loyalties in Afghanistan are fickle and change with fortunes and masters. This remains the scenario even today. Malik Jiwan owed his life to Dara Shikoh; else, he would have been reduced to a lifeless pulp under an elephant's foot years ago. But this mattered not an iota to the treacherous Afghan mountain dacoit. Dara was a gone case, a fugitive running for his life, and hunted by the Mughal sultanate. The new reality was that Aurangzeb was the latest *Badshah* of India. Jiwan wanted reward and position under the new master. He and his men made Dara and his son Siphir Shikoh prisoners and sent word of their capture to the pursuing Raja Jai Singh. One can only imagine Dara Shikoh's shock and despair. He, his son Siphir and two daughters were brought to Delhi as captives on August 23, 1659.

Aurangzeb ordered celebrations in the Mughal court and on August 29, Dara Shikoh the prisoner was paraded through the streets of Delhi in a most humiliating manner. In his heydays, the Shahzada Buland Iqbal would often ride through the streets on his elephant, a magnificent pachyderm from Sri Lanka. He was now clad in a coarse sack cloth, with feet chained, placed in an uncovered howdah of a small female elephant covered with dirt. The crowd wept and wailed as they saw their beloved prince now brought down to this abject, helpless state.

Most of Aurangzeb's lackeys now demanded that Dara be put to death because he was a "danger to the faith of Islam". These lackeys of course, parroted their 'opinions' when they knew where their master's inclinations lay. Jahanara, the eldest sister, like her father loved and doted on Dara, but she was a prisoner inside the walls of the Red Fort and could nothing. Roshanara the younger sister, viciously hated her eldest brother and had fanatically batted for Aurangzeb, functioning as his spy in the Mughal capital when he was in the Deccan plotting his march to seize the Mughal throne. Her insistence that Dara ought to be put to death was pitiless, and silenced any feeble voices pleading for mercy. Pliant Muslim clerics hurriedly signed a decree that Dara was a deviant from their faith, a friend of the infidels and himself a kafir, or even worse, a *murtad* (apostate). In the city, a mob, mostly Hindu, had revolted on August 30 and attacked the residence of the traitor Malik Jiwan. This incident served as a casus belli for Aurangzeb—Dara was a threat to both Deen (the faith) and Daulah (the state), argued Aurangzeb's minions, and had to be put to death forthwith. Not that Aurangzeb needed any urging or excuse; he had made up his mind to kill his eldest brother years ago. Dara made a feeble plea to Aurangzeb that he would pass his days quietly if he were allowed an ordinary residence with an attendant, but Aurangzeb's reply, written in his hand, said it all: "You first acted as an usurper, and were a mischief-maker" (British Museum archives/Ms. Addl. 1381, f.77a). The fate of Dara Shikoh had been sealed.

Aurangzeb passed immediate orders for Dara's execution and on the night of August 30, 1659, the man tasked with doing the gruesome deed, a heartless slave Nazar Beg and some minions entered Dara's cell. He knew his doom had arrived; his son Siphir Shikoh clung to his father's knees weeping and wailing, but was violently dragged away by Nazar's henchmen. Dara had kept a kitchen knife concealed under a pillow and suddenly grasped it, striking one of the henchmen with great force, twisting the small knife in his bones. He then valiantly fought his killers, using his fists to land blow after blow. It was a grim, futile final effort. The trained killers finished their job, decapitating the head of Shahzada Buland Iqbal Dara Shikoh, the favourite of his father Shah Jahan and sister Jahanara, and the eldest son of Begum Arjumand Banoo, aka Mumtaz Mahal. The cell room was covered in a pool of blood.

The severed head was sent to Aurangzeb, whose malevolence was satiated only when he sent it placed on a platter to the imprisoned Shah Jahan. For the father, this was the final wretched blow. Dara's headless body was placed on an elephant and paraded through the streets of Delhi a second time and buried in an unmarked vault somewhere near the tomb of Humayun without even the customary Muslim rites of washing and dressing a dead body, leave alone a *janaza* (Muslim funeral procession). The saga of Dara Shikoh was over and along with his demise, ended the possibility of what India and the subcontinent might have been if he and not his fanatical jihadi brother prevailed in the game of the Mughal throne.

Dara Shikoh's liberalism in religion and his philosophical explorations were undeniable. Yet, they were never reflected in the way he conducted his affairs. He apparently did not learn any lessons of *rajadharma* from his scholarly perusal of the Hindu texts like the Upanishads, *Ramayana* and *Mahabharata*. Had he done so, he would not have been so casual in his approach to kingly duties, nor would have relied solely on his idealism more than the inputs from officials and spies working on the ground. Trying his hand at the politically sensitive game of religious syncretism between Hindu and Islamic ideas and ideals so openly was always fraught with grave danger, especially so in Dara's age. It drew the ire of the fanatic and influential *ulema* in the royal court, while Dara made no effort to cement his own position as monarch. Comparisons are sometimes made between Dara and Shikoh and Akbar, but the latter championed an eclectic approach in his day more due to the compulsions of his public life and the sociopolitical realities of India. Moreover, Akbar was as the supreme leader of the empire and of *both* the political and religious aspects of his empire. He understood power, and never hesitated to wield it, unlike Dara. Nobody could dare raise a word against him as he publicly exchanged philosophical ideas and preached syncretic religious views with scholars and saints of Hinduism, Jainism, Zoroastrianism, and Christianity. After all, he was the emperor and pope at once. Unlike Jalaluddin Akbar, the significance of power, the means and ruthlessness to achieve and secure it, were lost on Shah Jahan's eldest son.

Dara Shikoh lost two military conflicts with his brother Aurangzeb, Samugarh in May 1658 and Deorai in April 1659, but it was really the Battle of Samugarh, ending in the unambiguous defeat of the former that erased for good whatever moderate strain Mughal India might have had. Samugarh on May 29, 1658 was the death of the Akbarian world, and with it, of any vestige, real or imagined, of a coexistence of two different worlds and outlooks. Aurangzeb had prevailed, but this was a victory that would consume him and his rule less than half a century later, and the Mughal Empire itself a century and half following that, in the same whirlpool of blood Aurangzeb had unleashed.

TREACHERY AND BETRAYAL—ALAMGIR'S INGRAINED CHARACTER

CHAPTER 08

So, who was Aurangzeb?

Shorn of politically correct jargon, one can describe him adequately in two words, the characteristics of which made their appearance itself time and again in the sixth Mughal emperor: treachery and betrayal.

Sir Jadunath Sarkar, who has done the most extensive work on 'Alamgir' Aurangzeb, describes the Mughal emperor as a person who pushed his self-assumed 'divine right' to breaking point. What we have seen so far of Aurangzeb unmistakably and undeniably confer on him the unescapable judgment: he was a bigot, a zealot and a tyrant.

History is not short of rulers, tyrants and tinpot dictators who shelter themselves in an extreme sense of righteousness, often bordering on the devout, to justify their numerous excesses. This has been, and is still being used, and has become particularly fashionable of late, in certain ideological circles, to portray the villains of our past as heroes. This is made to look even more palatable if the villain's objects of hate and those of the ideological posturers of today are the same. It then becomes easier to see why tyrants and Islamic zealots like Aurangzeb are the darling of today's Left and 'secular' crowd. The Hindu community is the target of the pathological hate of both. Leftist 'historians' have been in the forefront in defending Aurangzeb and trying to whitewash his actions by claiming them to be motivated by 'materialist' purposes, as though that is supposed to absolve him of any religious bias. Funnily, Aurangzeb himself never made any secret of his Islamist zealotry.

Aurangzeb's malevolent behaviour throughout his life offers us a clearer answer, and the one trait(s) of his character that stands out is treachery and betrayal. The scrutiny of his life reveals his repeated betrayal of the trust others reposed in him. This was second nature to Aurangzeb; arguably his *actual* nature. Adhering to the definition of betrayal as going against one's given word, or against a code of honour, Aurangzeb fits the bill of a treacherous betrayer perfectly. A brief look at the bio-data of his deeds paints the picture quite clearly.

The clearest instance of Aurangzeb's treacherous nature came to the fore during the war of succession between Shah Jahan's four sons for the Peacock Throne. In May 1658, Aurangzeb and his younger brother Murad defeated Dara Sikoh at the Battle of Samugarh. That clash sealed Dara's fate and handed Agra to Aurangzeb. The duo of Aurangzeb-Murad had won, or so Murad believed. In November 1657, he had already proclaimed himself emperor at Ahmedabad where he was appointed governor, after hearing that his father had taken ill. During the same year, he even received the Ottoman ambassador at Surat. Aurangzeb had promised to make him emperor, but asked for his help to fix the infidel Dara. Now that Dara was done and dusted, Murad really believed that his emperorship was an open and shut case. Aurangzeb was a pious Muslim and had told him that his actual interest was to 'purify' the Mughal domain of the apostate Dara, and after that he would hand over things to Murad and himself spend his days in religious pursuits.

Murad did not know his brother. When he found out, it was too late.

Aurangzeb now chose to act. En route from Agra to Delhi in pursuit of the fugitive Dara Shikoh, he made his army set up camp near Mathura and invited Murad to his tent for supper that night. The host put on his most gracious act. Accounts tell us that the puritanical Aurangzeb plied his younger brother with choice wine. The liquor took effect, and Murad began growing drowsy. One by one, the courtiers slunk away in the dark, with only one bodyguard in the tent. Just then, a beautiful slave girl came in and motioned the guard to leave. She then proceeded to massage the youngest Mughal *shahzada*.

After giving him a thorough 'massage' the slave girl left the tent—with Murad's sword that lay by his bedside even as he was lost in his dreamland. He woke minutes later to the sound of heavy feet marching in and the clanking of chains. When he opened his eyes, his hands were clasped in those very fetters. Murad knew that any resistance was asking for death. He was whisked away the next afternoon in a covered palanquin, so that his loyal troops wouldn't know of the whereabouts of their master. Leaderless and bewildered, they soon joined Aurangzeb's army. One brother had been put out of the way. Dara Shikoh had escaped to Delhi, while Shuja had retreated to Bengal. But Aurangzeb was now free to go after them without having to worry about his rear.

Murad, when he was posted as Governor of Gujarat, had murdered a diwan clerk Ali Naqi at Ahmedabad. After his falling into captivity, the murdered clerk's sons demanded justice for their father's killings; most likely, it was Aurangzeb who instigated them through officials to raise the howl. Murad was produced before a Qazi, and his reply to the charges was defiant: "If the emperor (Aurangzeb) choses to spare the life of this unfortunate being who was once his brother, I can assure him there would be no threat to his rule from me. If, however, he has made up his mind to take my life, of what use is even talking to such lowly creatures (the murdered Ali Naqi's sons)?" That was enough for the Qazi to announce the sentence of death on Murad. The youngest of Shah Jahan's sons was interred in a prison inside the fortress of Gwalior for three years, before his head was taken off in 1661. Thrones brooked no rivalry, and Aurangzeb's ill-gotten throne certainly wouldn't. This was the among the earliest of betrayals by Aurangzeb.

Seventh Sikh guru Har Rai, who had sided with Dara Shikoh (he was the Mughal prince's personal friend) was the target of Aurangzeb's ire. In 1661, after having snatched the Mughal crown three years earlier, Aurangzeb ordered the guru to present himself in court and apologize for 'such conduct'. Possibly suspecting foul play on the Mughal's part, the wise Har Rai sent his son Ram Rai in his stead. We do not have details of this in records, but this much is known that Ram Rai was held for months as a hostage, and intimidated enough by the Mughal clergy to rewrite a few lines of the holy Gurbani, which the ulema found 'offensive'.

Threatening and imprisoning a guest contravenes any decent code of honour and conduct. Those were alien things to Aurangzeb. Some commentators are wont to paint this episode as a masterly, tactical move to divide the Sikhs, but it fell flat. Guru Har Rai was incensed at what his son did, and promptly excommunicated him. However, Aurangzeb's behaviour remains unpardonable. This treatment of a host shows him up as a man who cared little for his given word.

Aurangzeb went on to display further evidence of his treacherous nature—not that any was needed—when Hindu Hriday Samrat Chhatrapati Shivaji Maharaj visited Agra as his guest. This must qualify as the most infamous of betrayals by Aurangzeb. Shivaji's military and political heft were increasing. He slew Bijapur's Afzal Khan in 1659 and decimated Aurangzeb's uncle Shaista Khan at Pune in 1663, besides inflicting a humiliating defeat on Shaista's army that had been sent to subdue him. Shaista Khan himself escaped death at Shivaji's hands by a whisker when the latter made a daring surprise raid at midnight on his childhood home the former had forcibly occupied. Shivaji had stormed the palace's bedroom where Shaista was resting and the Mughal commander had to jump out of the window to save his life, though Shivaji hacked off three of his fingers. Alarmed by the Maratha's growing stature, Aurangzeb was forced to send the ablest commander of his empire, Mirza Raja Jai Singh, who poured a huge army into the Deccan. Finding himself in a tight corner, Shivaji agreed to a truce and by the terms of the Treaty of Purandar concluded in 1665, agreed to a temporary vassalhood of the Mughal Empire.

Shivaji, however, made no unilateral or unconditional surrender at Purandar. He bluntly asked jai Singh that he would have to be excused from attending Aurangzeb's court. As Shivaji candidly told his Rajput interlocutor during the treaty negotiations, he simply didn't trust his boss. With good reason.

Shivaji was spot on in his assessment of Aurangzeb's character. The next year, i.e., 1666, Shivaji had to attend the Mughal court in Agra with his son Sambhaji. Mirza Raja Jai Singh's clout did not extend to getting a reprieve from court attendance to Shivaji, but he did exact a promise from his master that no personal harm should befall Shivaji, as the Maratha king would come to Agra only on Jai Singh's promise of safety. Aurangzeb was forced to give a verbal promise guaranteeing Shivaji's safety in the Mughal capital, as the veteran Jai Singh couldn't be trifled with, not even by Aurangzeb.

But the champion betrayer couldn't, and wouldn't honour his own word.

On May 12, 1666, Chhatrapati Shivaji Maharaj and his son faced the Mughal supremo in person, and in acrimonious interlude, insulted Alamgir in front of his *mansabdars* and other lackeys and stormed out of the court. For Aurangzeb, the presence of the dangerous Shivaji, who the Mughal had by now come to fear, in his capital was too good an opportunity to let go. The Hindu warrior-king and his son were placed under detention by Aurangzeb. Doubtlessly, he intended to murder Shivaji at an opportune moment, as openly doing so would have meant insulting Raja Jai Singh. Aurangzeb wasn't prepared to risk a Rajput rebellion. But this incident shows he cared two hoots about his own words.

Destiny had willed it otherwise. A mere four months into his captivity at Agra fort, Shivaji and his son made a most daring, almost unimaginable escape from Agra hidden in a box of sweets. But the incident only underscores

Aurangzeb's unchanging and odious propensity of dumping any and every promise and betray just about everyone, even his loyalists.

The year 1675 saw one of the dastardliest acts of betrayal by Aurangzeb. The victim was none other than ninth Sikh Guru Teg Bahadur. Aurangzeb had been viewing the Sikhs with suspicion and hostility for long. He had good reason to do so. Sikhism's scriptures called for inter-religious unity. But they had also militarized the Jat community. The Mughal emperor believed that the Jat would always be an enemy of the Mughals. When Guru Teg Bahadur decided to raise his voice in support of the Kashmiri Pundits, who were being subjected to merciless religious persecution by the Mughals, Aurangzeb decided to act.

Guru Teg Bahadur and his deputies were made hostage in Sirhind, subjected to the worst sort of torture imaginable in Delhi, and then finally executed. His deputies, Bhai Mati Das, Sati Das and Dayal Das were put to unspeakable torture before being killed, and the Guru offered his sheesh (head) but refused to convert to Islam to save his life. Chandni Chowk in Delhi is the place of Guru Tegh Bahadur's martyrdom, where the Gurudwara Sheeshganj Sahib today stands.

No amount of whitewashing can disguise Aurangzeb's crime. The fact is that Guru Teg Bahadur set out for Delhi with prior public notice; he and his deputies were unarmed. More to the point, the ninth guru nominated his son Gobind Rai as successor, who went on to be known as Guru Gobind Singh, the tenth guru. His father *knew* he wasn't coming back from this trip to the Mughal's capital. No need to guess why. Aurangzeb meant treachery.

The Rajputs of Marwar, Jodhpur particularly, had for long been a thorn in Aurangzeb's side, despite the House of Jodhpur having aligned with him. Their Maharaja, Jaswant Singh, had even led a military expedition in the North West Frontier Province. Jaswant Singh, though, siding with Dara Shikoh had fought Aurangzeb's forces in the Battle of Dharmatpur in 1658 on behalf of Shah Jahan's imperial army, albeit unsuccessfully. The relationship between him and Aurangzeb was already muddied. Jaswant Singh passed away at Jamrud (Afghanistan) in 1678, and the Mughal *badshah* wasted little time in marching against Jodhpur, demolishing temples there, and installing a puppet as the new Maharaja.

But fate intervened. One of Jaswant Singh's widows gave birth to an heir—Ajit Singh Rathore. The Rajputs now demanded that Aurangzeb recognize this infant as the rightful inheritor of the Marwar throne. Aurangzeb had no intention of honouring any promise, and deliberately dithered for months, forcing the Rajputs led by Durgadas Rathore, to bring the infant heir to Delhi.

Once again, Aurangzeb invited his adversary home, and true to his nature, he betrayed his guest. He demanded that the child be placed in his harem, and brought up as a Muslim. Affronted beyond belief, the valorous Durgadas did what any self-respecting Rajput would do—and refused to comply. The torturous impasse grew with each passing day, but the Rajputs weren't allowed to leave. In the end, they resolved to solve the problem themselves. Jawant's widow with her infant son Ajit broke out under cover of seventy warriors, who laid down their lives while the infant and his mother were spirited away. Many more Rajputs perished in valiant rearguard actions, but slew many pursuing Mughals, which eventually slowed the pursuers to a halt. The Jodhpur bloodline was saved, and honour too. Durgadas went on to become the nemesis of the Mughals in Marwar, and he and the grown-up Ajit Singh finally kicked out the Mughals from Jodhpur in 1707.

The record of Aurangzeb's acts of betrayal were repeated, wilful, dishonourable, and carried out with no remorse. His hatred, born of several reasons from insecurity to greed, justified almost anything. While hatred can be a fantastic defensive mechanism, it unfortunately also blinds one from the truth.

So it was with the sixth Mughal Emperor. Fate gifted him a life where he could have made a huge positive difference to the country he ruled over. But his innate nature cursed his era with an unforgettable hell. Whatever else one may choose to call him, Alamgir certainly wasn't great.

DEFEAT IN ASSAM—THE BEGINNING OF THE MUGHAL SLIDE

CHAPTER 09

Aurangzeb styled himself as Alamgir, meaning "Lord of the World". It could also be taken to mean Conqueror of the World, and so on in a similar vein. The bald truth is that Aurangzeb ended up a failure in the three major military campaigns of his long life and career; namely, against the Ahoms of Assam, the Rajputs and finally, the Marathas. The last of these not only ended in his military defeat, but also consumed his life in faraway Deccan and buried the Mughal Empire forever. Of these, his defeat in Assam was the first one, which we shall look at here briefly.

The Mughal Empire under Aurangzeb lost Assam to the Ahoms in 1671, briefly regaining control of the province before being finally kicked out in 1682. The Battle of Saraighat was the last battle in the last major attempt by the Mughals to extend their empire into Assam. Though the Mughals managed to regain Guwahati briefly later, the Ahoms wrested control in the Battle of Itakhuli in 1682 and maintained it till the end of their rule. In retrospect, the Mughal defeat in Assam was the beginning of a long slide under Aurangzeb's watch into its final oblivion. Saraighat is the place where the Assamese warrior hero Lachit Borphukan ended the Mughal dream of becoming the masters of northeastern India.

The Ahom kingdom had suffered repeated invasions by the Turkic and Afghan rulers of the Delhi Sultanate. and later by the Mughals. Clashes between the Mughals and Ahom had been going on since 1615-16, i.e., slightly before Aurangzeb was born. The Mughals had eyed Assam with a view to capturing the region. The Ahoms ruled major parts of Assam for nearly 600 years, between 1228 and 1826.

Background of the Mughal-Ahom Conflict

Nara Narayana was the last ruler of the undivided Koch Dynasty (it ruled parts of eastern India, primarily Assam and Bengal) of the Kamata Kingdom, which had risen in western Kamarupa sometime around 1257 AD. He succeeded his father, Biswa Singha. Narayana's rule saw the Koch kingdom attain cultural and political zenith. Narayana was a formidable ruler, and under the military command of his brother Chilarai, subjugated the entire Brahmaputra Valley, including the Ahom kingdom; he spread the Koch influence into the kingdoms of Kachari, Tripura kingdoms, Khyrem, Jaintia and others. This influence was halted when he faced the then Bengal sultan Suleman Karranni.

Nara Narayana passed away in 1587. At the time of his death, the Koch kingdom lay between the Mughal Empire in the west and south and the Ahom kingdom to its east. The Koch domain itself was divided into the western Koch Bihar and the eastern Koch Hajo, ruled by his son Lakshmi Narayan and nephew Raghudev respectively. Though originating from the same dynasty, these two kingdoms became bitter rivals. The Mughals aligned themselves with Lakshmi Narayan and the Nawab of Dhaka. In 1602, a governor of the Mughals attacked Raghudev's son Parikshit Narayan, at Dhubri, the westernmost corner of present-day Assam. Parikshit accepted defeat after fighting the Mughals in many battles, and was sent off to Delhi. His brother Bali Narayana sought refuge with the Ahoms, who wanted to keep the Koch kingdom as a buffer between themselves and the Mughals.

The first Mughal-Ahom battle took place when Jahangir was Mughal emperor, in 1615. The Mughals attacked the Ahoms, then under Pratap Singha. This resulted in a period of Ahom-Mughal conflicts with fluctuating fortunes. This period of warfare ended with the Treaty of Asurar Ali in 1639. The Treaty fixed Barnadi river in the north bank and Asurar Ali in the south bank of the Brahmaputra as the boundary between the Ahoms and the Mughals. The Kochs suffered a defeat at Pandu in 1641, which resulted in the Mughal occupation of Kamrup, mainly Guwahati and Hajo. But constant warfare had exhausted both sides, and they agreed to sign a treaty.

Mughal emperor Shah Jahan suddenly took ill in September 1657, triggering off a war of succession among his four sons, Dara Shikoh, Shuja, Aurangzeb and Murad Baksh in mid-1658. Pran Narayan, the then ruler of Koch Bihar, taking advantage of the Mughal strife, tried to occupy Koch Hajo, but the Ahoms were in no mood to give in. Their ruler Jayadhwaj Singha took Guwahati and pushed Pran Narayan back beyond Dhubri. In 1658, Aurangzeb snatched the Mughal throne by defeating his brothers Dara Shikoh and Mohammad Shuja. The latter was defeated by Aurangzeb's forces in the Battle of Khajwa in January 1659 and Aurangzeb's able commander Mir Jumla II pursued Shuja up to Bengal. Mir Jumla was then appointed the subedar of Bengal in 1660 and Aurangzeb, who had by then consolidated his grip on the throne, immediately ordered Mir Jumla to annex Assam again.

Mir Jumla marched in 1661 and defeated the Ahoms at successive encounters to finally take the Ahom capital Garhgaon. But Atan Burhagohain, an Ahom leader made effective use of *daga juddha* (guerrilla warfare) and the provinces rains cut off Mughal communication lines. It became impossible for Mir Jumla to consolidate Mughal rule in Assam despite his military success. Unaware of Mir Jumla's difficulties and unnerved by the defection of Baduli Phukan, Jayadhwaj Singha sued for peace, an opportunity Mir Jumla didn't let go of. The Treaty of Ghilajharighat in 1663 brought an end to Mughal occupation of Garhgaon, but the conditions of this treaty were so severe that the Ahoms resolved to reverse them.

Ahom monarch Jayadhwaj Singha passed away that year, heartbroken. On his deathbed, he exhorted his cousin and successor Chakradhwaj Singha to "remove the spear of humiliation from the bosom of the nation". Soon after, Chakradhwaja Singha took over the reins of the Ahom empire the same year. Immediately after the beginning of his reign, he began repairing the forts at Samdhara and Patakallangand and restored the Ahom army to a state of battle readiness. In March 1665 the king summoned an assembly of his ministers and nobles and ordered them to devise and adopt measures for expelling Mughals from Western Assam, declaring: "My ancestors were never subordinate to any other people; and I for myself cannot remain under the vassalage of any foreign power. I am a descendant of the Heavenly King. How can I pay tribute to these wretched foreigners?"

Early in 1667 Saiad Firuz Khan, who succeeded Rashid Khan as the thanedar of Guwahati, sent a strongly worded letter to the Ahom King, demanding the payment of the balance of the indemnity still outstanding. Instead of being unnerved, Chakradhawaj Singha's resolve only hardened on receiving this message. He would go to war with the Mughals, would free Assam of the *mlecchas* (impure foreigners).

A complete overhaul of the Ahom kingdom was undertaken. The kingdom's people who had dispersed following Mir Jumla's invasion were rehabilitated in the appropriate *khels*. Food and military productions were increased, new forts were constructed and garrisoned and an expeditionary army was organized under a new commander—Lachit Borphukan.

Necessary preparations were made as speedily as possible. By August 1667, a well-equipped army led by Lachit Borphukan was ready to wrest Guwahati from the Mughals. King Chakradhwaj gave valuable gifts to the commanders of the expedition and delivered to them the following message: "I desire that your wives and children, and the cows and Brahmins should be duly protected and preserved; and I should also acquire the prestige and reputation of having vanquished the Mughals. If you prove incompetent in the task of defeating the enemy at Itakhuli, you shall not be let off with impunity. And, do you think that there will paucity of Phukans and Rajkhowas like yourselves". Those stirring words were to have effect.

The Ahoms Prepare for War

Chakradhwaja appointed Borphukan as the new army commander in August 1667. Alliances were renewed with the Jaintia and the Kachari kingdoms. Mughal imperial demands were continually made during this period, but the Ahoms used tact and diplomatically rebuffed most of these, but when the new *faujdar* of Guwahati, Firuz Khan, forced the matter in March 1667, the Ahoms were compelled to move. In August 1667 the Ahom army, under Lachit Borphukan and accompanied by Atan Burhagohain, sailed downstream to retake Guwahati.

Lachit made Kaliabor, the old seat of the Borphukan, his base camp and advanced toward Guwahati along both banks of the Brahmaputra. Early clashes took place along the north bank the Deka. Borphukan retook Bahbari in early September 1667. The *Nausalia* Phukan and others traversed the south bank, moving on both land and water. This force captured Kajali, Sonapur, Panikhaiti, and Titamara forts between the Kapili River and Guwahati. The Ahoms then reached Guwahati, which was defended by five *choukies* on each bank of the Brahmaputra. The battle for Guwahati saw the Ahom army incur some loss, but they captured Shah Buruz and Rangamahal forts, a little north of the city.

The Itakhuli fort (at the site of the current Deputy Commissioner's bungalow) drew both the adversaries into an extended battle. The Ahoms besieged Joiduar and occupied Pandu; meanwhile, the Mughals sent reinforcements to block the Ahom advances, but Borphukan relentlessly besieged Itakhuli. His men launched a big attack on the night of November 4, 1667, scaling the walls with ladders. The siege of Itakhuli lasted two months, the fortress fell by the middle of November 1667. Most Mughal defenders were massacred, many surrendered but a few managed to escape. A huge booty of elephants, horses, guns, coins, war provisions, treasures and material fell into Ahom hands. The enemy was chased down to the mouth of Manas River, the old boundary of Assam and Mughal India. The Ahoms rescued and brought back the Assamese subjects who had been taken captives by the Mughals during Mir Jumla's expeditions. Upon receiving news of victory, Chakradhwaj proclaimed: "It is now that I can eat my morsel of food with ease and pleasure".

The Mughals managed reinforcements at this point and launched a retaliatory attack. The Ahoms deployed their naval forces and evicted them from their bases in Umananda and Barhat. The Mughal army fell into retreat, but was now pursued by the Ahoms. Firuz Khan, the Mughal commander managed to fortify the Manahmukh (the confluence of Manas River) and fend off the attackers for some time but finally surrendered and was taken prisoner. This ended the recapture of Guwahati, lending the Ahoms control their old Manas border once again. But this victory did not last long and they had to beat a strategic retreat.

Mughal supremo Aurangzeb learnt of this heavy defeat on December 19, 1667, which threw him into alarm. This was a serious blow to Mughal prestige and worse, threatened the Mughal presence in the east. Bengal of course, was still in Mughal hands, but the empire could not gloss over this defeat. He ordered Raja Ram Singh I, son of the veteran Mirza Raja jai Singh to recapture Guwahati. It was a huge Mughal force that proceeded eastwards—30,000 infantry strong, 18,000 Turkish cavalry, 15,000 archers (some of whom were the Koch, rivals of the Ahoms), 1,000 cannons and 40 ships. The Rajput commander left Delhi on December 27, 1667 and reached Rangamati in February 1669, a timespan that gives us a considerable idea of the distance he had to cover. He was accompanied by Rashid Khan, an ex-faujdar of Guwahati. But the Ahoms had anticipated a major Mughal invasion against them, and are said to have stationed their spies in Delhi. They tracked Ram Singh's movements right from the Mughal capital.

The Ahoms were thus aware of the larger numbers of the Mughal army and the weakness of the Ahom militia. The disadvantage would be further acute against the professional cavalry and mounted forces in open fields. Lachit Borphukan and other Ahom commanders decided to choose the terrain of the battlefield with care. The choice veered around to Guwahati. The city's terrain is hilly, on the way to the heart of the Ahom kingdom and without open fields. Mughal mobility would be considerably restricted here. The only way east was via the river Brahmaputra passing through it. The Brahmaputra at Saraighat, at its narrowest with a 1 km width, was ideal for a naval blockade. It was one of the soundest decisions Lachit made.

To check the Mughal advance, Lachit prepared a complex system of mud embankments in Guwahati. The plan was to make Guwahati impregnable by land, forcing the Mughals to use their navy, which was their weakest link. The chief Ahom commander knew well that the Mughal army was not good at naval warfare, and hence wanted to force them to take the river route. He set up his headquarters at Andharubali, the sandbanks between the Kamakhya and Sukreshwar hills. The deliberations of the war council were recorded and made into a manual.

The Mughal march reached the river Manas in March–April 1669 and the initial clashes between them and the Ahoms saw the latter suffer some reverses. It was then that Lachit decided on a strategic retreat to Guwahati. Three Rajkhowas were assigned the task of engaging the Mughal forces and retreating to Guwahati, keeping the Mughal forces in sight but beyond the reach of their weapons. When the Mughals drew closer, Lachit began sham negotiations with Ram Singh via the captured Firoz Khan, who had set up camp at Agiathuti, calling the Mughal Emperor the "Bhai Raja" (brother sovereign) to the Ahom king. After he was ready for the Mughal attacks, Lachit sent word to Ram Singh that Guwahati and Kamrup did not belong to the Mughals, since they were taken from the Koch. Lachit also conveyed that the Assamese were prepared to fight to the last.

A period of battles between the Ahom and Mughal forces in the region of Guwahati followed, with varied results with forts changing hands many times. By August 1669, Aurangzeb received information of the lack of progress his armies were enduring, and made arrangements with his maternal uncle Shaista Khan, then stationed as the Subedar of Bengal, to provide reinforcements to Ram Singh who was making rough weather of the Assam campaign. This period is also known for Atan Burhagohain's *dagga judha* (guerilla warfare). Ram Singh protested that these harassing campaigns lowered the "dignity of warfare", and withdrew from fighting in the period between October 1669 to March 1970. The Mughal army had by then been a year into its Assam campaign, but gained no particular military advantage.

Setback at Alaboi

The Ahoms suffered a major defeat in one of these battles. The delaying tactics, interspersed with guerilla attacks by the Borphukan drove Mughal commander Ram Singh to exasperation. He asked for a duel with the Ahom king and promised to withdraw from Assam with his army if he was defeated. Lachit informed Ahom monarch Chakradhwaj Singha about this proposal; the fiercely proud Ahom monarch rejected the offer outright. It was beneath his dignity to duel a mere servant who was not a Chhatrapati, i.e., one devoid of a royal canopy over his head. Taking umbrage at Ram Singh's proposal he ordered Lachit to confront the Mughals militarily. In a battle that became a de facto challenge, a contingent of 10,000 Mughals under Mir Nawab was to confront a force of 20,000 Ahom cavalry. Ram Singh's approach was psychological, marked by pride, chivalry and revenge. The Ahom approach, to cover their basic weaknesses, was based on diplomacy, deception and misrepresentation. So instead of 20,000, they sent in 40,000 and used a tactic they had deployed against Kochs, which had worked. The Ahoms dressed their vanguard archers and musketeers as Brahmins to make the Rajput warriors desist from killing them. Ram Singh, on the other hand, set a woman, Madanavati, dressed as a man, to command the vanguard to deny the Ahoms any glory in case they won. The battle took place in the fields adjoining the Alaboi hills about August 5, 1669.

The first phase went in favour of the Mughals. The units under Madanavati were successful in dispersing the first four lines of the Ahom vanguard with ease, but then the Mughal progress stalled. Borphukan had trenches dug to conceal his other lines. In the second phase of the battle, a Mughal diversion that attempted to cross the Brahmaputra was thwarted, and Madanavati was shot dead. The battle turned, and in the third phase, Mir Nawab's forces were routed. This defeat threw Ram Singh into a rage and let loose his veteran horsemen. It was a carnage; 10,000 Ahom soldiers were massacred.

News of the Mughal success at Alaboi reached Aurangzeb, who was pleased. He raised Ram Singh's *mansab* from 4,000 to 5,000. He was also ordered to occupy Guwahati soon. If that wasn't possible, the Mughal army was to devastate the land and plunder the people.

Diplomacy...Maneuvering...and Preparing

The Alaboi clash had taken place in late 1669. After the Mughals won this encounter, Ram Singh began diplomatic efforts. His proposal was for the Assamese to evacuate Guwahati and a return to the 1639 status quo (the Treaty of Asurar Ali) in return for a Mughal payment of 300,000 rupees. There was no Ahom response to this proposal. Ram Singh next attempted to bribe and create divisions among the Phukans (Ahom field commanders). In the meantime, King Chakradhwaj Singha passed away in March 1670 and was succeeded by his brother Udayaditya Singha. The long war had resulted in popular discontent in the Ahom kingdom. Ram Singh again put forward his proposal on the 1639 status quo settlement and this time the Ahoms appeared receptive. King Udayaditya, though displeased at this turn of events, left the decision to his commanders in Guwahati. In the meeting which included Lachit Borphukan, the only dissenter to the proposal was Prime Minister Atan Burhagohain, who displayed his statesmanship.

Atan Burhagohain unambiguously stated that there was no guarantee that the Emperor at Delhi, a treacherous person by nature, would abide by Ram Singh's assurance. Also, a settlement then would mean that the drain on the kingdom's resources would have been in vain. Further, what was the guarantee that once the Mughals take Guwahati, they wouldn't try to grab Garhagaon or even Namrup?

The Ahom Prime Minister was able to persuade the other commanders; Ram Singh's proposal was rejected. The Mughal commander's diplomatic games once again came to nought. Events were shaping up for a final showdown with Aurangzeb.

The Showdown at Saraighat

Meanwhile, Mughal reinforcements in the shape of war-vessels and *umraos* (imperial officers) reached Ram Singh, along with the Mughal admiral, Munnawar Khan. Mughal Viceroy Shaista Khan sent the message that Ram Singh had been sent to fight the Assamese, not make friends with them. Singh now made preparations for his final and direct assault on Guwahati and began moving along the northern bank. Near Sualkuchi, he was joined by ships with artillery and archers under five sardars. The Mughals had large boats, some carrying as many as sixteen cannons. The Mughal ambassador Paditrai had reported a breach in the embankment at Andharubali a few days earlier, and Ram Singh wanted to exploit this opening.

Meanwhile, demoralization had hit the Ahoms after their losses at Alaboi. If that weren't enough, commander-in-chief Lachit Borphukan and their admiral were both seriously ill, and the Nara Raja, the son of the Miri Sandikoi, was in command. An encounter both on land and water took place near Ashwakranta, where Laluk Borgohain Phukan, leading the Ahom land forces worsted the Mughals, but the Mughal boats compelled the Ahom boats to retreat to Barhila, north of Saraighat. The Ahom land army was now wary of being encircled and therefore opted for retreat. The battle reached a crucial phase, when the Mughals were beginning to inch closer to Andharubali. The Borphukan, as well as Nara Raja sent messages to inspire the soldiers. It looked as if there was a break in command and some boats began falling back to Kajali and Samdhara. Lachit Barphukan observed this from his sickbed in the gatehouse of the Itakhuli fort.

At this crucial moment in the battle, when the Mughals were about to land at Andharubali, Lachit sent orders via *katakis* to all the land and naval forces to attack. He also ordered seven war-boats for himself and had Nadai of Kharangi carry him to a boat. He shouted "The King has put all the people in my hands to fight the enemy. Shall I go back to my wife and children?" and pushed a few men into the water, himself heading towards the naval battle with six other war-boats.

Borphukan's entry had an electrifying effect on the Ahom soldiers. His flotilla, which looked small at first soon swelled with Ahom warships from all sides that smashed into the Mughal warships at Amrajuli on the north bank, opposite the Kamakhya hills. The triangle in the river, between Itakhuli, Kamakhya and Aswakranta was filled with men and boats. The Ahoms spanned the river over an improviso bridge of boats and resorted to a combined front and rear attack. The Mughal admiral Munnawar Khan, smoking a hookah was taken out by a gunshot from the back; his death threw the Mughals out of gear. They suffered the loss of three top-ranking *amirs*, and another 4,000 dead. The day of this decisive battle is not known for certain, but it happened in the middle of March 1671.

The retreating Mughals were now chased up to the river Manas, the Ahom kingdom's western boundary. Anticipating a counterattack, Lachit Borphukan set messengers at regular intervals, while Prime Minister Atan Burhagohain and other commanders stood ready for one. There was another battle at Darrang, in which the Mughals were worsted. Ram Singh, the defeated commander-in-chief, left Kamrup on April 7, 1671 for Rangamati. His army got no further chance to recover or regroup and Mirza Raja Jai Singh's son finally had an audience with Aurangzeb on June 25, 1676 to report news of the disaster the Mughal Empire had suffered at Saraighat. The Mughal defeat at Lachit Borphukan's hands effectively ended Ram Singh's career for good, as he was demoted in rank and order in the imperial Mughal court. As though to rub salt into his wounds, Lachit Borphukan and his king Udayaditya Singha after his victory at Saraighat openly declared Chhatrapati Shivaji to be their inspiration (*Shivaji Suraj*, by Anil Madhav Dave; Prabhat Prakashan, 2015). Ram Singh I, the son of Mirza Raja Jai Singh, was humbled by Shivaji's worthy legatees in the far east of India.

Eleven years after the epochal Battle of Saraighat, the Ahoms erased the Mughal hold on Assam for good. This was brought about in the Battle of Itakhuli, fought in 1682. The Ahoms pushed back Mughal control to the west of the river Manas permanently. The main battle was fought at a garrison island on the Brahmaputra, in which the Mughal faujdar Mansur Khan was put to defeat and the remnant of the Mughal forces pursued to the Manas. With this win, the Ahoms recovered Sarkar Kamrup from the Mughals.

What did Aurangzeb, the self-styled Alamgir, do about his empire's military debacle in Assam?

Nothing at all. By 1682, he was already two years into his campaign in the Deccan. He was caught up in a war with the Marathas from which he could not come back. He was in no position, materially or militarily, do anything about this defeat of his empire in India's northeast. But the enormous drain of resources in Assam was to cost him dearly in Rajputana and the Deccan. In retrospect, Assam began the slide of the Mughals into the abyss.

AURANGZEB'S RAJPUT WAR— THE RUIN BEGINS

CHAPTER 10

The Maharanas of the house of Mewar had resolutely stood against Islamic invaders for a thousand years. This was a saga of sheer sacrifice, unbending resolve and glory, besides being surreal; without the meticulously preserved annals of Mewar and brilliantly documentations of this chapter of India's history by James Tod and Shyamaldas, it would have been relegated to only folklore.

From Bappa Rawal in the 8th century to Raj Singh towards the end of the 17th century, the royal house of Mewar kept producing rulers and warriors who ceaselessly owed their allegiance to Hindu dharma and paid every conceivable price to live up to it.

Mewar forged alliances with friendly and like-minded kings to defend Hinduism and honour of the kingdom; at times, it stood alone in this war against an alien and intolerant ideology. It was befitting in a way that it fell on Mewar to write the penultimate chapter of this history of the Rajput war against the Mughals.

Raj Singh was crowned the Maharana of Mewar on October 22, 1652 AD. For the next 28 years till his death, Raj Singh changed the course of Hindu history in the subcontinent irreversibly. His life went on to become a saga of legends that are part of everyday folklore of Rajasthan and India.

War against the Mughal Empire under its zealot-in-chief, Aurangzeb, too began afresh in this phase. The sixth Mughal ruler had resolved to erase 'infidelity' from his domain by whatever means he conceived as not only necessary, but imperative to "defend the faith". In the ultimate analysis, all Aurangzeb achieved was to sink a substantial portion of the Mughal army in Rajputana, suffer ignominious defeat, make sworn enemies of a clan that once had been a dependable ally of the Mughal Empire, and above all, unwittingly lay the grounds for a pan-India Hindu alliance.

In the period Aurangzeb provoked religious warfare with all its attendant atrocities, Mewar was just recovering from a hellish pestilence, which had devastated the region. And a just retribution soon enough came forth on this

Mughal assault on the region. It was a retribution that visited the Mughal emperor with full force, and his successors too, ending only with the overthrow of their power.

Aurangzeb, whose army had suffered an ignominious rout at Saraighat in Assam at the hands of the Ahoms in 1671, had begun to realize that his dream of pan-India supremacy would not be uncontested. The rise of Shivaji and his many battle successes against the Mughals, his astounding escape from Aurangzeb's captivity in Agra (1666), the fall of Kondana (later renamed Sinhgad) in 1670 and Shivaji coronating himself as a Hindu emperor had thrown the sixth Mughal *Badshah* into consternation. Shivaji had not only overcome all military attempts against him by the Mughals and the Adilshahi Sultanate of Bijapur, but worse, had emerged as a pan-Hindu hero and inspiration to a hitherto defeated and despondent Hindu people. Aurangzeb's intolerant Islamic zealotry and his jihadi targeting of Hindus, particularly the destruction and/or desecration of temples, reimposition of *jaziya* and forced religious conversions of Hindus wherever possible slowly but surely began turning Hindu opinion against him. He had murdered his brothers, imprisoned his father and usurped the Mughal throne in 1658. He then strove with his unmistakable Islamic zealotry to wipe out 'infidelity', i.e., Hindu dharma and impose puritanical Islam on this land. But a mere 10 to 12 years into his reign, challenges in the north (Sikhs and Jats) east (the Ahoms), west (Rajputs) and south (the Marathas) arose inexorably. And the 'world-conquering' Alamgir failed on all fronts.

Aurangzeb's mighty attempt to stamp Mughal suzerainty over Assam was checked and defeated by the Ahoms under Lachit Borphukan in 1671. The Mughals could never set foot in Assam again. To the south of the Mughal Empire, Shivaji had arisen as the foremost threat to complete Mughal supremacy; the Marathas, moreover, were an unconventional, quick-thinking and quicker moving foe. To the Mughal west lay Rajputana, once the most dependable allies of the empire since the age of Akbar. The Rajputs had stood by the Mughals during the reigns of Jahangir and Shah Jahan as well. In fact, several Mughal successes were due to Rajput rajas and generals.

The most notable exception was the house of Mewar, which had never bowed to the Mughals. From Maharana Sanga who fought the invading Turk Babar to Maharana Pratap who defied Akbar, Mewar had never shrunk from displaying its steel when confronted with Mughal expansionist design and actions. In a twist of irony, this Mewar-Mughal conflict had stretched from grandfather to grandson on both sides; Akbar was Babar's grandson; his unvanquishable adversary Pratap was Sanga's grandson. And it fell upon Mewar and its intrepid Maharana Raj Singh to deliver the final Rajput assault on the Islamic zealotry of Aurangzeb that would weed out Muslim imperialism from Rajputana permanently. The Ahoms had landed the first mighty blow; the Rajputs would eviscerate Mughal notions of invincibility and the Marathas would finally bring the curtain down.

After Raja Ram Singh I's defeat at Saraighat, Aurangzeb's hope of extending Mughal rule further east of Bengal were extinguished for good, though Bengal continued to remain in Mughal hands. But it was a tenuous hold at best. Closer home, he now realized that eleven years after he had become emperor, he didn't really control all of north India. Any empire that desires control of northern India has to contend with the Rajputs. So did the Mughals in the reign of Akbar and Jahangir. The Mughals established peace with Rajputs through matrimonial or military alliances and made use of the Rajput valour and sword for their military endeavours in the subcontinent. The Rajputs are known for honouring their word. They did thus with Akbar, Jahangir and Shah Jahan; Rajputana became an important pillar for Mughal Empire in the north. Any damage to this fulcrum would sound the death-knell of their empire.

Aurangzeb either did not understand this political chessboard or chose to ignore it owing to his religious expansionism and military ambitions. How and why Aurangzeb irreparably damaged relations with Marwar and Mewar, the principal royalties of not just Rajputana but India in general, bears examination.

Seeds of this Mughal-Rajput conflict lay in the war of succession between Dara Shikoh and Aurangzeb. Though the latter disposed of his two other siblings Shuja and Murad as well, it was his enmity with Dara whose ripples and echoes traversed Rajasthan. The war of succession among Shah Jahan's four sons triggered military and diplomatic movements across the country. All the regional kings, chiefs, zamindars and *mansabdars* were expected to pick sides. Princes invested heavily in forging alliances with kings. For Aurangzeb, his coming clash with Dara also saw a cleavage in Rajput-Muslim relations within the Mughal system emerge for the first time. Dara managed to win many of the Rajput chiefs along his side, prominently the Rathods, Hadas,

Sisodias, Gaurs, Jhalas, Bundelas and Chandawats (Jadunath Sarkar, *History of Aurangzeb* Vol. 2, pp. 12–14). Auarangzeb's early conflict with Dara also played no inconsiderable part in shaping the former's religious policy in later years. Dara was tolerant of Hindus. Aurangzeb deposed him on the accusation of apostasy, and also had him done to death to justify his act. Shah Jahan's third son portrayed himself as a puritanical Muslim. After his crowning, he styled himself with radical Islamist titles like "Nasruddin" (Defender of the Faith) and "Shuja Bahadur Ghazi" (Courageous Slayer of Infidels/Hindus).

The house of the Rathods of Marwar ruled from Jodhpur, led by Maharaja Jaswant Singh. Previously, his forefathers Mota Raja Uday Singh and Sur Singh had won great respect at the Mughal court. The clan of Marwar was one of the most trusted by Mughal rulers. Jaswant Singh, wanting to continue his family legacy, offered his sincere services to Shah Jahan.

Following Shah Jahan's illness and semi-retirement in 1657, a war of succession broke out among his four sons. Jaswant Singh, a loyalist of Shah Jahan, sided with Dara Shikoh; in fact, he led the imperial Mughal army in its first clash with Aurangzeb's rebel forces at Dharmatpur near Ujjain in April 1658, but suffered defeat. Following Dara's defeat at Samugarh the very next month, Jaswant had no option but to side with Aurangzeb. He had a reason for doing so. He did not want Jodhpur to be overrun by the Mughals. Aurangzeb, for his part, did not want rivalry with a reputed and formidable Rajput kingdom. Their alliance thus hung on a lose strand of mutually defensive mentality, and by no means of their free volition. The inherent weakness of this alliance was shown up in the battle of Khajwa between Aurangzeb and his older brother Mohammad Shuja in January 1659. Jaswant Singh commanded Aurangzeb's forces, but not obtaining his desired commanding position in the battlefield, felt disrespected and angered. One night he fell upon Aurangzeb's camp from the back, killing many Mughal soldiers and fleeing to Jodhpur with whatever loot he could lay hands on.

Possibly, Jaswant Singh was making a statement here. Had this rebellion continued it could have shaken the Mughal throne. We do not know for certain, as Mirza Raja Jai Singh of Amer soon thereafter mediated between the two sides and managed to get Jaswant Singh back on Aurangzeb's side. For the next 18 years, The Raja of Jodhpur served Aurangzeb in various places like Gujarat, the Deccan and Afghanistan. Hindu chiefs in the north trusted him. His influence also kept a check on Aurangzeb's religious policies.

However, both Marwar and the Mughals weren't destined to be friends. As we have noted, it was an unnatural alliance in which trust never blossomed; mistrust and a barelt concealed hostility simmered. It was out in the open soon after the death of Jaswant Singh at Jamrud in Afghanistan while on a Mughal campaign. Aurangzeb now wished to dictate the succession of Marwar, although he had solemnly promised Jaswant Singh that he would recognize his successor's natural right to the throne of Marwar. But promises and treaties meant nothing to Aurangzeb. He not only dumped his promise to the late Jaswant Singh and refused to recognize his infant son Ajit Singh as the natural successor of the Marwar throne, but worse, imprisoned Jaswant's widow and the infant Ajit in Delhi, with the undisguised intent of converting them to Islam, and of course, usurping Marwar itself.

Jaswant Singh had a son, Prithviraj Singh, who was to be his designated successor. It is chronicled in the Marwar *khyats* that Aurangzeb, who was eyeing Marwar, presented Prithviraj Singh a poisoned dress, on wearing which Prithviraj died on May 8, 1667 at Delhi, in great pain. Prithviraj was an efficient leader and a brave prince. Jaswant could not get over the shock of his son's death, and was sunk in grief because he had no male heir who could seek revenge. But Rajput retribution wasn't long in coming.

The resistance was started by the Rajput nobles under the intrepid Durgadas Rathore, and later erupted into an all-out war between the Mughal empire and Rajputs of Marwar, who were supported by Mewar Rajputs. It lasted for almost thirty years, and its culmination was the end of Mughal rule over Rajputana.

Jaswant Singh was campaigning in Jamrud in Afghanistan when he died in December 1678. His elder son Prithviraj had been treacherously poisoned by Aurangzeb, thus leaving Jaswant no heir. Aurangzeb seized the opportunity to intervene by imposing his direct rule over Marwar. Soon after Jaswant Singh's death two of his queens each gave birth to male children. One of these sons died soon after his birth, leaving the other, Ajit Singh, as sole heir.

Aurangzeb ordered the infant Ajit to be brought to Delhi where he was kept in Noorgarh under house arrest. No Rajput had any illusions about what lay in store next. The Mughal emperor was out to convert Jaswant's widow and the infant Ajit to Islam, and also extinguish Marwar as an independent entity.

But it was the Mughal entity that had chosen its ruin in embarking upon war with the Rajputs.

A 20-year long struggle against Aurangzeb and the Mughal Empire now began in 1679, led by the intrepid Durgadas Rathod. Marwar, seemingly the weaker side in this war, actually had a strategic advantage. They were fighting in their homeland and knew the territory like the back of their hand and resorted to guerrilla war against Mughals. The principal parts of Marwar were soon recaptured by the Rajputs, and in the end, the house of Rathod inflicted a decisive defeat on the house of Timur.

The details of the battle are quite numerous, but the point worth noting is that Aurangzeb was lack of trustworthiness as a ruler and individual, and his jumping the gun to take advantage of vassal states the moment they were off guard proved disastrous. Looked at from a shrewd realistic angle alone, it was a political blunder.

And Jodhpur had not even been rebellious, unlike say, Mewar, which never bowed to the Mughals. A military move against a rebellious vassal kingdom is understandable. But this was not the case here, and Aurangzeb's move was driven solely by his religious zeal. Jaswant Singh of Jodhpur and Jai Singh Kacchwaha of Amer were two prominent Rajputs who were hugely significant Mughal allies. Also, both Rajput stalwarts kept Aurangzeb's religious policies in check. After death of Jaswant Singh there was no Hindu *mansabdar* of note in the Mughal court. Aurangzeb was now free; almost immediately, he re-imposed the *jaziya* tax on Hindus in 1679.

Coming to Mewar, since the days of Jahangir, peace had prevailed between them and the Mughals. The Ranas of Mewar paid their homage by sending gifts and tributes but never visited Delhi. The political relations were stable; the house of Mewar did not lose its honour as it was not completely subjugated, while the Mughals received their regular tributes. Aurangzeb's unique achievement was to destroy these relations in a short span of time.

Marwar till the time of Jaswant Singh was a Mughal ally, and thus Mewar's western part now touched Mughal territory directly. The kingdom was surrounded from all sides. It was evident that Aurangzeb wanted to subjugate Mewar too.

As the Ranas of Mewar were patrons of many temples, Aurangzeb's campaign had both military and religious ambition. He took possession of

Udaipur and destroyed many of its great temples. Bent on crushing Hindu pride, in Mewar alone, the sixth Mughal ruler destroyed 235 temples.

Maharana Raj Singh Sisodia decided to wage counter war against Aurangzeb. Mewar is a hilly region with tricky mountain passes. The people of of the kingdom knew their territory well and used techniques like cutting off supplies, attacking at night and destroying communication. Veteran Mughal warriors like Hasan Ali Khan were terrorized and refused to enter the hills of Mewar. We learn from Mughal records that Khan's army was lost for a fortnight in the hills west of Udaipur. Aurangzeb's plan to ravage Mewar to the core failed miserably. The Mughals lost two campaigns in succession, and this was a revelation of their approaching decay.

Personal misfortune lay in store for Alamgir in his war against the Rajputs. This first came forth in the form of a rebellion by Prince Mohammad Akbar, orchestrated by the Rajputs themselves. Akbar was a loved son and was thought of by his father as a possible successor. He was deputed in Rajputana by Aurangzeb, who wanted him to completely subjugate Rajputana. Instead, it were the Rajputs who influenced and subjugated Akbar's mind. Durgadas Rathod and Rana Raj Singh of Mewar instigated him to rebel against his father. They convinced him that his father was a bigot and his actions would shake the foundations of their empire (which of course, eventually came about). The Rajputs also demanded that Akbar capture the Mughal throne to himself become the emperor of India, and promised him military assistance in his endeavour. Akbar's rebellion failed in the end, but it was one of the most shameful things for Aurangzeb as an emperor and as a father. This came about because of his decision to persecute a war against the Rajputs.

In Aurangzeb's 50-year reign, Rajput-Mughal relations strained over several issues of which only some have been discussed above. After the death of Aurangzeb every Rajput state carved out its independent dominion. They began ruling as they had been ruling before the Turkic invaders came. It seemed as if the 150-year Mughal rule had left no political mark in Rajputana. It was because of leaders like Durgadas Rathod, Maharana Raj Singh and Maharaj Sawai Jai Singh that this seemingly impossible feat could be achieved. There was a time during Akbar's rule when the Rajputs were chivalrous protectors of Mughal Empire but during the later years the withering Mughals far from being able to count on the support from their once-dependable allies, actually had to fear their enmity.

The state of Mewar and the Mughals had concluded a treaty in 1616 AD, following Mewar witnessed uninterrupted tranquillity and prosperity for half a century. The peaceful interregnum helped it to replenish its resources and manpower to fight one final war with the Mughals, which eventually hastened the downfall of the Mughal Empire in Delhi.

Shah Jahan had grown old at the time of Raj Singh's ascendance to the throne of Mewar. A bloody war of succession broke out between his sons Dara Shikoh, Shuja-ud-Daula, Muhiuddin Aurangzeb and Murad Baksh.

The Mughals had no tradition of primogeniture, i.e., the systematic bequeathing of rule upon a ruler's death, to his eldest son. Instead, it was customary for sons to overthrow their father and for brothers to war to death amongst themselves.

The final outcome of the succession war would rest heavily when it came to the issue of whose side Mewar would tilt towards. All the four sons of Shah Jahan wrote letters to Raj Singh seeking help from him. Raj Singh was personally inclined to Dara Shikoh who was a liberal individual in matters of religion, and had even gotten the Upanishads translated into Persian. Besides, Dara was also acquired renown as a scholar and saintly figure.

Aurangzeb eventually outmanoeuvred and killed everyone who stood in the way of his ambitions. His father, his brothers, and even his sons who opposed him became his victims in his insatiable lust for power, which eventually destroyed the Mughal Empire itself.

Dara was defeated by Aurangzeb in the Battle of Samugarh (near Agra) in May 1658 and was finally put to death in 1659 AD. Murad, who had been Aurangzeb's ally and had fought alongside him, too was not spared. The luckless prince was imprisoned at Mathura and executed in Gwalior at the behest of Aurangzeb in 1661. Shuja had been the governor of Bengal, but grew ambitious and was eventually overcome by Aurangzeb's forces. He escaped eastwards to Burma and was killed there by the locals.

The policies of Akbar, Jahangir and Shah Jahan of aligning with the powerful Mewar dynasty in order to cement a strong foothold in India were abandoned by Aurangzeb to his peril. It is noteworthy that Shah Jahan and Jahangir had Rajput Hindu mothers and thus, belonged to the bloodline that made them relatively tolerant and wise to rule a nation as complex as India, which was 95 per cent Hindu.

Aurangzeb's unmixed Tartar blood brought no Rajput sympathies to his aid. On the contrary, every noble family of Rajasthan stood with Shah Jahan and Dara Shikoh in the Mughal war of succession. Aurangzeb's bigotry and evangelistic lust outweighed any policymaking and he began an unrelenting and self-destructive persecution of Hindus in general and Rajputs in particular.

Renewal of resistance to the Mughals after the treaty of 1616 AD between Mewar and the Mughals can be credited to Raj Singh. He was a deeply religious and aggressive Hindu monarch who not only wanted to regain every inch of Mewar, but also expand its horizons to all of northern and western India and eventually defeat the Mughals in Delhi.

Raj Singh began his work many years before Aurangzeb grabbed power in Delhi. He used *teeka daur*, the name given to hunting expeditions by Mewar kings, to slowly nibble away at the neighbouring kingdoms. He annexed Malpura in one such hunting expedition and thus expanded Mewar to the frontiers of Ajmer. This was a direct challenge to the Mughals. Shah Jahan, who was the Mughal king then, chose to look the other way amidst these adventures by Raj Singh and is quoted as saying, "Oh, it's just a piece of mischief by my nephew." Shah Jahan looked upon of Karan Singh, Raj Singh's grandfather, as his adopted brother.

However, after the Malpura episode, Raj Singh approached Dara Shikoh and sent his trusted nobles along with his son Sultan Singh to the court of Shah Jahan. Shah Jahan treated the boy Sultan Singh with love and respect and a temporary truce materialised between Mewar and Mughals once again. Raj Singh understood that a disunited Hindu leadership and an ill-conceived strategy to fight the Mughals would stymie the plan he had in his mind, and therefore decided to fortify Mewar further. He now reached out to the other princely states of Rajasthan, mainly Jodhpur, Bikaner and Jaipur to forge a Hindu alliance. He even dispatched emissaries to the intrepid Maratha leadership, which was emerging as a menace to Mughal rule and its bigoted emperor Aurangzeb. Raj Singh, along with Chhatrapati Shivaji, can therefore be credited as being a Hindu leader with a pan-Indian outlook. After Aurangzeb's move of reimposing *jaziya* in 1679, Shivaji in his letter to the Mughal cautioning against the likely ill-effects of such a step, included a taunt, challenging Aurangzeb to exact *jaziya* levy from Raj Singh, if he could.

As mentioned earlier, by 1659, Aurangzeb had eliminated all his three brothers. The magnanimous Dara, the hyperactive but indecisive Shuja and the impetuous Murad all met the same tragic end. Aurangzeb imprisoned his father Shah Jahan, who died a sad, broken man in January 1666. and thus began the final chapter of conflict between Mewar and the Mughals under the two most committed and ablest leaders on either side. It is shameful and tragic for Hindus of this subcontinent that the amazing saga of the Hindu victory over Mughals has been completely erased from our history. In the course of these 20 years of his vengeful reign, Aurangzeb was challenged and defeated by Raj Singh.

This is a saga of humongous significance, as it forced Aurangzeb to completely abandon his desire of conquest of Rajasthan and shift forever to Deccan. He had already sustained defeat in the Far East in Assam against the Ahoms. The Rajput war of Aurangzeb also demonstrated the abilities of Rajput kingdoms to forget their differences and forge alliances against a common enemy when Hindu Dharma was under siege. In that era, there was perhaps none better than Raj Singh of Mewar to be the protagonist of the culmination of this thousand-year-old saga of civilisational conflict between the great Hindu Dharma with a barbaric death cult.

Three events, all of equal significance, bear mention to be able to grasp the scope and build-up of the Rajput-Mughal conflict under Raj Singh.

The Nathdwara Episode

Aurangzeb in his religious zeal issued two *firmans* (orders) that brought him to a head-on confrontation with Raj Singh of Mewar. The Mughal ruler sent an order to the *Gosains* (Brahmin priests of the Krishna Temple of Mathura saying if they claimed divinity, they had to show him some miracle, else, he would destroy the Krishna temples of Mathura and Vrindavan. On October 10, 1669, the priests of Srinathji temple of Mathura, Damodarji, Bal Krishna, Vallabhji, and Ganga Bai took the *moorti* (icon) of Bhagwan Krishna and left for Rajasthan to seek shelter for the precious divine sculpture of Shri Krishna.

No other Rajput kingdom could muster the courage to pick enmity with Aurangzeb. On some pretext or the other, they politely asked the priests to seek shelter elsewhere. Finally, after traversing the entirety of Rajasthan, through Jaipur, Kota, Jodhpur, Boondi, etc., the priests approached Maharana Raj Singh of Mewar to seek shelter and protection from Aurangzeb to build a temple of Shri Nathji in Mewar. Raj Singh assuring the Brahmins of his protection, decalred, "Only when a lakh Rajputs have been beheaded can Aurangzeb touch the *moorti* of Shri Nathji."

Raj Singh accorded state protection to the *moorti* and the priests and asked them to choose a place of their liking to build a temple for Shri Nathji. The priests chose Sihaad village near river Banas about 50 kms north of Udaipur and on February 20, 1672, Shri Nathji's *moorti* was reinstalled at the village, which remains till date to be one of the most significant *teerth* (pilgrimage centres) for Hindus and Vaishnavites in particular, the Nathdwara.

Giving state protection to the priests of Vrindavan was the second major bone of contention in the already vitiated relationship between Aurangzeb and Mewar. Raj Singh chose to stand for honour and love of his dharma than to forsake it at the altar of fear and greed.

Aurangzeb wrote a letter to Raj Singh forbidding him from giving protection the priests and Shri Nathji's *moorti*. The Maharana completely ignored Aurangzeb's rantings and dispatched a large army to the village of Sihaad to prepare for a battle should Aurangzeb attack the temple. The nobles of Devgadh, Saloombar, and its neighbouring areas geared up for battle to protect the icon of the Hindu deity.

Raj Singh sent an emissary to the Rathore clan of Jodhpur to assist him in fighting Aurangzeb. A major battle took place near Nathdwara which has been detailed later in this chapter.

Alliance with Durgadas Rathore

It was as though destiny had started to tilt towards Hindu fortunes. During Aurangzeb's tenure, all three major kingdoms of Rajasthan were ruled by three very capable, brave and staunch Hindu rulers plus of course the Marathas in the Deccan. Raj Singh in Mewar, Jaswant Singh in Jodhpur, Mirza Raja Jai Singh of Amer (Jaipur) and Chhatrapati Shivaji Maharaj in the Deccan were a formidable quartet that thwarted and eventually buried Aurangzeb's ambition of the full-blown Islamisation of the subcontinent. Jai Singh and Jaswant Singh were devout Hindus but had become Mughal allies because of their ancestral loyalty. However, both were internally displeased at Aurangzeb's growing Islamic zealotry and adequately demonstrated it to him from time to time.

Aurangzeb's continuous conflict with Hindu kings all over India and with the Afghans in Afghanistan resulted in the mass-scale migration of Hindus from Mughal-controlled regions to Hindu-controlled areas. Cities were vacated by Hindus and small villages sprung up all along the countryside in rural India. A major economic slowdown began gathering pace and Mughal coffers started depleting.

Aurangzeb then planned to implement the *jaziya* or religious tax on the Hindus of the subcontinent. *Jaziya* is an Islamic practice of taxing non-Muslims under Muslim rule simply for adhering to their faith. Aurangzeb was also aware that as long as the Rajput kingdoms of Jaipur, Jodhpur and Mewar stood tall, his plan of implementing *jaziya* would invite rebellion from Rajputs, and the possible effacement of the Mughals from Delhi. He now planned the murder of Mirza Raja Jai Singh and Maharaja Jaswant Singh.

He ordered Jai Singh to go to the Deccan to quell a local rebellion and sent Jaswant Singh to fight in Afghanistan. On August 28, 1667, under the orders of Aurangzeb, Jai Singh was poisoned and thus eliminated. Besides his opposition to *jaziya*, Aurangzeb also held Jai Singh responsible for secretly helping his great enemy Chhatrapati Shivaji Maharaj.

In the same year, Aurangzeb presented Jaswant Singh's valorous son, Prithviraj Singh, with a poisoned *khilat*, an Arabic robe, which caused the latter's death. Jaswant Singh was shattered by the murder of his son because he had no male heir to Jodhpur (his eventual successor Ajit Singh was born after Jaswant's death in Jamrud, Afghanistan). For reasons unknown, Jaswant Singh still kept fighting for Aurangzeb. On December 28, 1678, Jaswant Singh too died, possibly poisoned and put out of the way by Aurangzeb.

Jaswant Singh's queen was pregnant at the time of his death but was forced by Aurangzeb to shift to Delhi and was confined with his queens. Aurangzeb also annexed the kingdom of Jodhpur under the pretext of the absence of a rightful heir at the time of Jaswant Singh's death. Jaswant's widowed queen delivered a son who was named Ajit Singh. Aurangzeb planned to forcibly convert both mother and son to Islam and raise Jaswant Singh's son as a Muslim.

And then arose a warrior from the deserts of Thar, who changed the entire course of the history of Marwar by unsheathing the sword of revolt against Aurangzeb. He was a warrior of such calibre that history had to attach the prefix of 'Veer' to his birth name—Durga Das Rathore (*Veer* is the Sanskrit word for brave). Durga Das was a simple soldier in Jaswant's Singh's army but rose to the level of a much respected and feared noble of Marwar. Before Jaswant Singh's poisoning, Durga Das promised to protect the unborn child of Jaswant Singh and one day coronate him as the Maharaja of Jodhpur.

How Durga Das lived up to his promise and eventually crowned Ajit Singh as the king of Jodhpur is an astonishing saga of chivalry, loyalty, intelligence and selflessness which needs another book to be narrated in its full detail and glory. Suffice it to say that Durga Das decided to extricate the infant Ajit Singh from the clutches of Aurangzeb and a brief account of that needs to be mentioned here because this one event of the rescue of the infant Ajit Singh catapulted Durga Das to the status of a true leader and protector of Jodhpur's dynasty. This act would also prove to be crucial as Ajit Singh grew up to finally weed out Mughal rule from Marwar and Jodhpur totally. This escape has been documented in detail in Marwar's annals and needs to be quoted for historical accuracy but also for the sheer poetry of the valour of each noble of Marwar who laid down his life protecting its legal and rightful heir.

When these brave men saw that nothing short of the surrender of all that was dear to a Rajput was desired by Aurangzeb, their first instinct was the preservation of their prince; the next was to safeguard their own honour and that of their late king Jaswant Singh. The means by which they achieved their objectives were mind-boggling.

The womenfolk of the Rathore contingent who were stationed with the Queen and infant prince were placed in an apartment filled with gunpowder and torched. All was over in an instant, instead of the long agony of *jauhar*. Once free of the bonds of family and love, Marwar's Hindu warriors had nothing to look forward to except a niche in the immortal temple of valour when the motto was, "Youth who died, to be by poets sung". The lust for this sacrifice is so intense that it often beggars description. The Rathore warriors and their companions wished to die gloriously rather than suffer everlasting ignominy.

Hidden in a basket of sweetmeats, Ajit was taken out of the Mughal palace and a contingent of about 500 Hindus of Marwar under the able leadership of Durga Das Rathore made oblations to their family deity Goddess Bhawani, took a double helping of opium and mounted their steeds to achieve the impossible.

Thus spoke Ranchor and Govind, the son of Jodha, and Chandrabhaan, the Darawut and the son of Raghunath, with the fearless Bharmal, the Ooda, Soojawat and Raghunath, "Let us swim", they exclaimed, "in the ocean of battle. Let us uproot these *Asuras* (demons) and be carried by the *Apsaras* (heavenly damsels) to the abode of the Sun."

As thus each spoke, Soojah the bard took the word: "For a day like this", he said, "You enjoy your fiefs to give in your Lord's cause, your bodies to the sword and in one mass to gain *swarga*. As for me who enjoyed his friendship and gifts, this day I will make his salt resplendent. My father's fame, I will uphold, and lead the death in this day's fight, that future bards may hymn my praise."

Durga Das, the son of Askaran Das, spake thus: "The teeth of Yavanas (impure foreigners) are whetted, but by the lightning emitted from our swords, Delhi shall witness our deeds; and the flames of our wrath shall consume the troops of the Shah" (*The Great Maharanas* by Omendra Ratnu).

To quote James Tod

> *"As Aurangzeb's troops approached, lances in hand, with faces resembling Yama (the deity of death), the Rathores and the rest of Hindus of Marwar rushed upon the foe. Wave followed wave in the field of blood."*

Shankar completed his chaplet in the streets of Delhi. Ratna contended with nine thousand foes. Dilloh, Darawut made a gift of his life to Dewas. Chandrabhan was conveyed by the Apsaras to Chandrapur. The Bhati was cut piecemeal and lay on the field besides the son of Sultan. The faithful Udawat appeared like crimson lotus. Sandoo, the Chaaran bard with a sword in both hands, was in front of the battle and gained the mansion of moon." Every tribe and every clan performed its duty in this day's pilgrimage to the stream of the sword, in which Durgadas ground the foe and saved his honour.

Five hundred Hindu warriors of Marwar made the final sacrifice, but slew close to ten thousand soldiers of Aurangzeb on this one day of August 1680 and ensured the survival of their valuable prince and the queens of Jaswant

Singh. Ajit Singh was taken to Maharana Raj Singh of Mewar by Durga Das. Raj Singh immediately granted protection to the infant heir of Marwar. Thus, a bond was cemented between the Sisodiyas of Mewar and the Rathores of Marwar. This was to prove instrumental in the final uprooting of Mughal rule from Rajasthan.

Durga Das took shelter in the Aravalis of Sirohi and Abu and continued the war against the Mughals. Aurangzeb's army had to sustain heavy casualties. There is an incident that deserves particular mention here.

Aurangzeb commanded pictures to be drawn of two of his most mortal foes, Shivaji Maharaj and Durga Das. Shivaji was drawn on a couch and Durga Das on horseback. Aurangzeb at first glance exclaimed, "I may entrap that fellow (Shivaji) but this dog is born to be my bane."

Aurangzeb even offered a bribe of forty thousand gold dinars to Durga Das, if he were to surrender Ajit to the Mughals. Durga Das laughed it off contemptuously. He kept the banner of resistance to Aurangzeb flying and outlived Aurangzeb to reinstate Ajit Singh as the Maharaja of Jodhpur.

After Aurangzeb's death in 1707 AD, Durga Das drove out the Mughal army from Marwar and crowned young Ajit Singh as its new Maharaja. Thus, the lionheart Durga Das fulfilled the promise he made to Jaswant Singh and retired from serving Marwar to die in solitude with a few loyal chieftains around him on the banks of Kshipra river, in the holy city of Ujjain on November 22, 1718.

Returning to Raj Singh, as narrated earlier, after the rescue of Ajit Singh from Aurangzeb's clutches, Durga Das kept the child prince of Marwar in the custody of Raj Singh for a few months. This too became a bone of contention between the Mughals and Mewar. The last act that evaporated all possibility of peace between Aurangzeb and Raj Singh was the implementation of the *jaziya* tax on non-Muslims of the subcontinent.

Jaziya, though, became a blessing in disguise for the Hindus of the subcontinent, as the mask of a tolerant Islam was fully thrown off by Aurangzeb. He was now using muscular force to convert Hindus to Islam, causing a massive rebellion not only in the troops serving the Mughal army under Hindu kings but also among the general Hindu populace.

Jaziya also ensured that Rajput kingdoms of Jodhpur, Jaipur and Mewar would begin to forget their differences and align with each other. Raj Singh was the pivot under whom the Rajput unity was crystallised. He also wrote letters to Chhatrapati Shivaji Maharaj and the tenth Sikh Guru, Gobind Singh, thus laying the foundations of pan-India Hindu resistance to Islamic rule over the country.

The cunning Aurangzeb knew that as long as Maharaja Jaswant Singh of Jodhpur and Mirza Raja Jai Singh of Amer were alive, any move to implement *jaziya* would mean immediate and unmanageable revolt by both these devout kings and would also push them both into the willing and waiting arms of Raj Singh of Mewar.

As has been narrated, Aurangzeb poisoned both these great Hindu kings of Jodhpur and Jaipur and then imposed the *jaziya* order on India in 1679 AD. Promulgation of *jaziya* immediately evoked a response from Raj Singh.

Following are random passages from the letter Raj Singh wrote to Aurangzeb, almost challenging him to attack Mewar if his love for taxing Hindus needed quenching:

"I have been informed that enormous sums have been dissipated in the persecution of the designs formed against me, your well-wisher; and that you have ordered a tribute to be levied to satisfy the exigencies of your exhausted treasury."

While your great ancestors pursued generous principles, wheresoever they directed their steps, conquest and prosperity went before them; and they reduced many countries and fortresses to their obedience. During your majesty's reign, many have been alienated from the empire, and further loss of territory must necessarily follow since devastation and rapine now universally prevail without restraint. Your subjects are trampled underfoot and every province of your empire is impoverished.

When indigence has reached the habitation of the sovereign and his princes, what can be the condition of the nobles? As to the soldiery, they are in murmurs; the merchants complaining, the Mohammedans discontented, the Hindu destitute, and multitudes of people are beating their heads throughout the day in rage and desperation.

At this juncture, it is told that you, jealous of the poor Hindu devotees, will exact a tribute from Brahmins, Samorahs, Jogis, Bairagees, and Sanyasis. If your majesty places any faith in your own books, by a distinct called divine, you will then be instructed that God is the God of all mankind, not the God of Mohammedans alone.

In fine, the tribute you demand from Hindus is repugnant to justify; it is equally foreign from the good policy as it will impoverish the country; moreover, it is an infringement of the laws of Hindustan.

But if the zeal for your own religion hath induced you to determine upon this measure, the demand ought, by requisites of equity, to have been made first upon Ram Singh (then king of Jaipur), who is an esteemed principle among the Hindus. Then let your well-wisher (referring to himself) be called upon, with whom you will have less difficulty to encounter; but to torment ants and flies is unworthy of a heroic and generous mind.

It is wonderful that the ministers of your government should have neglected to instruct your majesty in the rules of rectitude and honour."

Around the same time, Chhatrapati Shivaji Maharaj too wrote a letter to Aurangzeb challenging him to extract *jaziya* from Raj Singh of Mewar. The grounds for the final conflict between Mewar and Mughals were thus laid, which would conclude a great resistance to the Islamic invasion of India before the mantle of fighting the Mughals shifted to the great Marathas. This is a saga that establish the greatness of Mewar, by defeating the mighty Aurangzeb and forcing him to the plains of Deccan from where he never returned.

Raj Singh was the last great king of Mewar who militarily matched and defeated the Mughals conclusively. Raj Singh's progeny did continue the struggle but with the rise of Maratha power, the Hindu flag of resistance went into the hands of Shivaji Maharaj and the Peshwas. The crucial role of Raj Singh in weakening and pushing Mughal forces out of Rajasthan and thus laying grounds for the pan-India Hindu resistance cannot be overstated.

The account of the war between Raj Singh and Aurangzeb which was an enduring conflict lasting two years between 1679-80 AD and ended with Aurangzeb's army decimated, humiliated and driven out of Rajasthan completely, merits narration here.

The preparation Aurangzeb made for the conquest of Mewar resembled those of the conquest of a potent kingdom than for the subjugation of a local *zamindar* (the title by which the Mughals referred the local Hindu princes), a vassal of the so-called mighty Mughal empire on whose colossal spread, Mewar was but a speck. He called his son Akbar from Bengal, Azim from Kabul, and also Muazzam (the Mughal's heir) from Deccan. With this formidable array, Aurangzeb entered Mewar.

Raj Singh responded adequately to Aurangzeb's assault. He first sent emissaries to all big and small Rajput kings to appeal to their Hindu pride and amassed a massive army. Raj Singh's life and deeds inspired every Hindu youth of Rajasthan to enlist in massive numbers with a fierce determination to destroy a *vidharmi* (adherent of an alien creed) who was out to destroy Hindu Dharma.

The Bhils, Palindas and Palipats (lords of the passes) embarked with thousands of bows and hearts devoted to the cause of a Hindupat (chief of the Hindus). The red banner of Mewar was raised high and mighty against the most powerful and vicious sovereign anywhere in the world at the time by the Sisodiyas and Rathores, Maharana Raj Singh of Mewar. The first royal edict of the Maharana was to follow the centuries-old tactic of the 'scorched earth policy' of his great ancestors. The peasantry, the mercantile class, the shepherds, blacksmiths, entire villages vacated the plains and moved to the hills where, once again, the Bhils fed them and served them.

This caused extreme hardships for the Mughal army, as food supply had to be ensured from Ajmer which was regularly attacked and looted by Mewar's Hindus. Raj Singh divided his forces into three armies. He dispatched his eldest son Jay Singh to the crest of Aravalis, ready to attack the invaders from either side of the mountains. The younger son, Bhim Singh, was dispatched to the western side of Mewar around Abu to keep channels of communication open with Marwar and Gujarat. Maharana Raj Singh kept the main body of the Mewar army with himself on the left flank of Aravalis, ready to cut off any possibility of retreat by the Mughals.

Aurangzeb entered Debari, on the outskirts of Udaipur and instead of entering the valley where Jay Singh was waiting for him, sent his general Tyber Khan and his son Akbar to Udaipur with 50,000 troops. The Mughal emperor was possibly tipped off about the placement of Raj Singh's troops by an insider and this one move of Aurangzeb to stop Debari and not committing his entire army into the valley leading to Udaipur, saved his army from a complete wipeout.

Akbar advanced into Udaipur unresisted. Palaces, gardens, lakes and isles met his eye, but no living thing; there was an eerie silence all around. Akbar set up camp at Udaipur and instructed Taj Khan and Ruhilla Khan to start demolishing temples and destroying sculptures. More than 200 temples in and around Udaipur were razed to the ground. Numerous skirmishes took place around these temples where 20-50 Mewar Hindus were killed three times their numbers before being overwhelmed by the invading Mughals. The battle around the famous Jagannath temple was very fierce and deserves special mention.

The gatekeeper of the Royal Udaipur house was a warrior named Naru Barhath. As Raj Singh was vacating the palace and leaving for the hills, someone mocked Naru saying, "You have taken gifts for decades as the gatekeeper, won't you stay back and fight for the temple?" Naru sent his family with the Rana to the hills and stayed back at the gates of Jagannath temple with chosen warriors.

When Taj Khan and Rohilla Khan came to the Jagannath temple, Naru and his 20 men gave battle to an entire army of Mughals and killed close to 500 troops before being overpowered. Thus, the people of Mewar gave a foretaste of the things to come to the Mughals. Aurangzeb moved to Udai Sagar from Debari to rejoin Akbar. At Udai Sagar, Aurangzeb destroyed three beautiful temples of Shiva and Vishnu.

Raj Singh moved in with his troops and placed them in such a way that neither Aurangzeb could proceed further, nor could Akbar retreat from Udaipur. The Mewar maharana was a master war strategist and used his immaculate knowledge of Mewar's topography to his advantage. He pushed Akbar to commit a blunder and after weeks of waiting, Aurangzeb's son made the suicidal move. He chose the mountains and passes of Gogoonda as his exit and this was the worst choice he could make. Prince Jay Singh, along with his troops and the Bhil army waited precisely for this move.

To quote James Tod

> *"The allodial vassals of the mountains, along with Bhil auxiliaries, outstripped Akbar's retreat, and blocked up farther egress in one of the long-extended valleys termed as Naal, closed by natural ramparts on which they formed post of trees, and manning the crests from each side, hurled destruction on the foe; while the Prince, in like manner, blocked up the entrance and barred retrogression too. Death menaced them in every form."*

The trapped Mughal army was starved and was staring at annihilation when Prince Jay Singh showed mercy to them, admitting overtures from Akbar, confided in protestations to renounce the origin of the war and gave them guides to conduct them out of the trap to the defile of Jilwarra onwards to the eastern side till they reached the safety of the walls of Chittor. While Akbar was trapped in the Aravalis, another Mughal general, Diler Khan, approached from the west through Desuri pass from Marwar to rescue Prince Akbar.

Mewar's army allowed Diler to approach unopposed and when they were fully inside along an intricate gorge, Vikram Solanki and Gopinath Rathore, both gallant nobles of Mewar, attacked the Mughals. It was a desperate conflict at the end of which the Mughal contingent met complete destruction.

A huge amount of money and weaponry fell into the hands of the Mewar army. Their plan had worked out to perfection. With the Mughal army dissipated, trapped and partly destroyed, it was the right time for Raj Singh to attack Aurangzeb himself somewhere around the mountains between Udaipur and Chittor.

Tod quotes the British historian Robert Orme, who is credited to have many historical details of that period:

"The Mughal army advanced among the defiles with incredible labour, and with so little intelligence, that the division which moved with Aurangzeb himself was unexpectedly stopped by insuperable defences and precipices in front; whilst the Rajputs on one night closed the straits in his rear, by felling the overhanging trees; and from their stations above, prevented all endeavours of the Mughal troops, either within or without, from reversing the obstacles. Udeperri (this must have been Begum Udaypuri), the Circassian wife of Aurangzeb, accompanied him in the arduous war, and with her reticence and escort was enclosed another part of the mountains; her conductors dreading to expose her person to danger or public view, surrendered. She was carried to the Rana, who received her with homage and every attention."

Meanwhile, the emperor himself might have perished by famine, of which the Rana let him see the risque, by confinement of two days; when he ordered his troops to withdraw from their stations and suffer the way to be cleared.

As soon as Aurangzeb was out of danger, the Rana sent back his wife, accompanied by a chosen escort. The Rana's only request in return was that Aurangzeb should refrain from destroying the sacred animals of their religion; but the latter, who believed in no virtue but self-interest, imputed the generosity and forbearance of the Rana to the fear of future vengeance, and continued the war.

Soon after, he was again well-nigh enclosed in the mountains. The second experience of difficulties well beyond his age and constitution and the arrival of his sons, Azim and Akbar, determined him not to expose himself any longer in the field, but to leave the conduct of operations to his sons. Thus, the great clan of Rajputs of Mewar, ably assisted by the general population of Mewar and an alliance with gallant Rathores of Jodhpur under Veer Durga Das, nobly contested the palm of glory."

Aurangzeb had thus quailed before the fury of the Sisodiya-Rathore forces. Though equipped with superior firepower manned by European gunners, the Mughal army proved to be no match for the just cause and avenging steel of the Rajputs. Alamgir was humiliated, ignominiously defeated and compelled to a disgraceful retreat with an immense loss of men and equipment.

Raj Singh captured the imperial standard of Mughals, horses, elephants and immense state equipment. The humiliation of Aurangzeb and his sons by Raj Singh and his sons and his nobles did not end here but continued for two more years. Of the multiple battles fought, a few deserve special mention and are described briefly.

Aurangzeb retracted to the safety of Chittor and joined his sons Akbar and Muazzam there. Despite of the reverses and hardships endured by Aurangzeb and his army, he continued one act of barbarity very religiously and that was destroying Hindu temples. Even while retreating and nursing his wounds and contemplating how to respond to an ascending Rajput power, Aurangzeb is recorded to have destroyed 76 Hindu and Jain temples in and around Chittorgarh.

Meanwhile, a noble of Mewar, Sanwaldas Rathore (direct line of Jaimal Rathore) wrought havoc on the supply lines of Mughals from Ajmer to Chittor. This caused alarm to Aurangzeb with regard to his personal safety. Leaving the perilous warfare of Mewar to his sons, Aurangzeb retreated to the relative safety of Ajmer.

Foiled in his vengeance, personally disgraced, twice granted a pardon by the great Maharana himself, his women captured and returned, his armies depleted, his invincibility crushed, his religious zeal blunted, Aurangzeb, the Tartar, was pushed out of the sacred lands of Mewar by the pious and glorious blood of Bappa Rawal and Maharana Pratap Singh flowing in the veins of one of the greatest Maharanas of Mewar, Raj Singh.

Maharana Raj Singh is a Hindu warrior whose name finds no mention in the history curriculum of this unfortunate nation of ours. A Maharana who did not rest on the affluence and calm created by his father and grandfather, but chose to respond to the Islamic zealotry of Aurangzeb in kind and equal force.

Upon his return to Ajmer, Aurangzeb dispatched Rohilla Khan with 12,000 troops to capture or kill Sanwal Das. The Marwar troops came to the rescue of Sanwal Das and the joint army defeated the Mughals at Poor Mandal, pushing them back to Ajmer. While Rana and his elder son Jay Singh succeeded in destroying Aurangzeb in the east, the younger son Bhim Singh continued with his own pursuits in the west and made a powerful diversion against the Mughals by invading Gujarat and seizing it. Bheem also annexed the crucial state of Idar and mercilessly slew the Mughal vassal Hassan and his troops.

Bhim went on to Badnagar and Pattan and plundered them. Siddhpur, Mhourassa and other towns of western Gujarat shared the same fate. Bhim was advancing to Surat when Raj Singh recalled him out of benevolence to the local nawab and sultan, who sought mercy from Mewar's Maharana.

Bhim was a staunch Hindu prince and inflicted retribution for the Muslim plunder of temples with an equally furious demolition of mosques all over southern Rajasthan and northern Gujarat. Shyamaldas says in the *Veer Vinod*:

"The Maharana sent his son Bhim Singh with 4,000 horsemen to Badnagar in Gujarat where he demolished 300 mosques and extracted 40,000 rupees as penalty from the city dwellers and returned triumphant."

One episode of the vengeance of Hindus under the Maharana needs special mention after which we shall come to the three major battles fought by Maharana and his two sons, which led to the conclusive victory of Mewar and ended with Aurangzeb extending a hand of friendship to Raj Singh. A treaty ensued. This treaty not only ensured total safety and prosperity of Mewar, it also secured the freedom of Marwar from the clutches of the Mughals.

For two years, the intense Mewar-Mughal conflict for superiority went on with Raj Singh and his two sons and a dozen-odd noblemen of Mewar fought for Hindu supremacy over the murderous Aurangzeb who had bared all his *jihadi* fangs.

One such nobleman was a Brahmin civil minister of Mewar, Dayal Shah, who had shown great military acumen and loyalty to the Rana to have earned his trust. Dayal Shah headed a flying force that would indulge in 'shoot and scoot' tactics to harass the Mughals. Raj Singh sent a large contingent with Dayal Shah eastwards to Malwa and the latter ravaged the region up to Narbada and Betwa rivers.

James Tod describes Mewar's retribution by Bhim Singh and Dayal Shah against Islamic onslaught thus:

Contrary to the Rajput character, whose maxim is Parcere Subjectis, Mewar's military leaders were compelled by the utter faithlessness of Aurangzeb to retaliate against his excesses.

Dayal Shah ravaged Sarangpur, Dewas, Sarong, Mandoo, Ujjain, and Chanderi. Every Mughal opposer in these areas was put to the sword. To continue using the words of annals:

"Husbands abandoned their wives and children, and whatever could not be carried was given to the flames. The Qazis were bound and shaved and the Qurans thrown into wells."

For once, the Mewar army avenged themselves in the imitation of the Islamic tyrant, even on the religion of their enemies. Dayal Shah is said to have razed hundreds of mosques to the ground. He was unrelenting in his vengeful slaughter and turned Malwa into a desert. Once again, Malwa was ravaged to fill the coffers of Mewar, just as had happened at the time of Pratap when Bhama Shah did the same to Malwa, albeit on a smaller scale. Plush with the looted riches and weaponry from Malwa, Dayal Shah met the forces of Prince Jai Singh at the foothills of Chittor and fought a battle with Aurangzeb's son Azim near Chittor.

Jai Singh camped at Chittor with 13,000 horsemen and 26,000 soldiers when Dayal Shah joined him. The night before the decisive battle for Chittor, Mukhim and Ganga Shaktawat, Ratan Choondawat of Saloombar, Chandrasen Jhala of Sadri and Sabal Singh Chauhan of Baidla made powerful, motivating speeches to the Mewar army, which are recorded in the Mewar annals

Someday, in July 1680, the Mewar army sneaked around the fort at night and under the cover of rains, wiped out the Mughal force. The Mewar army returned to Prince Jai Singh with looted elephants, horses, *nagadas* (war drums), tents, weaponry, etc., which the prince distributed among the nobles and the men. Chittor was finally regained by the Rajputs after 500 years of bloodbath and sacrifices, never to be lost again.

Azim fled from Chittor with his wife and was hotly pursued by the Mewar army till he reached the safety of the fort of Ranthambore and sealed himself inside. Maharana Raj Singh, in the meantime, was stationed at the western frontiers of Mewar, touching Marwar. Raj Singh fulfilled his promise of protecting the infant Ajit Singh, the Rathore heir of Marwar by taking on the Mughals at Ganora, the chief town of Godwar. The Rathores under Durgadas fought jointly with Mewar against Aurangzeb. The Mughal army suffered decimation and had to exit both Mewar and Marwar after this battle.

Somewhere in north-central Mewar, Prince Bheem gathered his Sisodiyas and was joined by Rathores to fight a battle with Prince Akbar and his general Tyber Khan, whom they worsted in battle. This victory is mainly attributed to the moves of a Rajput chief who first looted 500 camels from the Mughals and then hurled flaming torches on them, unleashing mayhem on the Mughal camp. The pandemonium that ensued gave the apt opportunity to Mewar soldiers to attack and inflict a comprehensive defeat on the Mughals. The Mughal-Mewar conflict was premised on multiple reasons of hatred between the two powers and reached its culmination with the permanent expulsion of Aurangzeb and his sons from Mewar.

Aurangzeb was so overwhelmed by the ferocity of Mewar's valour that he never set his eyes or foot on the pious land of Mewar again.

Raj Singh and his nobles, along with the Rathores of Mewar dented the myth of Mughal superiority permanently and depleted the army and resources of the Mughals to such an extent that it took the Mughals years to replenish them. By then, they had to shift their focus to the Deccan to meet the looming Maratha challenge.

Aurangzeb, in his religious zeal, provoked a fight that spun out of his control and ended the Rajput-Mughal alliance of 150 years, which had been the main reason for the continuance of Mughal rule in Delhi.

With the twin states of Marwar and Mewar alienated and the Rajputs of Jaipur under Ram Singh remaining indifferent, Aurangzeb had no alliance left with the Hindus of the subcontinent to placate the Hindu masses. Hindus all over India rose in revolt against the temple destruction and *jaziya* imposition by this intolerant Mughal zealot. Aurangzeb's madness to Islamise India had thus led to an unparalleled consolidation of Hindu forces in India.

All this would have shaped the trajectory of the thousand-year-old Hindu-Muslim conflict in the subcontinent very differently, but for one more act of treachery by Hindus who were close to Rana Raj Singh.

On November 3, 1680, after the Mughals had been convincingly kicked out of Rajasthan and when Raj Singh was planning to terminate the very seed of Islamic rule in India, he sat down to have lunch with a Chaaran friend, Aaskaran, whom he used to refer to as his 'brother'. Both friends consumed rice porridge, '*Khichdi*', and minutes after that, both died due to their food being poisoned.

At 51 years of age, the great Maharana's life came to an abrupt and tragic end by the unchivalrous connivance between one of his insiders and his enemies.

Looking at Aurangzeb's record of poisoning the Rajput kings of Jodhpur and Jaipur and the conduct of his great-grandfather Akbar, eliminating his enemies is the similar deceitful manner, it can safely be assumed that Aurangzeb might have been behind the poisoning of Maharana Raj Singh, although we may never be able to prove this conclusively. Thus, the sun set on the greatest dynasty of kings to have ruled anywhere at any time in recorded human history.

References

1. Sir Jadunath Sarkar, History of Aurangzeb; Vol. 2, p. 146.
2. Sir Jadunath Sarkar, History of Aurangzeb; Vol. 3, pp. 325-325.
3. Sir Jadunath Sarkar, History of Aurangzeb; Vol. 3, pp. 371-373.
4. Sir Jadunath Sarkar, *History of Aurangzeb;* Vol. 3, pp. 268-267.
5. Sarkar, *History of Aurangzeb Vol 3*, pp. 337-339.
6. S.R. Sharma, *Religious Policies of the Mughal Emperors,* p. 174.
7. Sarkar, *History of Aurangzeb*, pp. 344-347.
8. Sarkar, *History of Aurangzeb* Vol. 3, pp, 356-358.
9. Veer Vinod, Vol. 2, pg 452.
10. *Veer Vinod, Vol. 2, p. 453.*
11. *Annals & Antiquities of Rajasthan; James Tod; Vol. 1, p.302*

WAR WITH THE MARATHAS—DISASTER, DEFEAT, DENOUEMENT AND DEATH

CHAPTER 11

The onset of the 17th century witnessed a phenomenal shift in the politics of not just northern India, but of the whole of the country and indeed, the Indian subcontinent. It would go on to shape India's destiny for the next century and a half, but more importantly, it was destined to write the epitaph of the Mughal Empire that had been founded a century and a half prior to its last strongman Aurangzeb's one-way journey to the place of the origin of this development—the Deccan.

Map 4 : Mughal empire in 1720s

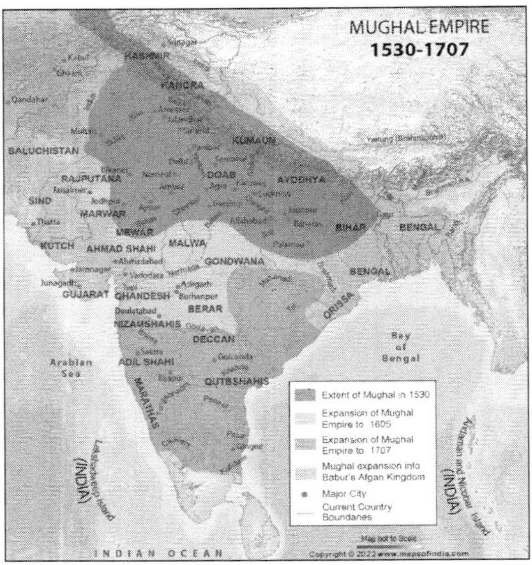

Till the 17th century, the country's southern arena, and particularly the Deccan was still out of the complete sway of the single sovereign of the north, i.e., the Mughals, who had managed to somewhat settle northern India from Gujarat to Bengal and Kashmir to Sind. Mughal Emperors since Akbar had long dreamt of conquering the Deccan, but it had remained a dream that was akin to the waves of the sea dashing against the immovable rocks of the shores.

Aurangzeb, who for unfathomable reasons was called the 'Great Mughal', had made up his mind to succeed where his predecessors had failed—and this endeavour of his, to complete the 'unfinished' business, dominated the history of southern India throughout the 17th century. In fact, his 'unfinished' business finished not only him but his much-vaunted empire as well.

The collapse of the Muslim Bahmani Sultanate, forty-seven years before the tragic fall of the Hindu Vijayanagar Empire (1565 AD) to the invading Bahamani constituents led to the establishment of the various Shahis, viz, the Nizamshahi of Ahmednagar and the Adilshahi of Bijapur. Ahmadnagar's Nizamshahi went extinct in the first quarter of the 17th century, a vacuum that was filled by Adil Shah of Bijapur. Akbar had prevailed against Ahmednagar in his time, but the Mughals had failed in annexing the kingdom and holding it for long. Jahangir and Shah Jahan in their times sought to fulfil the Mughal dream of absorbing the Deccan, and the best outcome had been a treaty between Bijapur and the Mughals in 1636 (Golkonda managed to retain its independence). Following the 1636 treaty between the Adilshahi sultanate and the then Mughal emperor Shah Jahan, Bijapur extended its sway from the west to the east coast. The capital city flourished, but this rise of the Adilshahi sultanate also contained the seeds of its decline and end.

The sultanate's earlier rulers had been hardy warrior-kings, but their successors were easily given to the life of the harem and the privileges of the durbar. Earlier conquests had been achieved by loyal slaves and servants, who were unwilling to tolerate these successors addicted to the sensuous pleasures of life rather than the toil and blood need to hold kingdoms and empires in that age. The Adilshahi threw up a child ruler and also a woman, who naturally commanded little or no loyalty—fighting men who stake their everything to win glories for their masters are not given to obedience of their laggard or wayward successors for long. The last great Adil Shahi sultan died in 1656. The other Deccan Muslim kingdoms were staring at an uncertain future; the ravenous Mughals of the north were waiting to absorb them. The absorption of the southern Muslim sultanates into the Mughal Empire might have happened as an inevitable corollary, but it was fated not to be. A new power arose in the Deccan, one that would not only thwart this seemingly inexorable drift, but also go on to rewrite the history of the Deccan, and later, of the Indian subcontinent itself.

This new power was the Marathas.

The Marathas have been part of the Deccan and the south since time immemorial, but had to contend with a dispersed existence since the 13th century. The Islamic invasions of the subcontinent and the downward turn in the fortunes of the Hindu kingdoms and empires that preceded the Muslim sultanates disaffected the Deccan inhabitants known as the Marathas as well; they were forced to become either subjects or at best, small-time vassals of wholly alien rulers, foreign in both ethnicity and religion. Till the 17th century, they lacked political organization and thereby the political status of their own. They needed a genius to unite their scattered castes and sub-castes and wield them into a nation. That man of history did arrive and when he did, he not only made the Marathas a formidable people, but also went on to create history by becoming the nemesis of the sixth and last Mughal of any consequence—Aurangzeb, the self-styled Alamgir.

That man was Shivajirao Bhonsale, whom the world knows as Chhatrapati Shivaji.

The Deccan is preponderantly marked by the Western Ghats, also known as the Sahyadri Range, which is a near-contiguous mountain range that separates the Konkan coastal region from the hinterland of Maharashtra known as the *desh*. The region of Konkan stretches from Mumbai to Mangalore. The Konkan region is noted for heavy rainfall and fertile land, plus its breathtaking beauty.

Crossing the Western Ghats and proceeding eastwards, the immediate region is a series of table-lands cut on every side by deep winding valleys. Hills and mountains of various heights, shapes and forms arise here, with steep sides often strewn with black boulders. There are ancient evergreen forests interspersing the region, which is otherwise extremely rugged. Eastwards of the Western Ghats, this part of Maharashtra is called Dang or Maval, and Mallad in the northern part of its neighbouring Karnataka. Hill-locked with deep ravines for the better part, this is the land that is rightly called the cradle of the Maratha Empire. Agriculture and cultivation are much tougher here; generally, the Deccan yields only a measure of subsistence to disproportionately larger amount of labour, The hardiness of the land has been transplanted by Nature on to its inhabitants.

The Maratha people had great and independent kingdoms prior to the arrival of the Muslims, whose expansionist movement of the 12th and 13th centuries had pushed the former to the western edge of the Deccan plateau by the early 14th century. Elsewhere, the sultanates of Ahmednagar and Bijapur flourished, but the Maratha people found refuge and safety in the inhospitable mountains and forests. Life in Maharashtra was—and in many ways still is—one that demanded and exacted hard toil. Nature in this region enforces a simplicity that does not lend itself to the pursuit of easy luxury. It was little wonder that the exaggerated aesthetics and polished manners of the northern milieu, brought on by Persianized interloping in India, could not take any root in this southern region of the country.

But Maharashtra produced several advantages like self-reliance, courage, perseverance, a simplicity steeped in sternness, straightforwardness of the rough kind, disdain for obsequiousness, social equality and pride for the dignity of the individual. 7th century Chinese scholar Xuanzang (more known as Hsiuen Tsang) who visited and lived in India during Emperor Harshavardhana's time had this to say about the Maratha people: "They are proud-spirited and warlike, grateful for favours and revengeful for wrongs". The soldierly nature of the Marathas was noted as early as the 7th century CE, when they were renowned as the Chalukyas. And it was Emperor Harshavardhana of the Pushyabhuti Dynasty, then the master of most of northern India, who discovered it the rather hard way; his southward expansion was halted on the banks of the Narmada and defeated by Chalukyan emperor Pulakesin II in 618-619 CE.

The fall of the Vijayanagara Empire in 1565 CE meant the extinction of the last Hindu empire in southern India. The fighting classes among the natives of the Maharashtra-Karnataka region, i.e., the Deccan clustered in small bands around different leaders and also lent their services for hire, i.e., as mercenaries. Many Maratha families rose to wealth, power and distinction, albeit as soldiers and commanders for hire in the services of the Muslim sultanates of Bijapur's Adil Shahi, Ahmednagar's Nizam Shahi and Golkonda's Qutub Shahi. Many Maratha dynasties have origins in the Kshatriya lineages of ancient India; Maurya, for instance is known as More in Marathi, Yadava as Jadhav, Yaudheya is Jedhe, to name a few; Pratiharas, who are today more commonly known as Parihar and Panwar in the north of India have become Pawars in Maharashtra. Then there are the Gurjaras, who are even today present as Gujjars in both the northern and southwestern parts of India.

One such family, the Bhonsales, originally lived in the Patas region of the district of Pune (Patas is today a railway station prior to Daund, the next immediate railway junction after Pune en route to the south). Towards the end of the 16th century, they had migrated to the village of Elur, within sight of the hill-fort of Devagiri (whose name was later changed to Daulatabad by the Muslim Tughlaq rulers) and the caves of Ellora. The early life of the Bhonsales was one of agriculture, but it wasn't long before they took to soldiering.

The decline of the Nizamshahi dynasty and the Mughal incursion into the Deccan towards the end of the 16th century opened the pathway for the rapid rise of the Bhonsales. The Mughals were the first to need these hardened and seasoned soldiers, and were not slow in winning over them with high *mansabs* (ranks) and handsome salaries. The early Bhonsales too did not baulk at changing their masters if the pay was better. The clan, and other Maratha clans to emerge in the region, entered the 17th century this way.

Shahji Bhonsale, the eldest son of Maloji Bhonsale was born in 1594 and when still adolescent or probably in boyhood, was married to Jijabai, daughter of a nobleman Lakhoji Jadhav Rao, who was the baron of Sindkhed. Shahji made his fortunes as a formidable soldier and commander, first in the service of the Ahmednagar Nizamshahi and after its decline and fall, in the offices of the Bijapur Adilshahi. Shahji also served the Mughals briefly during the reign of Shah Jahan before deserting them. He went on to become the king-maker among the Deccan sultanates, and went on to make much wealth and gain possessions of his own jagirs. To him was born the legendary Shivaji, who the Mughals learnt to fear and respect in the future; not least the Alamgir himself. Born in 1627 at Raigad, Shivaji single-handedly erased Mughal dominance in the Deccan, also slaying the hulky Bijapuri commander Afzal Khan in single combat in 1659 and decimating Aurangzeb's maternal uncle Shaista Khan's invading army in 1663 (Shaista Khan himself barely escaped alive, losing three of his fingers to Shivaji's sword-assault on him in the palace's inner chamber). Briefly pressed into submitting to a strong and preponderantly-resourced imperial Mughal incursion led by Mirza Raja Jai Singh of Amer in 1665, Shivaji proceeded to Agra in 1666 under the terms of the Treaty of Purandar but was treacherously imprisoned by Aurangzeb who saw this opportunity as a godsent opportunity to extinguish this growing Hindu threat for good.

It was not to be, as destiny had willed it otherwise. The blessed and mighty son of Goddess Bhavani was destined to have the final word.

Shivaji and his then adolescent son Sambhaji made an audacious—almost impossible—escape from Aurangzeb's captivity on August 18, 1666, concealing themselves in baskets of fruits and sweetmeats ostensibly to be distributed as alms among the poor and seekers. This daring escape from Aurangzeb's captivity not only shook the Alamgir's smugness and confidence in his military establishment, but also filled the Mughal emperor with a sense of foreboding. His hated Hindu foe had not only outsmarted him in his own den, but worse, had infused the Hindus of northern India with newfound confidence. Shivaji at the royal court in Agra showed absolutely no deference to Aurangzeb, but on the contrary, administered a stinging slap to Mughal prestige, right in the court, amidst the presence of the latter's *mansabdars* and other *durbari* lackeys. His daring escape, executed with contemptuous ease, was an insolent challenge to Aurangzeb. The Mughals were not invincible, and Shivaji proclaimed it loud and clear at Agra.

Nor was this to remain an aberration in Aurangzeb's control over his empire. Upon his safe return to Maharashtra after his unthinkable escape, Shivaji did not lay low, content with his smaller kingdom. Surat, the Mughal Empire's most prosperous city was counter-attacked and sacked for a second time by the Marathas in 1670 in response to the Purandar campaign against the Marathas (Shivaji had attacked and defeated the Mughals in Surat earlier in 1664, and also looted much treasure from the city), yielding much wealth.

Adding to the Mughal's consternation was the fact that Shivaji was not an enemy who, unlike most other Hindu adversaries of Islamic invaders and rulers of that medieval age, would fight battles of only defence. Waiting to be attacked first and then being trapped into battles against superior numbers backed by preponderant firepower, and going down in a blaze of defiant glory had generally been the Hindu story against Muslim conquistadors, with notable examples like Maharanas Kumbha, Sanga, Pratap and Raj Singh. The advent of the son of Shahji Bhonsale proved to be turning point. The Turkic encroachers in the country henceforth had to contend with a Hindu foe who would no longer be submissive, timid and resigned to his fate. He was prepared to confront them in battle for the sake of his existence, identity and pride. Worse, the Lion of the Sahyadris also showed that the Hindu would also not hesitate to attack, when needed. To the Hindu world in that age of persecution, Shivaji Maharaj appeared as the dawn of a new hope, the protector of Sanatana Dharma. Shivaji's kingdom and court, and later his son Sambhaji's, became the rallying point of Hindu opposition to Aurangzeb.

After his triumphant return from Aurangzeb's captivity, Shivaji engaged in a series of military campaigns to throw off with the constraints that the Treaty of Purandar had placed upon him. Under the treaty's terms, Shivaji had been forced to cede 23 of his forts to Aurangzeb, but he wasn't going to let these strategically located fortresses remain in the enemy's possession for long. In 1670, Shivaji attacked and captured Kondana, a militarily important hill fortress in the possession of Uday Bhanu Singh, a Rajput general in Mughal service; Tanaji Malusare, an intrepid and valorous Maratha commander wrested Kondana from Mughal control, although meeting a hero's death in the effort. The Mughal defeat at Kondana (later named Sinhagad) was a serious blow to Aurangzeb's dream of cementing Mughal presence in the Konkan to further his sway over the Deccan, a prize that had eluded the Mughals ever since the days of Jalaluddin Akbar. The fall of Kondana was no accident, either; the Mughal control over the fort had been ended in a Maratha offensive, and the Mughal army had been worsted in a commando-style Maratha assault on the fort.

Maratha power because of Shivaji's ambition in constant execution had grown exponentially, and Alamgir could no longer deny it. All attempts to crush Shivaji or bring him to heel had failed. Mughal armies sent under various commanders had proven unequal to the challenge, while Shivaji grew only stronger after each clash, with even a daunting setback at Purandar failing to quell him. The years between 1670 and 1672 saw a dramatic rise in Shivaji's power, with the Marathas raiding the territories of Baglan, Khandesh in northern Maharashtra and Surat (as mentioned above). Soon the Mughal-held forts of Aundha, Patta and Trimbak fell, with the Marathas next attacking Salher and Mulher near Nasik in 1672. Despite a 50,000-strong Mughal army well-supported by heavy cavalry and artillery being dispatched, a smaller Maratha army with light cavalry inflicted a humiliating defeat on Aurangzeb's forces, with 22 wazirs along with the Mughal army's commanders Ikhlas Khan and Bahlol Khan being taken prisoners by the Marathas. The fortresses of Salher and Mulher were captured by Shivaji. The Battle of Salher was also noted for another thing: all of Shivaji's clashes hitherto against the Mughals had been guerilla warfare making expert use of the mountainous and rugged terrain of Maharashtra. This was the first occasion both foes met in open battle, and the first time in nearly a thousand years a Hindu army went on the offensive against a Muslim adversary. The outcome was a rout for the House of Timur.

The Mughal defeat of 1672 meant that Aurangzeb's hold over the southern part of the Indian peninsula was more on paper than reality. As if to underline the reality, Shivaji crowned himself Chhatrapati in 1674 at Rajgad, a mere two years later, in a traditional Hindu ceremony. His coronation as monarch was consecrated by Gaga Bhatt, a Brahmin *purohit* (priest) from Varanasi; Aurangzeb could do nothing about it, except grudgingly acquiesce Shivaji's de facto independence. In fact, along with Englishmen, French, Dutch and Portuguese representatives, there was also a Mughal representative in submissive attendance at Rajgad. The Hindu monarch struck coins in his own names—this was a de jure statement of independence—and assumed the title of Chhatrapati, besides proclaiming his kingdom "Hindavi Swaraj". The phenomenon of Shivaji transcended that of any ordinary, rebellious Hindu warrior or chieftain. More than wresting territory from the Mughals and defeating them in battles, Shivaji had come to epitomize undying Hindu resistance to Islamic rule.

For Aurangzeb, the man from the Sahyadris, ten years his junior, had become a very personal, formidable and threatening enemy. In one of his own testimonies to Shivaji's power and influence on the events and history of his age, a newsletter of Aurangzeb's court in the year 1670 reports that the emperor Alamgir read a dispatch that had arrived from the Deccan, reporting some raids carried out by the Marathas and then remained silent. After the 1672 Mughal defeat, Aurangzeb lived in consternation because of the irrepressible challenge from the Deccan, but did not dare dispatch another military force to tackle Shivaji. The fate that had befallen previous Mughal generals who had marched against the Hindu king weighed heavily on the Mughal's mind. In the inner council of his court, he often anxiously asked whom he should next send against Shivaji—there wasn't any who was willing to volunteer for that sort of adventure. To this query, Mahabat Khan, one of Aurangzeb's generals, irreverently replied with a sneer, in contempt of the fanatic cleric Abdul Wahab's influence over the Badshah, "No general is necessary. A decree from the Chief Qazi (Wahab) will be sufficient to extinguish Shiva". The Persian king Shah Abbas II, who had beaten off both Aurangzeb and Dara Shikoh to wrest control of Kandahar in Afghanistan, sent a letter taunting Aurangzeb, "You call yourself a Padishah, but cannot subdue a mere zamindar like Shiva. I am coming to India with an army to teach you your business" (*Book of Aurangzeb*; Sir Jadunath Sarkar; Vol. IV, chapter 43, "Shivaji", page 188).

Chhatrapati Shivaji passed away in 1680, six years after his coronation as king.

The passing of that scourge of the Mughals brought no deliverance, happiness or even relief to Aurangzeb, though he must have felt elated in the immediate wake of the departure from the mortal world of his arch-nemesis. Far from it; Aurangzeb saw Shivaji's death as an opportunity to launch a war that he thought would extinguish the Martha threat for good. Chhatrapati Shivaji left for his heavenly abode in April 1680, and in the December of that year, Aurangzeb set out from Agra to subdue his greatest festering challenge.

The region southwards of the Narmada was known as the Deccan, though today's Deccan is smaller by geographical and sociocultural bandwidth. Alamgir Aurangzeb marched out from Agra and crossed the Narmada in December 1680.

He could not recross the Narmada to set foot again in northern India.

The Mughal-Maratha War from 1680 to 1707 was in every respect an epic war that altered the face of Indian subcontinent, epochally. It would be no exaggeration to call it the mother of all wars in India. When we take into account that the average life expectancy in that era was around 30 years, this war of 27 years can said to have spanned the lifespan of an entire generation. The total number of battles fought was in hundreds. It occurred over vast geographical expanse spanning four biggest states of modern India—Maharashtra, Gujarat, Madhya Pradesh and Karnataka. For time, expanse and human and material cost, this war has no match in Indian history.

It started in 1680 with the Mughal emperor Aurangzeb's invasion of Maratha empire and ended only in 1707 with Aurangzeb's death. The Alamgir threw everything he had into this war, only to lose it all. His own life was now reaching its inevitable phase of tragedy. He had by now become a man battling in vain against an irrepressible enemy and invisible but inexorable fate.

What makes the study of war more interesting is the understanding of politics behind it. Every war is driven by politics. Rather war is just one of the means to do politics. This war was not an exception.

Shivaji's tireless work for most of his life had shown fruits by the last quarter of seventeenth century. He had firmly established Marathas as power in Deccan. He built hundreds of forts in Konkan and Sahyadris and thus created a defense backbone. He also established strong naval presence and controlled most of the Western ports barring few on end of Indian peninsula. Thus tightening the grip on trade routes of Deccan sultanates, he strangled their weapons import from Europe and horses import from Arabian traders. These Sultanates launched several campaigns against Shivaji, but came a cropper.

On the northern front, while a few Rajput kings had accepted to be the vassals of Mughals, the House of Mewar had never bowed to the Mughals, not even in the day of the founder of the empire Babar. Aurangzeb had succeeded to the throne after brutal killing of his brothers and imprisonment of his father. He however, not only failed to quell Rajput resistance, but also led his empire into a ruinous war against this valorous Hindu community—a war that began the chain of events that were to culminate in the end of his empire. It was only matter of time before southern Marathas were in his cross-hairs. The reason for his implacable conflict with both was the same—both were Hindus who refused to yield to him and his bigoted religious way of life.

"The death of Shivaji was the mere beginning of Maratha history. He founded a Hindu principality—it had yet to grow into a Hindu Empire. This was all done after the death of Shivaji. The real epic opens as soon as Shivaji, after calling into being the great forces that had to act it up, disappears from the scene".

—Vināyak Dāmodar Sāvarkar

Shivaji's Passing

At the time of Shivaji's death in 1680, the Maratha Empire spanned an area far more than the current state of Maharashtra and had taken firm roots. Though it was surrounded by enemies from all sides; namely, the Portuguese on northern coast and Goa, British in Mumbai, the Siddhis in Konkan and remaining Deccan sultanates in Karnataka posed limited challenge each, none of them was capable of taking on the Marathas alone. The Mughal Empire with Aurangzeb at its helm was the most formidable foe.

Aurangzeb's life was a saga of unbridled religious fanaticism. The Rajputs and Sikhs in northern India had already been irreparably alienated because of his intolerant policies against Hinduism. After his blood-soaked succession to the throne, life for Hindus in his kingdom was nothing short of a living hell. Taxes like the hated *jaziya* were reimposed on Hindus. They were forbidden from riding palanquins or mounting a horse. Hindu temples were destroyed by the dozen and forcible conversions were unleashed on the *kafirs* (infidels). The imposition of Sharia, the Islamic law, on the entire country was Aurangzeb's dream project, in which however, he failed disastrously, though not for want of trying. The fanatical drive for Islamization angered all Hindus; Rajputs, once staunch military allies of the Mughal Empire, now gave him the cold shoulder in his Deccan campaign, as they weren't willing to shed the blood of fellow-Hindus. Aurangzeb's treacherous murder of Guru Tegh Bahadur aroused the Sikhs to take up arms. Under Tegh Bahadur's son Gobind Singh, who became the tenth guru of the Sikh Panth, they became inveterate foes of the Mughals. The Sikh-Mughal enmity and wars continued beyond Aurangzeb's demise and ended only with the erasure of Mughal control of the Punjab in the late 18th century.

In September of 1681, after somehow settling into a costly and even humiliating stalemate with the royal house of Mewar, Aurangzeb began his journey to Deccan. The disastrous Mughal defeats to the Ahoms in Assam and debilitating show of the Mughal war machine in Rajputana did not dampen his resolve to pursue yet another war. The burning objective of his life remained only one—to extinguish the Maratha confederacy that was not even fifty years old. The Mughal supremo had fielded an enormous army numbering half a million soldiers; these numbers were more than three times that of the then Maratha army. He had plentiful artillery particularly heavier cannons, horses, elephants, not to forget huge wealth in royal treasuries. Aurangzeb's plan in the Deccan was to team up with the Portuguese, English, the Siddis of Janjira, the Golkonda and Bijapur Sultanates to surround the Marathas from all sides and thus form a death trap for his enemy. To an outside observer, the prediction of the outcome of such vastly one-sided conflict would have seemed a foregone conclusion. The perfect storm was headed towards Maratha confederacy.

The Deccan then became a ground of enormous death and destruction for what seemed like eternity. The ensuing war, by all conventional calculations, should have been a fairly quick victory for the Mughals. But its culmination was an unimaginable epoch that defied all logic. The Marathas were lacking in resources on nearly all fronts, and it were they who triumphed in this war. And at the expense of all his treasure, army, power and life, it was be the invading emperor who learnt a very costly lesson—that the will of people to fight for their freedom should never be underestimated, nor could be extinguished. Aurangzeb died in the Deccan a defeated, broken man after a futile quest of nearly three decades. He never got to see Agra or Delhi again.

The Maratha War—the First Phase (1680-1689)

Chhatrapati Shivaji Maharaj passed away in 1680. His death set off a brief power struggle in the royal family, chiefly between his two sons Sambhaji and Rajaram, at the end of which Sambhaji prevailed to become the next Maratha king. At around this time, Aurangzeb's northern military adventures—he had lost disastrously in Assam and was evicted from Mewar after a failed invasion—had become stuck. The Mughal however, had not taken his eyes off the biggest threat to his empire, and contemplated a final push in the Deccan. Vanquishing the Marathas, he reckoned, would give him the mastery of all of India.

Chhatrapati Sambhaji was aggressive in his military outlook and in 1681, attacked Janjira, though this attempt ended in failure. One of his generals Khan Jahan was sent to the south and laid siege to the fortress of Ahivant in May 1680, but the Maratha resistance there was firm and unyielding; the Mughals gained no success in this siege. The Marathas waited out the monsoon before commencing any reprisal, but Sanbhaji sent a message to Khan Jahan promising to give him battle in the open after the rains. By October, the two Maratha divisions marched to Surat (Gujarat) and Burhanpur (Madhya Pradesh), while a third one sauntered into Khandesh in the north, drawing the Mughals there. The Marathas then retreated, but this was only a tactical ploy.

The Marathas struck again at Burhanpur in January 1681. A 20,000 strong cavalry under Hambir Rao fell upon this rich and populous town. The Mughal subedar there was totally unprepared for such a contingency and simply locked himself up in the fort. Lakhs of rupees worth of booty was forcibly taken from every suburb of the town. Many terrified Mughal officials killed their wives and daughters and then themselves fell, desperately fighting the Marathas. This was the beginning of fear the Mughals were to experience, a fear that Hindus had endured for centuries—the fear of an invading army. Only, the roles had now been reversed. The Maratha sack of Burhanpur continued for three whole days, yielding the treasure of many past generations. Upon hearing of the Maratha raid on Burhanpur, Khan Jahan made a forced march towards Aurangabad, but his army soon ran into the roughness of the jungles and innumerable hills on the way. The Marathas had already reached their stronghold of Salher, while Khan Jahan's force reached Burhanpur too late.

At the same time, Hussein Ali Khan, one of Aurangzeb's generals, attacked northern Konkan. Sambhaji was then forced to leave Janjira and turn his attention to Hussein Ali Khan. The latter was pushed back by the Maratha king to Ahmednagar. By this time, 1681 had long ended and the summer, followed by the monsoon of 1682 was upon the geography. Rains in western Maharashtra, especially the Konkan, are often torrential, and in this instance, both belligerents had to halt their major military operations, though skirmishes continued. Ramsej, near Nasik, was besieged by Shahabuddin Khan in March 1682, but a gallant Maratha defence of the fort rendered the Mughal siege a failure. Aurangzeb for his part, did not remain inactive. He tried to sign a deal with the Portuguese to allow Mughal ships to harbour in Goa. This move, had it been successful would have enabled him to open another supply route to Deccan via the sea, but Sambhaji obtained news of it. He attacked the Portuguese territories and pushed deep inside Goa. Viceroy Alvor was however, able to defend the Portuguese headquarters in this Maratha-Portuguese clash.

The Mughals were primarily a land power, with no real ability or experience of war at sea. It is doubtful that Aurangzeb's forces would have been able to present any threat to the Marathas from the western coast. The Mughal lord had by now readied a massive army that had started gathering on Deccan's borders. It was apparent that the south of India was headed for one huge conflict. Sambhaji understood the seriousness of this Mughal move and therefore abandoned his offensive against the Portuguese to turn around to face the Mughal threat developing in the east. It was now late 1683, and Aurangzeb moved to Ahmednagar. He divided his forces in two and put his two princes, Shah Alam and Azam Shah, in charge of each division. Shah Alam was to attack southern Konkan via the Karnataka border while Azam Shah would invade Khandesh, the northern parameter of the Maratha territory. The plan was to use a pincer strategy, whereby these two divisions would to encircle the Marathas from the south and north to isolate them. But more importantly, the Mughal emperor had already spent two and a half years in the Deccan and had accomplished nothing of note.

Aurangzeb by this time had already begun experiencing a domestic and mental crisis apart from a growing Maratha challenge, which wasn't going away anytime soon. His son Prince Mohammad Akbar, fed up with his father's religious fanaticism and unending zealotry, had rebelled. Akbar first joined the Rajputs, seeking refuge with Durgadas Rathore and then met and courted the friendship of Sambhaji, who agreed to maintain him on a substantial yearly pension. Akbar's rebellion came as a shock to Aurangzeb. It totally shook his faith in his family and dear ones. From then on, Aurangzeb became even more suspicious, watchful, capricious and self-contradictory. The confidence of old began deserting him. By April 1682, less than two years into his Deccan campaign, reports from Surat spoke of how the Mughal emperor "has with him a great army, with which he sits still and attempts nothing, being under great jealousies and fears, thinks himself hardly secure". In May 1683, Aurangzeb repeatedly proposed going back to Agra, leaving either Khan Jahan or his son Prince Azam in charge of the Deccan war, but both declined this onerous responsibility, and with sound reasons.

Akbar's rebellion petered out and he left to settle in Persia, leaving his very young son and daughter in Rajput hands. Upon hearing of his son's flight to Persia, Aurangzeb is caustically remarked, "Let us see who dies first; he or I". The sixth Mughal emperor drew no affection, leave alone inspiring any trust from even his near and dear ones.

The beginning of the Mughal campaign went smoothly enough for them. Shah Alam crossed River Krishna to ingress into Belgaum. From there, he took a northern detour to enter Goa and started marching further northwards via the Konkan, crossing Ramghat and reaching Sawantvadi. As he pushed further, his army encountered continuous harassment by the Marathas. They ransacked his supply chains and reduced his forces to starvation. Finally, Aurangzeb sent Ruhulla Khan for his rescue and brought him back to Ahmednagar. The first pincer attempt failed, but not before the Marathas cut off many remnants of the retreating army, looting them at many places and cutting down many of them. What began as a smooth campaign ended as a painful retreat of stragglers.

The monsoon of 1684 had begun. Shahabuddin Khan, another of Aurangzeb's generals was given the title of Ghaziuddin Khan. He directly attacked the Maratha capital at fort Raigad. Maratha commanders successfully defended Raigad. Aurangzeb dispatched Khan Jehan for help, but Hambeerrao Mohite, commander-in-chief of Maratha army, defeated him in a fierce battle at Patadi. Another division of the Maratha army attacked Shahabuddin Khan at Pachad, inflicting heavy losses on the Mughals.

In early 1685, Prince Shah Alam attacked the south again via the Gokak-Dharwar route. But Sambhaji's forces harassed him on the way without respite. Finally, he had to give up. The Mughals had failed to close the loop a second time.

In April 1685 Aurangzeb put a new strategy in place. He decided to consolidate his power in the south by launching expeditions against the sultanates of Golkonda and Bijapur. Both were kingdoms under Shia Muslim rulers and the Alamgir had no love lost for them. They had long-standing treaties with the Mughal Empire, but treaties, promises and commitments had never mattered to Aurangzeb. He suffered no pangs of conscience in consigning Mughal treaties with both sultanates and attacked them. Aurangzeb's offensive against these southern Deccan sultanates was an opportunity for Marathas, who launched their own offensive on the north coast. Bharuch in Gujarat was attacked. A Mughal army was sent to combat the Maratha invaders, but they were able to evade the Mughal forces and came back with minimum damage.

On Aurangzeb's freshly opened southern front, things were proceeding rather smoothly. Bijapur fell in September 1686. King Sikandar Shah was captured and imprisoned. Golkonda agreed to pay a huge ransom, but after receiving the money, Aurangzeb showed his true nature. He dumped the treaty in the dustbin and attacked the kingdom in blatant treachery. Soon, Golkonda fell as well in 1687. King Abu Hussein of Golkonda was captured and met the same fate as Sikandar Shah.

The Marathas had tried to win Mysore through diplomacy. Kesopant Pingle, brother of Moropant Pingle (Shivaji's teacher and mentor) was in charge of the negotiations, but the fall of Bijapur to Mughals had turned the tide. Mysore now displayed reluctance to join Marathas. But Sambhaji proved successful in courting several Bijapur sardars and winning them over to join the Maratha army.

After the fall of Bijapur and Golkonda, Aurangzeb turned his attention again to his main target—the Marathas. His first few attempts proved unsuccessful in making any major dent. But in December 1688, the Mughal emperor had his biggest jackpot. Sambhaji was captured at Sangmeshwar (the place lies between Chiplun and Ratnagiri) due to treachery by one Ganoji Shirke. Aurangzeb gave him option of converting to Islam, which he contemptuously refused. Upon his refusal, Aurangzeb, blinded by his victories, handed Sambhaji the most barbaric torture conceivable. Sambhaji was paraded on a donkey. His tongue was cut, eyes were gorged out. His body was cut into pieces and fed to dogs. Aurangzeb and his army exulted at the end of Sambhaji Raje, who had been a terror to the Mughals. They had not been able to defeat him on the battlefield even once. This cruel torture of Sambhaji revealed that Aurangzeb had not shed his barbarism even an iota.

Many in the Deccan and Maharashtra did not like Sambhaji because of his ruthless and uncompromising ways, and thus till now had been indifferent to the Mughal-Maratha conflict. But this barbaric death of the Chhatrapati Shivaji's son, who refused to forsake his dharma even under the pain of death, now aroused the wrath of all Hindus in the Maratha domain. Maratha generals converged on Raigad. The decision was unanimous. There would henceforth be no more peace offers to the enemy. The Mughals would be repelled at all costs. Rajaram succeeded his slain older brother as the next king of the Marathas. He began his reign by a rousing speech on Raigad. All Maratha generals and councilmen united under the flag of new king. The second phase of the epic war with the Mughals now began.

The years 1689-90 seemed to Aurangzeb his supreme moment of triumph. The sultanates of Bijapur and Golkonda, which had defied Mughal overlordship since the period of Akbar, had fallen to him. His hated and unvanquishable enemy Shivaji had long departed. His son Sambhaji, who had terrorized the Mughals, had been captured and tortured to death. The Marathas seemed done and over with by end of 1689. He was seemingly the master of all of the south.

It was however, the proverbial calm before the storm.

Aurangzeb's assessment and smugness proved to be his most fatal blunder. In September 1689, along with a leading Maratha general Dhanaji Jadhav, Santaji Ghorpade, a valorous, intrepid and powerful Maratha warrior attacked one of Aurangzeb's top generals Sheikh Nizam, who had thrown a siege around the fortress of Panhala. Nizam's army was roundly defeated and his treasure, horses and elephants fell into Maratha hands. Then during 1689-1690, Santaji and Dhanaji were directed to prevent Mughal army in Maharashtra from chasing and entering Karnataka after Maratha ruler Rajaram left for the fortress of Jinji in Tamil Nadu. They succeeded in this task and were able to slow down and engage the Mughals in harassing skirmishes. In December 1690, Santaji and Dhanaji were promoted as leading Maratha generals, and were placed respectively under the supervision of Ramchandra Pant Amatya and Shankar Narayan Sacheev.

On May 25, 1690, Sarza Khan alias Rustam Khan, a Mughal nobleman and commander, was soundly defeated and captured near Satara jointly by

Ramchandra Pant Amatya, Shankraji Narayan, Santaji and Dhanaji. This was a major setback to Aurangzeb. In July 1692, for his great victory, Rajaram rewarded him with the Deshmukhi (fiefdom) of Miraj.

In March 1693, the Maratha commanders, under the leadership of Santaji Ghorpade launched the single most daring attack on Mughal army at any point in the history of the House of Timur. They not only attacked the army at Desur, but sacked the tent where the Aurangzeb himself slept. Aurangzeb was elsewhere in his daughter's tent, and was thus fortunate to escape death, but his private force and many of his bodyguards were massacred.

This huge triumph was followed by a negative development for Marathas. Raigad fell to treachery of Suryaji Pisal. Sambhaji's queen, Yesubai and their son, Shahu, were captured. The Mughal forces, led by Julfikar Khan, continued this offensive further south. They attacked fort Panhala, which was then rather poorly defended. The Maratha *killedar* (master of the fort) of the fortress gallantly defended it and inflicted heavy losses on the attacking Mughal army. Panhala finally surrendered, but only after Aurangzeb himself had to come with a substantial force.

The next Mughal move was likely to be on Vishalgad and the Maratha ministers had foreseen it. They made their king Rajaram leave Vishalgad for Jinji, which would be his home for next seven years. Rajaram travelled south under the escort of Khando Ballal and his men. The queen of Bidnur gave them supplies and free passage. Harji Mahadik's division met them near Jinji and guarded their onward journey to the fort. Rajaram's queen was escorted out of Maharashtra by the Tungare brothers. She was transported to Jinji by a different route. Ballal and Mahadik tirelessly worked to gather the scattered diplomats and soldiers. Jinji became new Maratha capital, breathing new life into the Maratha army.

Rajaram's successful escape threw Aurangzeb into consternation. The war with the Marathas was become tougher and tougher as time wore on; his hopes for an easy victory had already evaporated. His next move was to keep most of the Mughal army in Maharashtra while a small force would be dispatched to track Rajaram to try and bring him to heel. But the two Maratha generals, Santaji Ghorpade and Dhanaji Jadhav would prove more than a match for the Alamgir.

The advancing Mughal forces sent by Aurangzeb to keep check on Rajaram were first intercepted and destroyed by Dhanaji and Santaji, thus relieving the immediate danger to the Maratha king. Both then joined Maratha commander Ramchandra Bavadekar in Deccan. Bavdekar, Vithoji Bhosale and Raghuji Chavan had by then reorganized most of the Maratha army after its defeats at Panhalgad and Vishalgad.

The year 1691 had entered its ending phase. Bavdekar, Pralhad Niraji, Santaji, Dhanaji and several Maratha sardars met in the region of Maval and reformed the Maratha strategy. Aurangzeb had taken four major forts in Sahyadris and was dispatching Julfikar khan to subdue the fort of Jinji. The Marathas planned accordingly; Santaji and Dhanaji were to launch offensives in the east that would tie down the rest of the Mughal forces, but also keep them scattered. Others would focus in Maharashtra and would attack a series of forts around southern Maharashtra and northern Karnataka to divide the newly-won Mughal territories in two. This would pose significant challenges to enemy supply chains. Thanks to Shivaji's vision of building a navy, the Marathas could now extend this divide into the sea, choking off any supply routes from Surat to the south.

By early 1692 the renewed Maratha offensive was under way in keeping with the execution of the fresh plan. Commanders Shankar Narayan and Parshuram Trimbak recaptured Rajgad and Panhala. Rohida fell to a Maratha assault in early 1693, led by Shankar Narayan and Bhosale. Sidhoji Gujar wrested Vijaydurg. Soon thereafter, Parshuram Trimbak took Vishalgad. Kanhoji Angre, a young Maratha naval officer that time, took fort Kolaba.

While this was in work, Santaji and Dhanaji were launching swift raids—akin to what the Nazi war machine would do two and a half centuries later in Europe—on the Mughal armies on the eastern front. This was something Aurangzeb had not expected. The Marathas had lost one king, Sambhaji, and the second, his successor, had been driven into refuge far away. Conventionally speaking, the Marathas should have been suing for peace. Far from it; they were undaunted and actually were on offensive. From Khandesh in the northern part of the state, Ahmednagar in the centre, to Bijapur to Konkan and southern Karnataka, Santaji Ghorpade and Dhanaji Jadhav wrought havoc on the Mughal army. Encouraged by their successes, the duo hatched a new action plan to attack Mughal forces near Jinji. Dhanaji Jadhav attacked Ismail Khan and defeated him near Kokar. Santaji Ghorpade attacked Ali Mardan Khan at the base of Jinji and captured him along with 1,500 horses and six elephants. He was taken to Jinji and held to ransom. Ali Mardan Khan managed to secure his own release by paying the ransom of one lakh *hun*, which his brother-in-law Ali Qadir somehow raised (*Book of Aurangzeb*; Sir Jadunath Sarkar; Vol V, pg 62. With the flanks cleared, both Santa and Dhana joined hands and laid a second siege around the Mughal siege at Jinji.

Julfikar Khan, who was in charge of the siege of Jinji, left the campaign on his emperor's orders and marched back. Santaji followed him to north, but suffered a defeat by Julfikar's forces. Santaji then diverted his forces to Bijapur. Aurangzeb sent another general Kasim Khan to tackle Santaji. But Santaji made a swift midway counter-attack on Kasim with a brilliant military manoeuvre near Chitaldurg and forced him take refuge in the Dunderi fort. The fort then fell under a Maratha siege supervised by Santaji. It ended only when most Mughal soldiers inside were close death by starvation and Kasim Khan himself committed suicide. Aurangzeb, learning of this disaster, sent Himmat Khan to reinforce his besieged army at Dunderi. Himmat Khan carried heavy artillery, but Santaji lured him in a trap in the forests near Dunderi. The Marathas launched a sudden, ambush attack on the advancing Mughals, the ambush erupting in a fierce battle. The skirmish ended when Himmat Khan was shot in the head and died. All his forces were routed and Santaji captured a big cache of weapons and ammunition.

The year 1695 had arrived. By now, Aurangzeb beheld the grim realization that the war with the Marathas he had kicked off was much more serious than he thought. His enemy was no longer a bunch of forest and mountain brigands, as he had contemptuously dismissed them. They were an increasingly dominant force, and it was the imperial Mughal army that had begun to recoil from them. He regrouped his forces and rethought his strategy. Julfikar Khan was given an ultimatum by his emperor to either finish the Jinji business or be stripped of his titles. Julfikar tried to tightened the siege. But the Marathas had defeated and captured a Mughal commander Ismail Khan during the 1693 campaign and after their victory, proclaimed their authority over Kadapa and Kanjivaram, a region that was called the 'Hyderabadi Karnataka' in the old days. The Mughal battle against the Maratha counter-siege of Jinji consumed a lot of their resources. They failed to prevent Rajaram's escape from Jinji. The Maratha king was safely escorted to Deccan by Dhanaji Jadhav and the Shirke brothers. Haraji Mahadik's son took the charge of Jinji and bravely defended it against Julfikar Khan and Daud Khan till January of 1698. Rajaram had ample time to reach Vishalgad.

Jinji did fall, but it had blown a gaping hole in the finances of the Mughal Empire. The losses incurred in taking Jinji far outweighed any gains. The fort had done its work. For seven years the three hills of Jinji had kept a huge Mughal army occupied. It had driven a deep orifice into Mughal resources. Not only at Jinji, the royal treasury was bleeding everywhere and was under tremendous strain. Aurangzeb and his durbar looked eagerly to the huge sum of money sent faithfully by the Mughal subedar of Bengal every month. In fact, it was the treasure from Bengal that kept the Mughal war effort in the Deccan somehow going. But it was going nowhere.

The Marathas would soon witness an unpleasant development, all of their own making. Dhanaji Jadhav and Santaji Ghorpade had a simmering rivalry, which was somehow kept in check by the councilman Pralhad Niraji. But after Niraji's death, Dhanaji grew bold and attacked Santaji. Nagoji Mane, one of Dhanaji's men, killed Santaji. The news of Santaji's death was sweet news to Aurangzeb and the Mughal army. For years, Santaji Ghorpade had been their terror. He had defeated and killed many Mughal commanders; others had to secure their freedom after paying heavy sums as ransom. To be ransomed off is the ultimate disgrace for any warrior, but that was what the Mughal generals in the Deccan had been reduced to by the Marathas.

But Santaji's tragic death brought no relief to the Mughals. The army of the Dynasty of Timur was no longer the force it was once feared. Several of Aurangzeb's experienced generals advised him against the, kept the war on. It was much like Alexander on the borders of Takshashila and Kekaya. The Macedonian's Indian adventure had ended in ignominy and retreat.

The Marathas again consolidated and a new counter-offensive began. Rajaram made Dhanaji the next commander in chief. The Maratha army was divided in three divisions. Dhanaji would himself lead the first, Parshuram Timbak the second and Shankar Narayan the third. Dhanaji Jadhav defeated a large Mughal force near Pandharpur. Shankar Narayan defeated Sarja Khan in Pune. Khanderao Dabhade, who lead a division under Dhanaji, took Baglan and Nashik. Nemaji Shinde, another commander with Shankar Narayan, scored a major victory at Nandurbar.

The war in the Deccan, for Aurangzeb, had now become an unending saga of defeat after defeat. Aurangzeb himself took charge and launched another counter offensive, this time besieging Panhala and attacking the fort of Satara.

Satara was defended by a seasoned commander, Prayagji Prabhu, who held out for a good six months, but surrendered in April of 1700, just before the onset of the monsoon. This foiled Aurangzeb's strategy to take as many forts as possible before the monsoon. This long-drawn-out campaign could bag only Satara.

Come March 1700, and the Marathas had to endure another grievous development. King Rajaram breathed his last. His queen Tarabai, the daughter of the gallant Maratha commander-in-chief Hambeerrao Mohite, took charge of the Maratha army. Daughter of a braveheart, Tarabai proved her true mettle for the next seven years. She carried the struggle on with unflinching valour. This was the third phase, and was to prove the last phase of the prolonged war against Aurangzeb, with the Marathas under the leadership of Tarabai.

The 18th century had now dawned. It was the year 1701. In the Mughal camp, the signs of strain and an impending defeat were now impossible to ignore or wish away. The grey-haired veteran Asad Khan, Julfikar Khan's father, counselled Aurangzeb to end the war and turn around, even if it meant negotiating with the Marathas. The Deccan War, which had commended in 1680, had already taken a monumental toll, much larger than originally planned, on the Mughal Empire. And serious signs were emerging that the 200 years old Mughal empire was crumbling and was in the middle of a war that was not winnable. The number of Mughal *amirs* and commanders unwilling to stay on in the Deccan was growing, although few dared voice their feelings openly. One Mughal *amir* is said to have openly offered a bribe of one lakh rupees to the Mughal emperor in the presence of his courtiers, to be allowed to go back to Agra. This gentleman promised to arrange for "more, if this is not enough". It is said that Aurangzeb could only stare helplessly at the *amir* who had offered this bribe in return for being allowed to quit and go home.

The Mughals were indeed bleeding heavily, both in men and treasury. But Aurangzeb kept pressing on, without any end in sight. Queen Tarabai had now taken charge, when the sixth Mughal emperor chose to embark on a siege of the fort of Parli (Sajjangad). Parshuram Trimbak defended the fort until the rains and then made a quiet retreated at the break of monsoon. The Mughal army was dealt heavy loss by flash floods in the rivers around. These same tactics were followed by Marathas at the next fort Aurangzeb ventured into, Panhala. The tactics were repeated at Vishalgad, but the Mughals either did not learn anything or were simple incapable of adapting.

By 1704, Aurangzeb somehow gained Torana and Rajgad. He had won only a handful forts in this offensive, but he had expended several precious years, losing a huge portion of the Mughal army. It was becoming increasingly clear even to him that after 24 years of constant war, he was no closer to defeating Marathas than he was the day he began. Worse, some of his commanders like Zulfiqar Khan were in secret parleys with the Marathas. In 1693, after lengthy negotiations with Rajaram, Julfikar Khan was granted a safe passage out of Jinji. It is a widely known fact that Julfikar Khan deliberately delayed the capture of Jinji going along with his father Asad Khan's plan to carve a territory for himself, similar to the by then defunct Adilshahi and Qutubshahi states in the south. They hoped and expected the octogenarian Aurangzeb to conk off soon either due to old age or be overthrown by his impatient sons for the throne of Delhi. The ensuant chaos of succession at the Mughal court would ensue to provide them with the opportunity to annex the southern territory, especially Golconda in Hyderabad.

But then why single out Aurangzeb's commanders alone? His youngest son Kam Baksh too was in secret negotiations with the Marathas. Aurangzeb had him put under severe surveillance when he suspected that Kam Baksh was up to something fishy. His second son Azam too was in his own negotiations with the Marathas. Aurangzeb gave him marching orders to proceed to Malwa, but Azam deliberately made heavy weather of his posting, ensuring that the Mughal under his command covered a mere four miles in ten days. Nasik was all he reached. Obviously, he didn't want to be too far away when his old father kicked the bucket, as he was apprehensive that his elder brother Muazzam would grab everything. There wasn't much love lost between them.

The Marathas were preparing for a final counter-offensive. It gathered momentum in the north. Tarabai proved a most worthy leader of the Marathas. It would indeed be no exaggeration to state that if any single individual can be credited with destroying Aurangzeb in the Deccan, it ought to be Queen Tarabai. To his great dismay, his enemies were the ones seeking him out, and they no longer restricted the fighting to Maharashtra. Mughal provinces fell in the north were attacked, and they fell one after another. The Mughals were in no position to defend; the royal treasuries had been sucked dry by Aurangzeb's incessant warring and no armies were left in reserve. The year 1705 gave the now tottering Mughal emperor a taste of things to come. Two Maratha armies crossed the Narmada. One, under Nemaji Shinde struck as deep north as Bhopal. The second, led by Dabhade paid a visit to Bharuch in the west. Dabhade with his 8,000 men attacked and defeated Mahomed Khan's forces numbering almost 14,000. This threw the entire Gujarat coast wide open for Marathas. They immediately tightened their grip on the Mughal supply chains.

In Maharashtra, despondency was increasingly shrouding Aurangzeb. Military victories against the Marathas were now becoming a distant dream. Whatever forts his commanders could win were only through bribery. They, for their part, were desperate to show some results. One Bidar Bakht offered a huge sum of money to Parashuram, the kiladar of Khelna, to be allowed to occupy the fort, so that he might be known as its captor. The Maratha commandant did so and planted the Mughal garrison's glag on the ramparts and quietly vacated Khelna along with his garrison. By the command of the Mughal emperor, none hindered them. Khelna was a fortress the Mughals tried their best to take by force, but ended up losing six thousand men, and in the end were able to occupy it only through bribery.

Aurangzeb could capture only one Maratha fort by the strength of Mughal arms, which was Torana in February 1704. All other Maratha forts the Mughals had occupied had been accomplished through bribery. The Mughal emperor now began negotiations with Marathas—the writing on the wall was becoming clear to even him—but broke off the talks abruptly and marched on a small kingdom called Wakinara, ruled by the family of Naiks. This Wakinara dynasty traced their lineage to the royal family of the deceased Vijaynagar Empire. They had never seen eye to eye with the Mughals and had sided with Marathas. Dhanaji marched into Sahyadris and won almost all the major forts back in short time. The Satara and Parali forts were taken by Parshuram Timbak. Shankar Narayan recaptured Sinhgad. Dhanaji then turned around and took his forces to Wakinara. He helped the Naiks at Wakinara sustain the fight, and the latter fought very bravely. Wakinara did fall finally, but the royal family of Naiks successfully escaped with minimum damage.

No further good news would come Aurangzeb's way. His last years were already upon him, and they were filled with nothing else than sadness and desolation, apart from the thick air of defeat that hung over the Mughal camp. His lifelong endeavour to be the master of all of India was coming crashing down, leaving a trail of disruption and anarchy throughout his empire. His own health had broken down irreparably. Preserved records of the court newsletters give readers pathetic glimpses of the weak, old Alamgir ordering the screen of his bedroom tent to be drawn aside a little, while officers, horses and men were marched in the courtyard below for inspection, like in the old days. It was the Mughal emperor's way of keeping up the pretence of normalcy. The daily durbar had been Aurangzeb's regular practice ever since he had grabbed the Mughal throne in 1658, but was now a pale shadow of what it once had been at Agra.

Everywhere Aurangzeb looked around in his makeshift tent durbar, he could find only a motley crowd of young, inexperienced, pliant, incapable, weak, sycophantic and greedy *mansabdars* who had no more stomach to fight the marauding Marathas, but who were ever ready to engage in intrigue, and did not hesitate to display their mutual jealousy and petty rivalries. Aurangzeb's listless stare met faces and figures who shrank from responsibility, evaded glances and would look here and there, afraid to speak even the plainest of truths. All of his older, more capable nobles had passed away, some of them perishing in the battlefield. An entire generation of Mughals had been born in Maharashtra and had reached adulthood, a generation that hadn't ever seen Agra or Delhi. The sole companion of Aurangzeb's youth still with him was the veteran Wazir Asad Khan, father of Julfikar Khan, and even he was thirteen years Aurangzeb's junior. The sixth Mughal emperor had made a lifelong fetish of his austere, puritanical lifestyle, which had put off most who had to approach him. There had never been much of a human touch in him, and now, at the fag end of his life when he ardently needed some of it, none was forthcoming.

Things worsened on the domestic front as well. Aurangzeb's sole companions outside the durbar and its clutter were his second daughter Zeenat-un-Nisa, who herself was now an old woman, and his last wife Udaipuri Begum, whose intelligence was just a notch above than an animal's. Kam Baksh, Aurangzeb's youngest surviving son by Udaipuri, had been his father's favourite, but was in talks with the Marathas to carve out something for himself after his old father passed on. Aurangzeb's second son Azam had plotted the murder of his younger brother, who somehow managed to survive the first attempt. Azam had planned to kill even his older brother Prince Muazzam. Kam Baksh had to be guarded day and night by one of Aurangzeb's faithful commanders Sultan Husain.

Further bereavements closed in thick and fast. Aurangzeb's much-loved daughter-in-law Jahanzeb Banu died in Gujarat in March 1705. Mohammad Akbar, the emperor's son had rebelled against his father, first joining the Rajputs and then the Marathas before fleeing to Persia. He died there in 1704, though news of his death reached Aurangzeb in the Deccan only in 1705. His older daughter Zeb-un-Nisa, a poetess had ended her days in prison at the fort of Salimgarh in Delhi in 1702. She had spent the last 21 years of life in confinement, imprisoned by her father, who had suspected her of having an affair with one Akil Khan Razi, son of the governor of Lahore in the 1660s. Zeb-un-Nisa had also supported her brother Mohammad Akbar in his rebellion against their father, which invited her imprisonment in 1681 and confinement till death. Gauharara Begum, Aurangzeb's sole surviving sibling among his numerous brothers and sisters, passed away in 1706. When news of her passing reached Aurangzeb in the Deccan, he pathetically cried his heart out, "Gauhar and I alone were left among Shah Jahan's children". In May 1706, his daughter Mehr-un-Nisa and her husband Izid Bakhsh (son of Murad, one of the brothers Aurangzeb had murdered) died together in Delhi. Buland Akhtar, a grandson (son of the rebel Akbar) died in the next month in June. Next to go were two more of Aurangzeb's grandchildren, shortly before Aurangzeb's own death, but his wazirs were merciful enough to withhold these tragic developments from an emperor who was clearly sinking.

Desolation, defeat and anarchy reigned everywhere around Aurangzeb, who by now had shed all hopes and was planning to retreat to Burhanpur from Ahmednagar where he then was. News of a huge Maratha army of over fifty thousand advancing towards the Deccan Mughal capital had been received. Dhanaji Jadhav, Nima Scindia, Dado Malhar, Ram Nimbalkar and others fell on the retreaters and in a swift and ferocious attack, dismantled the rear guard of the imperial Mughal army. Julfikar Khan somehow rescued the emperor and they reached Burhanpur without any further disaster. In the northern part of the state, the Mughal defenders in Khandesh reached an understanding with the Marathas. Meanwhile, Gujarat had fallen; the Mughal defenders of Baroda threw it open to the Marathas. Aurangabad, which had been the emperor's Deccan capital for a number of years, was being frequently visited by the ravaging enemies. No Mughal commander or *mansabdar* now dared venture out to tackle them. Food and grain for both man and animal were becoming scarcer by the day.

It was February 1707. Aurangzeb, then encamped at Bhingar, not far away from Ahmednagar, had an attack of feverishness, the bouts of which had been rather frequent over the last few years. He recovered somehow and resumed attending the daily durbar, determined not to let go of his 'grip' on the affairs of the state. In reality, the state was existent only on paper. The Marathas were here, there and everywhere. If that wasn't bad enough, his over-ambitious and violence-prone son Azam too was reported to be hovering around in the vicinity. On 9th February, Aurangzeb appointed his youngest son Kam Baksh the subedar of Bijapur and sent him away, himself bursting into tears even as the imperial band played a farewell tune. The strife among his sons brought back to him vivid memories of how he had deposed his father Shah Jahan and killed his brothers to forcibly take the Mughal thrown. His karma of years long gone was now coming back to haunt him.

Four days after sending away Kam Baksh, Aurangzeb, now all alone, was again seized with fever. His obstinacy though, refused to leave him; he still insisted on coming to the court room and saying his daily prayers five times a day in full congregation. On February 19, one of his lieutenants Hamid-ud-Din Khan sought the advice of astrologers to ward off any evil influence on his Jahanpanah. The emperor had to donate an elephant, said the astrologers. The dying Aurangzeb sanctioned the ritual, but then, true to his calling, had an attack of majahabitis (religiosity). "Giving away of an elephant as charity is a Hindu custom. Instead, give Rs. 4,000 (the price of the elephant) to the Chief Qazi for distribution among the poor and then consign this heap of dust (his person) to dust."

It was during these last few days of his life that Aurangzeb dictated two letters to his sons Azam and Kam Baksh, depicting his pathetic state of both body and mind. The badshah entreated both to cultivate brotherly love, peace and moderation, and spoke of the "vanity of all earthly things" (both letters are reproduced at the end of this chapter). Another paper was said to have been found under his pillow after his death, in which he proposed a peaceful partition of his empire—rather, what still remained in Mughal hands—among his three surviving sons.

Alone, lost, defeated, depressed, bankrupt, and far away from home, Aurangzeb stepped out of his bedroom on the morning of March 3, 1707. He began his morning prayer, counting the beads of his rosary as his lips moved mechanically. One bout of unconsciousness took over but he somehow recovered to continue his prayer, till a second unconsciousness took hold. It was the final one. Muhiuddin Mohammad Aurangzeb, boss of the Mughal Empire, self-styled Alamgir had died a sad and lonely death. His son Mohammad Azam arrived a day later at the camp after the customary mourning, made arrangements for the deceased's body to be sent away to Khuldabad near Aurangabad, now renamed Chhatrapati Sambhaji Nagar. A low simple tomb, in deference to Aurangzeb's wishes today stands as monument to the burial site of the sixth Mughal emperor, who was responsible for laying an indelible dividing land between his subjects of differing faith, and in the eventual analysis, seeding the pernicious Two-Nation mindset among a substantial segment of his co-religionists down the years that would one day erupt in the form of the Partition of India and its still-continuing aftermath in the subcontinent.

The decay of Indian civilization in the medieval age under Alamgir Aurangzeb was inescapably clear in just about every field, but particularly so in the intellectual and industrial fields. The exceptionally prolonged life of Aurangzeb—he died at age 90—only accentuated the decline. A rather left-handed admission of this reality can be found in the writings of Mughal court hagiographers who began wistfully recalling the 'glorious' age of Akbar to Shah Jahan, as Aurangzeb's regime wore on with all its colourlessness and puritanical harshness. The Mughal regime was one where sycophancy of the emperor and his dynasty, not talent, was rewarded. Bigotry and vice increasingly tightened their grip. The ruin of the administration was chiefly instrumental in dragging the Indian people down, along with the downturn in the empire's fortunes. There was no justice for Hindus from the depredations of Aurangzeb's licentious officials. It was only the advent of Shivaji in the south, and the Rajputs, Jats and later the Sikhs in the north that drove fear into the empire. Any economic surpluses generated, mostly from agriculture was eaten up by the empire's insatiable hunger for opulence, wantonness and war. The wars themselves became increasingly unwinnable and finally consumed the empire itself.

Thus ended a prolonged and gruelling period of India's history. The Mughal empire fragmented and disintegrated soon after. The Deccan heralded the rise of a new sun, the Maratha Empire that would go on to bring the subcontinent under the sway of the saffron flag, from Attock in today's Balochistan to Cuttack in Orissa.

2.5 million men of the Mughal Empire perished in this 27-year war against the Marathas. Aurangzeb's army had huge artillery, cavalry, muskets, ammunition and giant wealth from royal treasuries to support this quest. When one looks at the sheer numbers, the Deccan war was by no means a fair game.

The main features of Aurangzeb's strategy were:

Use of Overwhelming Force to Demoralize the Enemy

This tactic had proved successful in Aurangzeb's other missions. He therefore, used the same in Maharashtra as well. On several occasions giant Mughal contingents were used to lay siege to a fort or capture a town. Only, the traditional Mughal way of war came a cropper in the Deccan.

Aurangzeb was not unaware that the forts in Sahyadri formed the backbone of Maratha defence. His calculation was to lay a tight siege of fortresses, demoralizing and starving the people inside and finally making them surrender the fort, something he had successfully done to force his father Shah Jahan to surrender the Agra Fort.

Forking or pincer movements, using large columns of infantry and cavalry was another Mughal tactic of war. Aurangzeb had skillfully and very effectively employed this to take Dara Shikoh by surprise in the Battle of Samugarh in 1658. A large number of infantry and cavalry was essential to any pincer movements, which had proved effective and almost fatal against the Mughals' adversaries in the plains. It failed miserably against the Marathas, whose unique method of warfare eclipsed the Mughal war strategies. The Marathas had an unbeatable advantage, geography, which they thoroughly utilized to the hilt. Their military moves were planned considering the terrain and the weather.

The main features of the Maratha way of war were:

A Combined Offensive-Defensive Strategy

Throughout the war, Marathas never slackened on offensive warfare. This served two purposes. The facts that the Maratha army carried out offensive attacks in Mughal-held land made them the psychological equals of the Mughals who were the invaders in Maratha land, even though Mughals were a much bigger force numerically when the Deccan war began in 1680. This stymied the Mughal morale early on, while acting as a morale- booster for the Marathas. Secondly, Maratha's offensive strikes in the form of lightning raids often heavily damaged enemy supply chains, taking a heavy toll on the Mughal army. Fortresses formed the backbone of the Maratha's defence. Thanks to Chhatrapati Shivaji, every fort had provision of fresh water. The total number of forts was almost 300, the conquest of which were beyond the capabilities of Aurangzeb's army, its large size notwithstanding.

Strategic Fort Defence

The Marathas were experts in fort warfare. The strategy of defence using forts had two components. The first was the right play of the strategic forts. In modern warfare, a country can have some strategic assets like aircraft carrier, presence of which needs a substantial change of plans on the part of one's enemy. And then there are tactical assets, like tanks and large field guns, which matter from battle to battle, but can be effectively countered by the enemy without making big plan changes. Similarly, there are strategic forts, like Raigad, Janjira, Panhala and Jinji. Then there are number of tactical forts like Vishalgad, Sinhgad, Rajgad, etc.

Raigad, by its very nature, is large daunting fort. Built in 11th century by the descendants of the Mauryan Empire, it served as an anchor to various kingdoms. Its cliffs are very high, more than 1,200 feet from base. It has abundant fresh water supply. Raigad, like Jinji could be defended for years at a stretch. No contestant could claim Sahyadri and Konkan as theirs without winning Raigad.

Aurangzeb knew difficulties in winning Raigad by war. He therefore, managed to win it by using an insider traitor, Suryaji Pisal. Had the Marathas retained Raigad, Aurangzeb's task, and losses, would have been much tougher. The Marathas lost Raigad early and could not win in back till much later. But they utilized the remaining two forts, Panhalgad and Jinji superbly. Panhala is strategic because of its location on the confluence of multiple supply chains. The Marathas defended it as long as they could and tried to regain it at the earliest when it wasn't in their hands.

The second component of defensive fort warfare is matching movements with weather. Forts are an asset during the rest of the year, but are a liability in monsoon as it costs a lot to carry food and supplies up. Also, the monsoon in coasts and ghats is severe in nature and no major military movement is possible. Thus, the Marathas would often fight till monsoon and surrender the fort just before the rains. Before surrendering they burnt all the food inside, thus making it a liability in every way. Often, the Marathas would surrender an empty fort, but would later snatch it filled with food and water. These moves demoralized the Mughals.

The Offensive of Evasive Raids

The Marathas were the first Hindu adversaries the Mughals encountered who did not hesitate to go on the offensive attacks, unlike earlier Hindu opponents who would fight mostly defensive battles, with mostly disastrous results. These Maratha offensives would be launched in regions from which the Mughal army was far away. They rarely engaged the Mughal army in open fields till later part of the war. If situation seemed difficult, they would retreat and disperse and thus conserve most of their men and arms for another day. The rivers Bhima, Krishna, Godavari and the mountains of Sahyadri, divide the region of Maharashtra in several north-south corridors. When the Mughal army traversed the south through one corridor, the Marathas would course along the north through another and launch attacks there. This went on changing gradually and in the end, the Maratha forces began engaging the Mughals head on.

Noted historian Sir Jadunath Sarkar makes an interesting observation. In his own words, "Aurangzeb won battle after battle, but in the end, he lost the war. As the war prolonged, it transformed from a war of weapons to war of spirits. Aurangzeb was never able to break Maratha spirit."

What the Marathas did was a classic example of asymmetric defensive warfare. The above observation of Sir Jadunath conceals an interesting fact about this asymmetric defense. Is it really possible to lose most of the battles and still win the war? The answer is yes.

One of the most famous warriors in ancient Indian history seemed to have arrived at the same conclusion above. In the Bhishma Parva of the Mahabharata, the Kuru grandsire Bhishma imparts sound advice on war to Emperor Yudhisthira with a famous quote: "The strength of an army is not in its numbers".

For centuries, the mountains and valleys, towns and villages of Deccan had gotten used to being a pawn in the game of power. They changed hands as kingdoms warred with each other. They paid taxes whoever was in a position to extract them. For the most part they remained in a sleepy slumber, just turning and twisting in their bed.

Once in a while, they sent their sons to fight in battles without ever asking why exactly the war was being launched. At other times, they fought amongst themselves. They were divided, confused and did not have high hopes about their future. This was the condition of Deccan when Shivaji launched his first expedition to take the fort of Torana in 1645. By the time of his death mere 35 years later, he had transformed Deccan from a sleepy terrain to a thundering volcano.

Finally, here was a man whose vision of future was shared by his people. This was the vision of a modern "nation-state". Perhaps the most important factor that distinguishes Shivaji's vision is that it was unifying. His vision went beyond building an army of proud warriors from warrior castes. It included people from all rungs of society sharing a common political idea and ready to defend it at any cost. That, in essence, was the secret of the Hindu victory in this long civilizational war, and Aurangzeb's defeat and the virtual end of the Mughals. Shivaji himself had quit the mortal world when Aurangzeb stepped into the Deccan, thundering at Agra, "I shall bury those *kafirs* (Marathas) or be buried there myself". The Alamgir kept his word. He did not die a peaceful and content death in the safe environs of his capital Agra, but was buried in Maharashtra, his saga ending in defeat and ignominy.

Shivaji's vision went far beyond creating a kingdom empire for himself in Maharashtra. It envisioned a confederacy of states against what he clearly saw were foreign invaders. He was trying to build an alliance of Hindu kingdoms. He went out of his way to convince Mirza Raja Jaisingh to quit Aurangzeb. He established relations with the dethroned royal family of Vijaynagar for whom he had tremendous respect. He attempted to unify the sparring Hindu power centres.

Other Hindu powers did respond, albeit a bit late. The Rajputs in Rajasthan, the Nayaks in Karnataka and the rulers of Mysore, the royal family of Vijaynagar were of valuable help to Shivaji and later to the Marathas. It was a huge step towards a nation winning its soul back.

Map 5: India under Maratha Rule

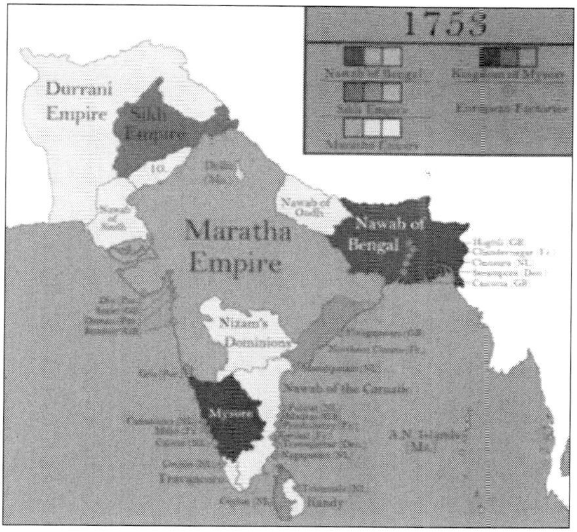

References

1. *History of the Mahrattas* by James Duff – http://www.archive.org/details/ahistorymahratt05duffgoog
2. *Shivaji and His Times* by Jadunath Sarkar – http://www.archive.org/details/cu31924024056750
3. *A History of the Maratha People* by Charles Kincaid – http://www.archive.org/details/historyofmaratha02kincuoft
4. *Background of Maratha Renaissance* by N. K. Behere – http://www.archive.org/details/backgroundofmara035242mbp
5. *Rise of The Maratha Power* by Mahadev Govind Ranade – http://www.archive.org/details/RiseOfTheMarathapower
6. *Maratha History* by S. R. Sharma – http://www.archive.org/details/marathahistory035360mbp

CHAPTER 12

AURANGZEB AND PAKISTAN

It is no surprise that Muhiuddin Mohammad Aurangzeb, the sixth Mughal emperor is viewed with admiration in Pakistan, India's neighbour that came into existence as a result of a violent partition of the subcontinent on August 14, 1947, exactly one day prior to India's independence from British colonial rule. Partition claimed over a million lives on both sides of the border, displaced at least ten million, and 77 years later, its aftermath continues to bedevil history and ties between Hindus and Muslims, apart from leaving behind a troubled subcontinent that continues to struggle with its tortuous legacy.

In Pakistan, Aurangzeb is regarded as a hero who not only fought and expanded the frontiers of the Islamic Mughal empire, but also strove hard all his life to purify the faith of non-Muslim, meaning Hindu, influences that had crept in, and thereby establish the 'perfect' Islamic state on earth. He is depicted as a pious Muslim who reintroduced Islamic laws by banning music and levying *jaziya*. a true believer who removed corrupt practices from religion and the court, and once again purified the empire. The fact that Aurangzeb's puritanical zeal eventually resulted in the disintegration of his empire is glossed over in most Pakistani textbooks.

While Akbar in India is touted as a tolerant ruler who treated his Hindu subjects with equality, encouraged interfaith dialogue and also abolished *jaziya*, in Pakistan, he is viewed with scepticism because of his experiments with different religious philosophies and his attempt to forge a religion of his own, the *Din-e-Ilahi*. In puritanical Islam, this is considered a human's attempt to intervene with the word of God, which is blasphemy. Pakistan has blasphemy laws that mandate the punishment of death to anyone in that country accused of insulting the religion, Prophet or the Quran. Not surprisingly, most Pakistani history textbooks extol Aurangzeb and either make only a cursory mention of Akbar, or in some cases, do not mention the third Mughal ruler at all! Thus, these textbooks jump from Humayun (Akbar's father) to Jahangir (Akbar's son and successor).

In recent years, the return of nationalist consciousness and consequent politics in India has led to a review of the Mughals and other Muslim dynasties before them, not as natives but invaders and colonizers. Briefly, this is the rise of Hindutva. This looking anew at history now sees even Islam as a foreign religion and the Mughal monuments, including the Taj Mahal, as occupiers' relics. The 1947 Partition continues to be debated, particularly its influence on Hindu-Muslim relations against the backdrop of the history of the medieval period.

There is understandable historical resentment as Hindu India re-evaluates the Muslim invasions and forcible settlements that spanned several centuries. On the other side, Pakistan prides itself in being a Muslim country; its founder Mohammad Ali Jinnah demanded a separate homeland for the Muslims of the subcontinent on the grounds that Hindus and Muslims are incompatible by history, culture, food and social upbringing and therefore cannot coexist. Partition between India and Pakistan, formally effected in August 1947, continues to deepen. This is not surprising, as India and Pakistan reconnect to their different identities. Except for religion, Bangladesh shares a much more cultural and linguistic history with India than Pakistan. As such, the India-Bangladesh alliance is much more authentic than the Pakistan-Bangladesh partnership.

In the early 16th century, the Muslim descendants of Tamerlane and Genghis Khan, who later came to be known as the Mughals, invaded the Indian subcontinent via Afghanistan and established the Mughal Empire that lasted from 1526 to 1857. But the Muslim conquest of the subcontinent began in much earlier, in 712 BC, when the Muslim Arabs landed in Sind, also the year Muslim Arabs entered Spain. For 800 years before the Mughals arrived, various Muslim dynasties wrought much bloodshed to gain control the subcontinent. For the first five centuries, i.e., from 711 to 1192, the invaders could not penetrate the subcontinent in any decisive way. This was due to unrelenting Hindu resistance. The hordes of Hejaz swept over the Mediterranean and Spain in 80 years, but had to spend five centuries before they could reach the Indian hinterland. It was only in 1206 that the Muslim invaders established what is known as the Delhi Sultanate, which was not one single dynasty, but five of them that came and fell in succession; namely, the Slave Dynasty, the Khiljis, Tughlaqs, Sayyids and the Lodis from 1206 to 1526, all of Afghan and Turkic origin, before Babar of Samarqand invaded India and finished off the Lodis.

The territory the Mughals ruled spans both India and present-day Pakistan. However, the point to be noted here is that since 712, Pakistan has been under constant invasions, occupation, ethnic settlement by foreigners, i.e., Islamic invaders, and religious cleansing. Incessant invasions forced Hindus to quit Lahore and other cities in northwestern India. The violent Partition of 1947 was thus a work in slow but steady progress, albeit centuries before 1947.

Situated next to Iran, Afghanistan, Turkestan, Kazakhstan, and Uzbekistan—the bastion of invaders—northwestern India, now transmogrified as Pakistan, has been the stepping stone for adventurers from the west, from Alexander of Greece and Macedonia (323 BC) to the Mughals. All roads to the invasion of the subcontinent passed through the region that today comprises Pakistan. The repeated conquests of centuries have made Pakistan fundamentally a settlement territory for invaders and their progeny. Pakistan's mindset towards every invader can therefore, be summed up as "Welcome, but keep going east". The 1947 break from Bharat, as a Muslim country, can be likened to a fruit that becomes ripe and eventually falls off the tree.

While waves of Islamic invasions laid the grounds for India's northwest becoming, religiously and culturally, an entity separate from Hindu Bharat, Pakistan's relates to the various Delhi sultanates and the Mughal Empire, particularly its sixth emperor, Aurangzeb. The Pakistan military names some of its missiles acquired from China and/or North Korea after the Muslim invaders who invaded India. One particular missile named Babur, the Mughal dynasty founder. These names are deliberate attempts to connect Pakistan with Muslim conquerors. It is this mindset that makes Pakistan resonate with Aurangzeb.

The irony is that Akbar, generally viewed as the greatest of the Mughal emperors, was born in Amarkot, Sind, a territory that presently is in Pakistan, while their hero Aurangzeb was born in Dahod, Gujarat, which is in India. Mughal and other dynastic architectural monuments exist in and around Lahore, which is a city that welcomed the northwestern invaders with open arms. Indeed, Lahore became a favourite capital for them, also going on to become one of the three capitals of the Mughal Empire, the other two being Agra and Delhi. These medieval monuments are reportedly degenerating into ruins through neglect, but very few Pakistanis express any concern about them, except the Badshahi Mosque.

It shouldn't be difficult to guess why. The Badshahi Mosque was built in Aurangzeb's reign, on his orders.

Pakistan self-imposed historical vacuum beggars description. The Islamic influence has made Pakistanis, especially the country's ruling elites and clergy, idealise 7th century Arabs as their forefathers, though the Arabs have nothing remotely to do with the ancestry of Pakistanis. If anything, Pakistanis, especially those working in the Gulf states are treated by Arabs as slaves or at best, labourers. Also, for all its professed love of the Ghaznavis, Ghoris, Timurs and Babars, Pakistanis in either public or the academia show little enthusiasm connecting with the pre-Mughal Muslim dynasties as their forefathers. But the country's ruling elites most definitely display what can be termed a 'Mughal syndrome'. The eulogization of Aurangzeb must be seen in this light.

There can also be no denying that Aurangzeb, a puritanical, zealot and intolerant Muslim ruler who had no qualms in persecuting his Hindu subjects through his religious policies became a hero for the Muslim community of India as a result of his lifelong actions. They admired him for being the ruler who 'restored' the prestige of Islam, defending it against enemies. This process only gathered pace when the Two-Nation Theory became a cornerstone of the Pakistan movement.

After Partition, Pakistani historians supporting the state ideology in the Two-Nation Theory reconstructed the historical narrative by critically examining Akbar and Aurangzeb. I.H. Qureshi condemned Akbar and his religious policy as being against the interest of the Muslims of India. He accused Akbar of being the major cause of the downfall of the Mughal empire as he had granted concessions to the Hindus, thereby alienating the support of the Muslims. To promote the image of Aurangzeb and to popularize his policies, 'Alamgir Day' was observed on May 3, 1965 under the patronage of Dairah-e-Muin-al-Marif.

In Pakistan's academia, M.D. Zafar's *A Textbook of Pakistan Studies* is one of the examples of how the country sees itself as a legatee of Aurangzeb. Zafar in his work, mentions Akbar's Din-e-Ilahi and Muslim cleric Sheikh Sirhindi's resistance to it and notes that "The spirit of Pakistan asserted itself". Under Aurangzeb, Zafar declares, "the Pakistan spirit gathered in strength"; his death "weakened the Pakistan spirit".

The 'Mughal syndrome' can loosely be described as the combined mindset of the Muslim dynasties that invaded the subcontinent, including the Mughals and the Delhi Sultanate's five dynasties. From Ayub Khan to Imran Khan and now Shahbaz Sharif, Pakistan's prime minister at the time of writing this book, Pakistani rulers have adopted these behaviours, and have been addicted to it.

THE Mughals, like prior Muslim dynasties who invaded India, were unmistakably and undeniably foreigners. Moreover, they aspired to foreignize—read Islamize—India. Consider cuisine. From food, language, customs and of course jihadi iconoclasm against Hindu temples and dharma, this was the saga of the 700 years of their rule.

Babar, the Mughal founder, wrote a line in Persian, "*Babur b'aish kosh ka alam dobara niest*" (Babar, live it up as you'd never see this world again), a line that many Pakistanis not only recite, but their ruling elites translate it into real action. Muslim invaders invaded the subcontinent to plunder, and when ensconced, taxed the people to pay for their opulence. Aurangzeb was indeed pious by comparison, but piety is no barrier to lavishness. Akbar and other Mughal Emperors established harems to house multiple wives and concubines. Their *ulema* (clergy) generously 'interpreted' the law to allow four wives and unlimited concubines, including Hindu women captured in battles.

For the mighty and the powerful, the law itself is a concubine.

In the pursuit of this *ayyashi* (wanton sensual enjoyment), Pakistan's ruling elites do mimic the Mughals. Prime minister Zulfiqar Ali Bhutto, who talked of 'Islamic socialism' in the 1970s, came from a rich family, lived like a nawab, and wore custom-made suits. Only a mindset of *ayyashi* can yoke socialism with a nawabi lifestyle. Like Babar, Bhutto loved drinking. And yet, in true Aurangzeb-style, in the name of 'pure' Islam, Bhutto declared in the constitution a sizeable Pakistani community, the Ahmediyas, to be non-Muslims, opening the way for their persecution. Pakistani scientist Abdus Salam won a Nobel prize in physics but had no recognition in Pakistan because he was an Ahmediya. In fact, his grave was desecrated after his death.

Takht ya takhta—either the throne or the funeral bier. Throughout the period of Muslim rule in India, succession happened not through primogeniture but by a contest of arms, overthrow, capture, exile, and murder. The transition from one ruler to the next within the same dynasty, or from one dynasty to the other, was without exception filled with violence. Strangely, in making their grab for the throne, Muslims did not hesitate to collaborate with Hindu kings and generals. Takht (throne) ya (or) takhta (gallows) perfectly the history of more than ten centuries of Muslim dynasties, including the Mughals.

Uzbeg invader Babur defeated the Lodi Sultanate (1451–1526) and killed its ruler Ibrahim Lodi to end their dynasty and set up his. Khusru, a beloved son of Emperor Jahangir, rebelled against his father to usurp the throne. Jahangir did not kill the son but blinded him as punishment. When Emperor Shah Jahan fell ill, his sons fought a bloody war of succession for the throne. The victor was Aurangzeb, who slaughtered his brothers and imprisoned the father for nearly eight years until he died in prison. Little wonder the spirit of Aurangzeb lives on in Pakistan; its short history has been marked by regular power-grabs and overthrows of the incumbent. Three different constitutions beginning with 1956 (a full nine years after Pakistan coming into existence), 1962, and then 1973 have been made, unmade, amended, unamended, and suspended with and without lawful authority. Elected prime ministers have been booted out of office, exiled, and hanged. Within three years of its independence, Pakistan's first prime minister Liaquat Ali Khan, was gunned down in broad daylight. This chaos looks abnormal only in the absence of historical context, but it is customary if viewed in light of the Muslim dynasties. Of course, Aurangzeb did not invent usurpation or the bloody transfer of power, but he certainly sanctified it.

Takht ya takhta is no less true about Pakistan's judiciary. Judges who write opinions to challenge the military dynasty face corruption cases, just as politicians do. Judges are helpless in retrieving people who 'disappear'. They can offer little assistance when the journalists who expose the dynasties are abducted, imprisoned, or murdered. Judges are threatened with consequences and removed from office if they take on any dynasty. The freedom of the judiciary is subject to the supremacy of the self-styled Babar-Aurangzebian dynasties.

Whether it accepts it or not, Pakistan is the continuation of the Sultanate, the Mughal Empire and particularly the Aurangzeb mindset. Mutiny, capture, exile, takeovers, and even murder to acquire the throne is an inherent part of the Pakistani state and polity. Behind the veil of democracy, Pakistan is nothing but feudal and dynastic, a continuation of the Delhi Sultanate and the Mughal Empire. Concepts like the rule of law, peaceful succession, and the constitutional supremacy have no place there. Its ruling elites are wedded to *ayyashi* and habitually engage in the game of *takht ya takhta*. The country does not have the wherewithal to counter the historical gravity of the Mughal syndrome.

HINDU TEMPLES—TARGETS OF AURANGZEB'S JIHADI ICONOCLASM

CHAPTER 13

The list of some of the major Hindu temples that Aurangzeb destroyed throughout India—both while he was still a *shehzada* (prince) and after he became the emperor—need little elaboration. Muhiuddin Mohammad Aurangzeb was a jihadi who hated Hindus and their dharma—as simple as that. No amount of secular whitewashing, as has become the trend in recent times or image-remaking public relations exercises by makeover artists can alter this sordid truth. We briefly present here the episodes of the destruction of each temple, verbatim from primary sources. These include Sir Jadunath Sarkar's seminal volumes on Aurangzeb (*Book of Aurangzeb*), William Crooke's *Handbooks*, De Graaf's chronicles, Aurangzeb's own *farmans*, accounts by Charles Stewart, *Akhbarat*, and the *Masir-i-Alamgiri*.

The Hindu temples destroyed, demolished and desecrated by Aurangzeb described in this chapter are only a brief list, a sort of ready reckoner, given the manner in which Aurangzeb has been elevated almost to sainthood by the secular mafia in India masquerading as historians.

Hindu Temples Destroyed by Aurangzeb as a Shehzada

1. The temple of Chintaman, situated close to Saraslipur, and built by the jeweller Sitadas, was converted into a mosque named Quwat-ul-Islam by order of the Prince Aurangzeb, in 1645. He slaughtered a cow in the temple.

2. "In Ahmadabad and other *parganas* of Gujarat in the days before my accession [many] temples were destroyed by my order" — Aurangzeb's own testimony.

3. "The village of Satara near Aurangabad was my hunting-ground. Here, on the top of a hill, stood a temple with an image of Khande Rai. By God's grace I demolished it, and forbade the temple dancers (*murlis*) to ply their shameful trade."

4. Aurangzeb's order to the Subedar of Gujarat: "In the city and parganas of Ahmadabad (i.e., Gujrat), the Hindus following their superstitious customs light lamps in the night of Diwali…It is ordered that in bazars there should be no illumination at Diwali."

Temples Destroyed by Aurangzeb after he became Emperor

1. "It has been decided according to our Islamic canon law that no new temple should be allowed to be built."
2. "The temple of Somnath was demolished early in my reign and idol worship (there) put down. It is not known what the state of things there is at present. If the idolators have again taken to the worship of images at the place, then destroy the temple in such a way that no trace of the building may be left, and also expel the worshippers from the place."
3. "On Dec 19, 1661, Mir Jumla entered the city of Cooch-Bihar, which had been evacuated by its king and people, and appointed Sayyid Mohammed, Sadiq to be chief judge, with directions to destroy all the Hindu temples and to erect mosques in their stead. Mir Jumla himself with a battle-axe broke the image of Narayan."
4. "The Emperor learning that in the temple of Keshav Rai at Mathura, there was a stone railing presented by Dara Shikoh, remarked, 'In the Muslim faith it is a sin. even to look at a temple, and this Dara had restored a railing in a temple! This fact is not creditable to the Muhammadans. Remove the railing. By his order Abdul Nabi Khan (the *faujdar* of Mathura) removed it."
5. Nov 20, 1665: "As it has come to His Majesty's knowledge that some inhabitants of the *mahals* appertaining to the province of Gujarat have again built the temples which had been demolished by imperial order before his accession...therefore, His Majesty orders that the formerly demolished and recently restored temples should be pulled down."
6. April 9, 1669: "The Emperor ordered the governors of all the provinces to demolish the schools and temples of the infidels and strongly put down their teaching and religious practices."
7. May 1669: "Salih Bahadur, mace-bearer, was sent to pull down the temple of Malarna [Sawai Madhopur, Rajasthan]."

8. Sep 2, 1669: "News came to Court that according to the Emperor's command, his officers had demolished the temple of Vishwanath at Benares."

   Kashi Vishwanath has particularly been the target of unrelenting jihadi attacks shortly after Islamic invaders entered India. It suffered its first attack in the 12th century by Qutb al-Din Aibak. The temple's peak was damaged in the attack; puja ceremonies however, continued there even after that tragic event. History records that the destruction of the most sacred among Hindu temples was carried out under the orders of Shahbuddin Mohammad of Ghori.

   The Kashi Vishwanath Mandir was the victim of another jihadi sultan, Sikandar Lodi (1489–1517). Evidence points to the fact that Sikandar Lodi was responsible for the invasion of Kashi Vishwanath. But it was in 1669 CE, that the sacred Hindu temple dedicated to Lord Shiva witnessed the ultimate assault upon it, by Mughal tyrant Aurangzeb. He demolished the temple and replaced it with the Gyanvapi masjid. The remains of the erstwhile mandir can still be seen in the foundation, the columns, and the rear part of the mosque. This was done deliberately in order to humiliate the Hindus. The Kashi Vishwanath Temple complex, which stands today, is adjacent to the disputed mosque complex and where devotees can do puja and prayers, was built by the great Ahilya Holkar of Indore in 1780.

   We have the Islamic record of *Maasir-i-Alamgiri* as evidence for this criminal act of iconoclasm. It states that on April 9, 1669, Aurangzeb had issued a *farman*, "to governors of all the provinces to demolish the schools and temples of the infidels and strongly put down their teachings and religious practices." The same is also mentioned in the *Varanasi Gazetteer* which was published in the year 1965. It is clearly stated on page number 57 that on April 9, 1669, Aurangzeb issued a decree to his governors to destroy the Hindu temples and schools in Kashi (Varanasi).

   The Kashi Vishwanath temple, of course, is just one of many Hindu temples destroyed by the Mughal emperor Aurangzeb in his absolute hatred for Hindu culture and faith. The Islamic record of *Maasir-i-Alamgiri* describes many other instances of Aurangzeb's fanaticism.

9. January, 1670: "In this month of Ramzan, the religious-minded Emperor ordered the demolition of the temple at Mathura known as the Dehra of Keshav Rai. His officers accomplished it in a short time. A grand mosque was built on its site at a vast expenditure. The temple had been built by Bir Singh Dev Bundela at a cost of 33 lakhs of rupees. Praised be the God

of the Great Faith of Islam that in the auspicious reign of this destroyer of infidelity and turbulence, such a marvellous and seemingly impossible feat was accomplished. On seeing this strength of the Emperor's faith and the grandeur of his devotion to God, the Rajahs felt suffocated and they stood in amazement like statues facing the walls. The idols, large and small, set with costly jewels, which had been set up in the temple, were brought to Agra and buried under the steps of the mosque of Jahanara, to be trodden upon continually."

10. "Emperor Aurangzeb partially destroyed the Sitaramji temple at Soron; one of his officers slew the priests, broke the image, and defiled the sanctuary at Devi Palan in Gonda."
11. April 7, 1670: "News came from Malwa that Wazir Khan had sent Gada Beg, a slave, with 400 troopers, to destroy all temples around Ujjain." But this was one iconoclastic adventure that badly misfired; a Rawat of the place resisted the attackers and slew Gada Beg with 121 of his men.
12. "Order issued on all *faujdars* of *thanas*, civil officers (*mufasaddis*), agents of *jagirdars*, *kroris*, and *amlas*, from Cuttack to Medinipur on the frontier of Orissa: The imperial paymaster Asad Khan has sent a letter written by order of the Emperor, to say, that the Emperor learning from the newsletters of the province of Orissa that at the village of Tilkuti in Medinipur a temple has been (newly) built, has issued his august mandate for its destruction, and the destruction of all temples built anywhere in this province by the worthless infidels. Therefore, you are commanded with extreme urgency that immediately on the receipt of this letter you should destroy the above-mentioned temples. Every idol-house built during the last 10 or 12 years, whether with brick or clay, should be demolished without delay. Also, do not allow the crushed Hindus and despicable infidels to repair their old temples. Reports of the destruction of temples should be sent to the Court under the seal of the *qazis* and attested by pious Shaikhs."

Mathura and Vrindavan—Special Targets of Alamgir's Hatred

When Aurangzeb plundered the holy city of Mathura, he destroyed the famous and one of the most revered Keshav Rai temples in January of 1670. This temple marked the place where Lord Krishna had taken birth, one of the most important temples in the Vedic tradition. Aurangzeb, true to his jihadi nature, he built a mosque in its place.

It is stated that the beautifully adorned deities were transported to Agra and placed beneath the steps leading to the mosque of Nawab Begum Sahib (Jahanara) so that they could be trampled by Muslims. Mathura's name was changed to Islamabad after having destroyed the very foundation of deity worship.

Gobind Dev Temple—Desecrated Only for the Badshah's Ego

However, the desecration of Gobind Dev temple in Vrindavan is unique; it was neither complete nor was it converted into a mosque. The structure was cut into half—horizontally. And why? Because whenever Aurangzeb happened to be in Delhi or Agra, at night he would see a *mashaal* (flaming torch), lighting up the sky. Now, how could any light shine higher than his? It had to be put out once and for all, felt the emperor. By 1669 he lost his patience, sent his men and had the Gobind Dev temple cut in half, four storeys reduced to two. On the truncated roof he had a *mehrab* erected so that he could pray there on his visit.

Probably, no other desecrated temple had been the subject of so much repair and refurbishment by British rulers. Of supreme importance was the fact of the temple being "restituted" to Hindu devotees. It was the greatest act of *shuddhi*, or purification, although performed before Swami Dayanand Saraswati reintroduced Vedic procedures. For this act of restitution, F.S. Growse, the magistrate of Mathura district in the 1870s, certainly deserves a place in the hall of Hinduism. The Gobind Dev temple is indeed massive; its plinth is 105 feet by 117 feet. It is estimated that the original height was about 110 feet, without which it would not have been possible to see the *mashaal* or torch either from Agra or from Delhi. The temple was built in 1590 AD by Maharaja Mansingh of Jaipur.

The temple is also unique for several other reasons, but on that, a little later. For the satisfaction of its desecrators, the sanctum sanctorum was destroyed. Fortunately, the idol of Shri Krishna or Govind had been removed to Jaipur by the priests in anticipation of Aurangzeb's coming in 1670 AD; the Mughal was already notorious as an iconoclast. The roof of the truncated edifice was to be reserved for *namaz*. No sooner had the *mehrab* been constructed, as illustrated in the photograph in *History of Indian and Eastern Architecture* by James Fergusson, Aurangzeb inaugurated it himself by offering prayers.

All except two statuettes were defaced, including the one at the door of what is now the temple, after crossing the foyer hall. The destruction was not confined to the upper floors. It extended to hundreds of statuettes that even today adorn the temple walls—outside as well as inside, the ceilings or doors. The iconoclast overlooked two small statuettes, one of Shri Krishna and the other of Radha, on the outside on the left as one faces the temple.

An American historian of Indian architecture, George Mitchell has concluded that the original sanctum sanctorum was destroyed. In his own words, "Once the *garbhagriha* has been torn down, there was little point in further wreckage... It seems to me that only those with some understanding of the ritual significance of the *garbhagriha* would have been capable of desecrating a temple in this careful manner."

The Gobind Dev temple finds mention in Aurangzeb's decree of April 1669. It said: "Eager to establish Islam, (Aurangzeb) issued orders to the governors of all the provinces to demolish the schools and temples of the infidels and with the utmost urgency put down the teaching and the public practice of the religion of these disbelievers." The great temple of Gobind Dev fell victim to iconoclastic vandalism within a year of the decree. Its inner sanctum and its superstructure were almost entirely destroyed. The main hall was also damaged. Sculpted figures on the *dwarasakha* were literally defaced.

According to an article in the *Calcutta Review* quoted by Growse: "Aurangzeb had often remarked about a very bright light shining in the far distant south east horizon and in reply to his enquiries regarding it, was told that it was a light burning in a temple of great wealth and magnificence at Vrindavan. He accordingly resolved that it should be put out and soon after sent some troops to the place who plundered and threw down as much of the temple as they could and then erected on the top of the ruins a mosque wall where, in order to complete the desecration, the emperor is said to have offered up his prayers."

Incidentally, the canopy standing on four pillars, which must have acted as a shed for the burning torch or *mashaal*, is lying on the ground at the back of the present sanctum sanctorum. It was so fixed, presumably by Growse in the 1870s. It has no relevance to the temple's architecture. This reinforces the belief that this canopy belonged to the top of the once towering temple.

While Aurangzeb's ego might have been gratified, the desecration took with it what is described by Fergusson as one of the most elegant temples in India, and the only one perhaps, from which a European architect might borrow a few hints. Growse added that "It is not a little strange that of all the architects who have described this famous building, not one has noticed its most characteristic feature—the harmonious combination of dome and spire—which is still quoted as the great crux of modern art, though nearly 300 years ago the difficulty was solved by the Hindus with characteristic grace and ingenuity." Fergusson, in his *Indian Architecture*, speaks of this temple as "one of the most interesting and elegant in India, and the only one, perhaps, from which a European architect might borrow a few hints. I should myself have thought that 'solemn' or 'imposing' was a more appropriate term than 'elegant' for so massive a building, and that the suggestions that might be derived from its study were 'many' rather than 'few;' but the criticism is at all events in intention a complimentary one."

A 19th century architect, Henry Hardy Cole, who had toured India widely, wrote: "I am not sure that the restoration of the upper most parapet is correct and think that it would have been better to leave the superstructure, as it appeared when I first saw it, with all the evidence of Aurangzeb's destructive hand."

A number of motives have been attributed to the many Islamic invaders who desecrated temples, such as looting of treasures, subduing the populace by arousing dread, "conveying to the populace that a sultan had replaced the raja". There is, however, no other instance of a temple being desecrated because it defied the fragile ego of an emperor drenched in hate for those not subscribing to his worldview.

Delhi's Kalka Temple

In September 1667, Aurangzeb issued a similar 'Farman' (decree) for the demolition of the _Kalka Temple in Delhi, dedicated to the Mother Goddess. The reason stated in the decree was that Hindus were gathering in large numbers at the temple. This was enough reason for the Mughal tyrant to order his hundreds of soldiers to go and demolish the temple.

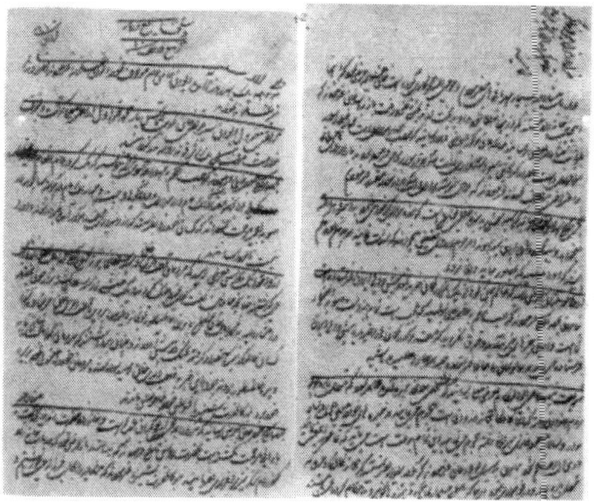

Figure: Copy of Aurangzeb's *Farman*
Source: True Indology

According to legends, when a Brahmin priest of the temple noticed the demolishers, he drew out his sword and killed one of them. He then turned around and attacked the Qazi who was leading the demolition squad inside the temple. The Brahmin was ultimately caught and stoned to death.

The present Kalkaji Temple was built over the ruins of an earlier temple dedicated to Goddess Kali shortly after Aurangzeb's death in 1707. Two *Akhbarat* dated September 3 and September 12, 1667, provide details regarding the demolition of the temple upon Aurangzeb's *farman*.

The Sita-Rama temple at Soron, as well as the Devi Patan temple in Gonda, were both destroyed in the same year. Acting on Aurangzeb's orders, the local ruler of Malwa dispatched 400 soldiers to destroy all of Ujjain's temples.

Furthermore, according to Muraqat-i-Abul Hasan, Aurangzeb ordered his soldiers and assistants from Cuttack, Orissa, and on to Medinipur in Bengal to destroy every house with a Hindu deity that had been built in the last 12 years. Aurangzeb further ordered that if any temples were reconstructed, they should be demolished again completely so that Hindus could not revive worship at the sites.

According to two *Akhbarat* dated March 28 and May 14,1680, temples in the even the loyal and friendly state of Amber, such as the famed Temple of Jagdish at Goner in Amber, were not spared Aurangzeb's religious fervour. It bears reiteration here that Amber was ruled by Mirza Raja Jai Singh, a most loyal Rajput ally of the Mughal Empire.

CONCLUSION

The Post-Aurangzeb Mess and Collapse

The Mughals 'emperors' who followed Aurangzeb were weak and could not hold the Mughal empire together. The decline of the empire led to the rise of many autonomous states within India. The Marathas had already become virtual masters of the south and Gujarat.

After Aurangzeb's death in 1707, his eldest surviving son Mirza Muhammad Muazzam, who assumed the title of Bahadur Shah became the emperor following a succession war with his brothers. He was 64 when he ascended the Mughal throne. In his father's lifetime, Muazzam had tried to organize a rebellion to overthrow him, a plan that possibly had the support of the Marathas. Nothing much came out of it, but Aurangzeb then on placed his son under surveillance.

Aurangzeb had died without appointing a crown prince or a designated successor. Muazzam was governor of Kabul and his younger half-brothers Muhammad Kam Bakhsh and Muhammad Azam Shah were the governors of the Deccan and Gujarat respectively. In yet another replay of the age-old Mughal fratricide for the throne, all three sons intended to grab the Mughal crown, and Prince Kam Bakhsh began minting coins in his name. Muazzam defeated Azam Shah in the Battle of Jajau near Agra in June 1707. Azam Shah and his son Ali Tabar met their death in this battle. Muazzam ascended the Mughal throne, but he was aged 64 in June 1707. He then marched to the Deccan and defeated and killed his younger brother Kam Bakhsh in a battle near Hyderabad in January 1708.

In the beginning, Bahadur Shah attempted to exercise more control over Amber and Marwar, but only ended up giving them high *mansabs*. He failed to defeat the Rajputs. He also granted the *sardeshmukhi* of Deccan to the Marathas but failed to give them the *chauth*. The Marathas were thus left dissatisfied. He also tried to pacify the Sikhs by befriending Guru Gobind Singh, but later, put down a rebellion by Banda Bahadur, Gobind Singh's successor, and put the latter to death, which only intensified the Sikh uprising against the Mughals. Failing in health, Bahadur Shah died in 1712, and the Mughal empire plunged into rebellion once again.

A war of succession began as Bahadur Shah reached his deathbed in 1712. The most powerful prince at the time of his death was his second son Azim-us-Shan, who had been the subedar of Bengal. Jahandar Shah, Muazzam's eldest son, was the weakest, with little-to-no military power or funds, but was supported by Julfikar Khan, who was a powerful nobleman. In the ensuing struggle for succession, Azim-us-Shan was defeated and killed and Jahandar ascended the Mughal throne in March 1712.

With Jahandar Shah began the era of puppet kings, as his accession did not enjoy support. He was regarded as an illegitimate ruler. He sought to consolidate his rule by rewarding his supporters and punishing his opponents, killing many and leaving their bodies to rot before burial. While his handler Julfikar Khan sought to establish amicable relations with the Marathas, Rajputs and Sikhs to restore peace in the empire, its finances were in deterioration, thanks largely to Aurangzeb's failed wars. Resentful of Julfikar's influence, Jahandar now conspired against him, stoking further chaos.

During this Mughal ruler, during his reign married a *tawaif* (courtesan) Lal Kunwar, who was considered to be of lowly origins. But she became his favoured wife, and subsequently her family gained unprecedent power and status. Jahandar Shah himself was no less a slave of feasts and entertainments.

Jahandar Shah's rule was challenged by his nephew Farrukhsiyar, son of the defeated and slain Azim-us-Shan. Farrukhsiyar found powerful support in the Sayyid brothers, Husain Ali Khan and Abdullah Khan, administrators of Azim-us-Shan who had been thrown out by Jahandar. With their resources and political connections, Farrukhsiyar assembled a rebel army and advanced on the throne. The underpaid imperial army was defeated in battle near Agra in early 1713. In almost a replay of Dara Shikoh's defeat and flight in 1658, the defeated Jahandar fled to Delhi and sought refuge at the house of Julfikar Khan and his father Asad Khan. However, the two imprisoned him and turned him over to Farrukhsiyar, in the hope of securing the victor's favour. But Farrukhsiyar had both Jahandar Shah and Julfikar Khan executed, with Jahandar Shah being beaten to death and then beheaded on 11 February, 1713. His body was paraded around Delhi in parts, hanging upside down from two elephants, before being buried in Humayun's tomb.

Farrukhsiyar, also spelled Farrukh Siyar, then became the tenth Mughal emperor from 1713 to 1719, after deposing and killing his uncle jahandar Shah. He was an emperor only in name, with all effective power in the hands of the courtier Sayyid brothers, who were the real power. Farrukhsiyar's close aides sowed suspicion in his mind that the brothers might usurp the throne, but the Mughal king could not confront them, as the Sayyid Brothers maintained control of the strongest part of the army, and thus had become de facto rulers of the empire. Farrukhsiyar's regime was marked by cruelty towards the Jats and Sikhs, who had risen in rebellion against Mughal authority. The hated *jaziya* tax, which had been abolished by Bahadur Shah, was reimposed by this Mughal ruler. The Sayyid brothers, the puppeteers behind the throne, followed a policy of religious moderation, but Farrukhsiyar was now increasingly suspicious of them. He plotted their overthrow, but they acted first, deposing and blinding him before executing him in 1719. The Sayyid brothers too, did not survive for long; they were murdered the following year by Muhammad Shah and fellow conspirators. Muhammad Shah went on to become the next Mughal *Badshah*. There were two Mughal 'emperors' in quick succession after Farrukhsiyar's fall. Mirza Rafi ud-Darajat was briefly the tenth Mughal ruler. He was the youngest son of Rafi-us-Shan, the nephew of Azim-us-Shan and a grandson of Bahadur Shah I. Rafi ud-Darajat died on 6 June 1719, either of tuberculosis or was murdered, serving as 'emperor' for three months and six days. He was succeeded by Rafi ud-Daulah as emperor Shah Jahan II two days later.

Rafi-ud-Dowlah was the second son of Rafi-us-Shan, and a grandson of bahadur Shah I. He is believed to have been eighteen months older than his brother Rafi-ud-Darajat, but details of his marriage, if any, or whether he had any child or not are unknown. The second Rafi, or Shah Jahan II ascended the throne on 6 June 1719 after the death of Rafi-ud-Darajat. He too was suffering from tuberculosis just like his younger brother, and was physically and mentally unfit to perform the duties of a ruler. Rafi-ud-Dowlah died on 17 September 1719.

After the quick coming and departure of these two Rafi sahibs, Mirza Nasir-ud-Din Muhammad Shah, born Roshan Akhtar became the thirteenth Mughal 'emperor' from 1719 and had a long stint of nearly thirty years, up to 1748. He was the fourth son of Bahadur Shah. He was chosen by the Sayyid brothers and ascended the throne at the young age of 16, under their strict supervision. Muhammad Shah's reign was marked by the rapid and irreversible decline of the Mughal Empire, the crowning ignominy being Persian invader Nadir Shah's invasion of India and the sack of Delhi in 1739. The course of events not only shocked and mortified the Mughals themselves, but also other foreigners, including the British. It was in Muhammad Shah's time that Hyderabad, Awadh, Bengal and Mysore broke away from the Mughal Empire and became independent states.

Ahmad Shah Bahadur, also known as Mirza Ahmad Shah or Mujahid-ud-Din Ahmad Shah Ghazi, was the fourteenth Mughal emperor, born to Muhammad Shah. He succeeded his father to the throne in 1748, at the age of 22. At the time of his coming to power, the Mughal Empire's decline was proceeding apace. Ahmad Bahadur's administrative weakness and a major defeat to the Marathas led to the rise of the usurping Imad-ul-Mulk, a wazir who deposed and later blinded him along with his mother. Ahmad Shah Bahadur spent the remaining years of his life in prison and died in 1775. In his lifetime, he had also lost Orissa to the Marathas.

Mirza Aziz-ud-Din Muhammad, the son of the murdered Jahandar Shah, known more by his regnal name Alamgir II, became the fifteenth Mughal emperor from 1754 to 1759. He was raised to the throne by Imad-ul-Mulk after the latter deposed Ahmad Shah Bahadur in 1754. On ascending the throne, he took the title of Alamgir and tried to follow the approach of the original Alamgir, i.e., Aurangzeb. But he was 55 at the time of his accession to the throne with no experience of administration and warfare, as he had spent most of his life in jail. He was a weak ruler, with all powers vested in the hand of his wazir Imad-ul-Mulk.

In 1756, Ahmad Shah Durrani invaded India a second time, captured Delhi and plundered Mathura. The Marathas became more powerful and dominated the whole of northern India. This was the peak of the Maratha expansion, which ate away what remained of the Mughal Empire, already weak with no strong ruler. Relations between Alamgir II and his usurping wazir Imad-ul-Mulk had now deteriorated, culminating in the murder of Alamgir II by Imad-ul-Mulk.

Next to sit on the Mughal throne was Shah Jahan III, originally called Mirza Muhi-ul-Millat, as the sixteenth Mughal emperor, albeit briefly. He was the eldest son of Muhammad Kam Bakhsh who was the youngest son of Aurangzeb. He was placed on the Mughal throne in December 1759 as a result of the raging intrigues in Delhi, again, with the intervention of Imad-ul-Mulk. But not for long; Shah Jahan III was later deposed by Mughal chiefs, acting in the name of the exiled Mughal Emperor Shah Alam II.

Shah Alam II , whose birth name was Ali Gohar, or Gauhar, was the seventeenth Mughal emperor and the son of Alamgir II. He became the emperor of a crumbling Mughal Empire. His power was so depleted during his reign that it led to a saying in Persian, *Sultanat-e-Shah Alam, Az Dilli ta Palam*, meaning, "The empire of Shah Alam is from Delhi to Palam" (Palam is a suburb of Delhi).

Shah Alam had to contend with many invasions, mainly by the Emir of Afghanistan Ahmed Shah Abdali, which led to the Third Battle of Panipat (1761) between the Maratha Confederacy and the Afghan Empire led by Abdali. In 1760, the invading forces of Abdali were driven away by the Marathas, led by Sadashivrao Bhau, who deposed Shah Jahan III, the Mughal puppet 'emperor' of Imad-ul-Mulk, and installed Shah Alam II as the rightful emperor (1760 – 1772).

Shah Alam II, though considered a rightful emperor, was unable to return to Delhi until 1772, which he could only under the protection of the Maratha general Mahadji Shinde. He also fought against the East India Company in the Battle of Buxar in 1764, but worsted. The Buxar defeat forced the Mughals to cede the diwani of Bengal, Bihar and Orissa to the East India Company, cementing their foothold in India after the Battle of Plassey in 1757. Shah Alam II was blinded in 1788, when he was a prisoner of Ghulam Qadir. The Marathas killed Qadir and rescued Shah Alam II, restoring him to the throne in 1788, but occupied and ruled Delhi for the next two decades until the decline of Maratha power and its deposition by the British. The Jats and Sikhs defeated the Mughals in the battlefield during the tenure of the second Shah Alam, who had to live under Maratha protection till his death in 1806.

Mirza Mahmud Shah Bahadur, known more by his regnal name Shah Jahan IV, was the eighteenth Mughal emperor for a brief period in 1788 after Shah Alam II was deposed by Ghulam Qadir. Mahmud Shah Bahadur was the son of a former Mughal Emperor, Ahmad Shah Bahadur. Shah Jahan IV was allegedly put to death in 1790 by order of Shah Alam II, supposedly for usurping his authority in 1788. He left behind two daughters.

Akbar II, also known as Akbar Shah II, the second son of Shah Alam II, was the nineteenth Mughal emperor from 1806 to 1837. Akbar had little de facto power due to the increasing British influence in India through the East India Company. He sent Ram Mohan Roy as an ambassador to Britain to plead against the manner of his treatment by the East India Company, and gave him the title of Raja. During his regime, in 1835, the East India Company discontinued calling itself the subject of the Mughal Emperor and issuing coins in his name. The Persian lines in the company's coins to this effect were deleted.

Akbar II is credited with starting the Hindu-Muslim unity festival *Phool Walon ki Sair*. He presided over an empire that was in effect limited to the Red Fort in Delhi, though Delhi's cultural life as a whole flourished during his reign. His attitude towards East India Company officials, especially Warren Hastings, to whom he refused to grant an audience on terms other than those of subject and sovereign, although honourable to him, increasingly frustrated the British, who regarded him as merely their pensioner. Akbar II passed away in 1837.

Bahadur Shah II, born Mirza Abu Zafar Siraj-ud-din Muhammad, usually referred to by his poetic title Bahadur Shah Zafar (Zafar meaning victory), was the twentieth and last Mughal emperor and an Urdu poet. He was the second son and the successor to his father, Akbar II, who died in 1837. Zafar was a titular emperor, as the Mughal Empire existed in name only and his authority was limited only to the walled city of Old Delhi (Shahjahanabad). Following his involvement in the Indian Mutiny of 1857, the British deposed him and exiled him to Rangoon in British-controlled Burma in 1858, after convicting him on several charges. The title of Empress of India was subsequently assumed by Queen Victoria.

Bahadur Shah Zafar's father, Akbar II, had been imprisoned by the British and he was not his father's preferred choice as his successor. One of Akbar Shah's queens pressurized him to declare her son, Mirza Jahangir, as his successor, but the East India Company exiled Jahangir after he attacked their residence in the Red Fort, paving the way for Bahadur Shah to assume the throne. With his defeat, his three sons too were killed by the victorious East India Company, and the Mughal Empire, the House of Timur, ended as it had begun in 1526—in a pool of blood.

Map 6: Decline of Mughal

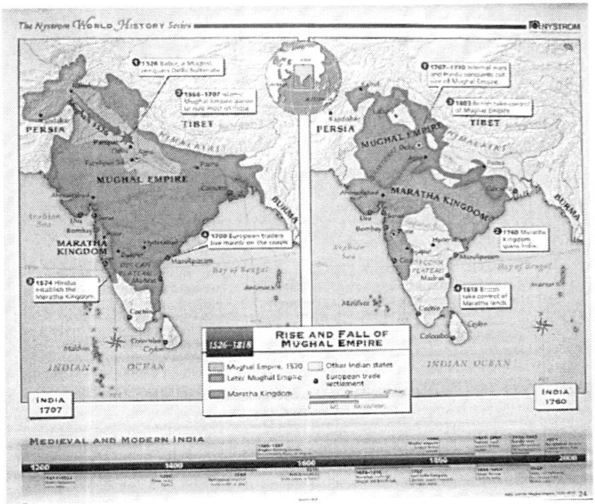

AURANGZEB'S FINAL LETTERS TO HIS SONS

To Shah Azam Shah

"Peace be upon you!

My heart is near thee. Old age is arrived: weakness subdues me, and strength has forsaken all my limbs. I came a stranger into this world, and a stranger I depart. I know nothing of myself, what I am, and for what I am destined. The instant which passed in power, hath left only sorrow behind it. I have not been the guardian and protector of the empire.

Life, so valuable, has been squandered in vain. I had a patron in my own dwelling (conscience), but his glorious light was unseen by my dim sight. Life is not lasting; there is no vestige of departed breath, and the past has departed but of the future there is no hope.

The fever has left me; nothing of me remains but skin and bone. My son Kam Baksh, though gone towards Bijapur, is still near; and thou, my son, art yet nearer. The worthy of esteem, Shah Aalam, is far distant; and my grandson Muhammad Azeem-o-Shan, by the orders of God, is arrived near Hindustan (from Bengal).

The entire imperial army, the camp and followers are like me: bewildered, perturbed, separated from God, helpless and alarmed, are, like myself, full of affliction, restless and in a state of trepidation like quicksilver. Separated from their lord, they know not if they have a master or not.

I brought nothing into this world, and, except the infirmities of man, carry nothing out. I have a dread for my salvation, and with what torments I may be punished. Though I have strong reliance on the mercies and bounty of God, yet, regarding my actions, fear will not quit me; but, when I am gone, reflection will not remain. Come what may, I have launched my vessel to the waves. Though Providence will protect the camp, yet, regarding appearances, the endeavours of my sons are indispensably incumbent. Give my last prayers to my grandson Bidar Bakht, whom I cannot see, but the desire affects me. The Begum (his daughter) appears afflicted; but God is the only judge of hearts. The foolish thoughts of women produce nothing but disappointment. Farewell! farewell! farewell!

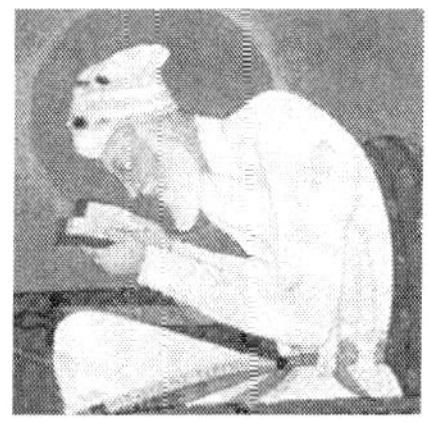

TO PRINCE KAM BAKSH

"My son, nearest to my heart. Though in the height of my power, and by God's permission, I gave you advice, and took with you the greatest pains, yet, as it was not the divine will, you did not attend with the ears of compliance. Now I depart a stranger, and lament my own insignificance, what does it profit me? I carry with me the fruits of my sins and imperfections. Surprising Providence! I came here alone, and alone I depart. The leader of this caravan hath deserted me. The fever, which troubled me for twelve days, has left me. Wherever I look, I see nothing but the Divinity. My fears for the camp and followers are great; but, alas! I know not myself. My back is bent with weakness, and my feet have lost the power of motion. The breath which rose, is gone, and left not even hope behind it. I have committed numerous crimes, and know not with what punishments I may be seized. Though the Protector of mankind will guard the camp, yet care is incumbent also on the faithful, and my sons. When I was alive, no care was taken; and now I am gone, the consequence may be guessed. The guardianship of a people is the trust by God submitted to my sons. Azim Shah is near. Be cautious that none of the faithful are slain, or that their miseries fall upon my head. I resign you, your mother and son, to God, as I myself am going. The agonies of death come upon me fast. Bahadur Shah is still where he was, and his son is arrived near Hindustan. Bidar Bakht is in Gujarat. Hyaut al-Nissa, who has beheld no afflictions of time till now, is full of sorrows. Regard the Begum as without concern. Udaipuri, your mother, was a partner in my affairs, and wishes to accompany me in death; but everything has its appointed time."

"The domestics and courtiers, however deceitful, yet must not be ill-treated. It is necessary to gain your views by gentleness and art. Extend your feet no lower than your skirt. The complaints of the unpaid troops are as before. Dara Shikoh, though of much judgment and good understanding, settled large pensions on his people, but paid them ill, and they were ever discontented. I am going. Whatever good or evil I have done, it was for you. Take it not amiss, nor remember what offences I have done to yourself; that account may not be demanded of me hereafter. No one has seen the departure of his own soul; but I see that mine is departing."

References

1. Book of Aurangzeb; Sir Jadunath Sarkar;Vol V, page 143.
2. Book of Aurangzeb; Sir Jadunath Sarkar;Vol V, page 197.

सल्तनते शाह आलम
अज दिल्ली ता पालम।

Here lies the Sultanate of Shah Alam
Whose sway is from Delhi to Palam

Persian Invader Nadir Shah's scathing observation of the state of the so-called Mughal Empire when his army sacked Delhi in 1739 AD.